Guide for Audit Committees

Under Federal Securities Law

Third Edition

James Hamilton, J.D., LL.M.

CCH INCORPORATED
Chicago

A WoltersKluwer Company

Guide
for Audit
Committees

Under Federal Securities Law

Third Edition

EDITORIAL STAFF

James Hamilton, J.D., LL.M.
Leslie Stoken

ISBN: 0-8080-1371-8

4025 W. Peterson Ave.
Chicago, IL 60645-6085
1-800-248-3248
http://business.cch.com

FOREWORD

The Sarbanes-Oxley Act is the most sweeping reform of the federal securities laws since the New Deal. The Act establishes a comprehensive framework to modernize and reform the oversight of public company auditing, improve the quality and transparency of corporate financial statements, and strengthen the independence of auditors. The Act also essentially federalized corporate governance by making it clear that senior corporate managers and directors are responsible for the climate they create.

The seminal principle underlying the regulation of audit committees is that they have a special role to act independently to ensure that the interests of the shareholders are protected in relation to the production of accurate and fairly presented financial statements and internal control over financial reporting. The audit committee's oversight job is a difficult, detailed, and demanding one.

The Sarbanes-Oxley reforms have placed audit committees at the center of federal corporate governance. The Act makes audit committees directly responsible for the hiring of the company's outside auditor and the oversight of the audit function. In addition, the audit committee must approve both audit and non-audit services. Audit committees must also be composed of independent directors, at least one of whom should be a financial expert.

The independent accounting firm performing the company's financial audit must report to the audit committee such important items as the critical accounting policies and practices to be used and all alternative treatments of financial information within GAAP that have been discussed with management. Audit committees also occupy a pivotal role in the corporate attorney up-the-ladder reporting regime.

The guidebook provides detailed discussion of how the Sarbanes-Oxley Act and SEC rules implementing the Act impact audit committees. It also discusses the interaction between audit committees and the Public Company Accounting Oversight Board, which was established by Sarbanes-Oxley to oversee the firms that audit the financial statements of public companies. Importantly, the guide examines the issues surrounding internal control reporting under Section 404 of Sarbanes-Oxley. The guide also looks at how the revised NYSE and Nasdaq listing standards affect audit committees. Finally, best practices are discussed, including the Breeden Report and the U.K. Combined Code on Corporate Governance.

June 2005

TABLE OF CONTENTS

8

CHAPTER 9—IMPROPER INFLUENCE ON AUDITS

CHAPTER 10—ATTORNEY REPORTING DUTIES

CHAPTER 11—BEST PRACTICES AND GUIDANCE

CHAPTER 12—OTHER CONSIDERATIONS

10

SELECTED LAWS AND RULES

SARBANES-OXLEY ACT PROVISIONS

SEC REGULATIONS

CHAPTER 1

INTRODUCTION

¶ 101 Background and Overview

The audit committee is the most established and clearly defined of all board committees. It is the primary link between the company's board of directors and its outside auditors. Audit committees play a critical role in the financial reporting system by overseeing and monitoring participation in the process by company management and the independent auditors. The committee's role fits into the larger picture of corporate governance because it lies at the core of the financial reporting process. The SEC wants the audit committee to act as a watchdog for the company's shareholders. (Release No. 34-15547 (SEC 1979), 16 SEC DOCKET 951.)

The Sarbanes-Oxley Act of 2002 essentially federalized corporate governance for the first time. The Act placed the audit committee at the center of corporate governance reforms designed to improve the accuracy of audited financial statements. The Act's provisions relating to audit committees are discussed throughout this work, and are reproduced at ¶ 2001 - 2008. For its part, the SEC has issued extensive rules for audit committees, both prior to and following Sarbanes-Oxley's enactment. Selected SEC rules affecting audit committees are reproduced at ¶ 3001 et seq.

These developments have heightened awareness of the audit committee as an extension of the full board and the first among equals between the committee, financial management, and the outside auditors. Put another way, the audit committee is one of the three pillars of financial reporting, with the other two being the financial executive and the independent auditor. All three pillars are needed to maintain the foundation on which the success of the capital markets has been built. (Remarks of former SEC Chief Accountant Lynn Turner before the Colorado Society of CPAs, Dec. 15, 2000.)

But note that, even after passage of the landmark Sarbanes-Oxley Act, the federal securities laws do not actually require a company to have an audit committee. The listing standards of the primary U.S. securities exchanges, however, do mandate that companies have audit committees.

¶ 102 Audit Committee's Role

Accurate financial reporting is the lifeblood of the securities markets. The U.S. Supreme Court has recognized that, by certifying the public reports that collectively depict a company's financial status, the independent auditor assumes a public responsibility transcending any employment relationship with the client. The independent public accountant performing this special function owes ultimate allegiance to the company' creditors and stockholders, as well as to the investing public. This public watchdog function demands that the accountant maintain total independence from the client at all times and requires fidelity to the public trust. (See *U.S. v. Arthur Young & Co.* (US S. Ct. 1984) 465 U.S. 805.)

Over the years, the audit committee has become a crucial player in the corporate governance of public corporations. The development of the audit committee is a recognition that accounting guidance alone is not enough to assure that financial statements will be properly prepared. It takes good oversight by the board of directors and especially the audit committee of the board. (Remarks by former SEC Deputy Chief Accountant John Morrissey, General Audit Management Conference, March 21, 2000.)

For public companies, audit committees have become an essential means through which corporate boards of directors oversee the integrity of the company's financial reporting process, system of internal accounting controls, and the financial statements themselves. Among other things, an audit committee serves as the board's principal interface with the company's auditors and facilitates communications between the company's board, its management, and its internal and independent auditors on significant accounting issues and policies.

In addition, Congress and the SEC have asked audit committees to play a more active role to ensure that investors receive a balanced, complete, transparent picture of the company's financial condition and results. The Commission has been a particular advocate of effective and independent audit committees.

Audit committees oversee and monitor management and the independent auditors in the financial reporting process, and thereby play a critical role in assuring the credibility of financial reporting. Audit committees can facilitate communications between a company's board of directors, its management, and its internal and independent auditors on significant accounting issues and policies. They can provide a forum separate from management in which auditors can candidly discuss any concerns. By effectively carrying out their many functions and responsibilities, audit committees help to enhance the reliability and credibility of financial reports.

Former SEC Chairman Arthur Levitt captured the essence of what audit committees can be at their best when he said that qualified, committed, independent and tough-minded audit committees represent true guardians of the public interest. These are the board members who, in the first instance, oversee a process that collects, verifies, and disseminates information about a public company's performance to the marketplace. (Remarks of SEC Chairman Levitt at the Audit Committee Symposium, June 29, 1999.)

Oversight Role

In the world of financial reporting, audit committees are cast in an oversight role. Audit committees bring business judgment to bear on the financial matters within their purview. It is not the role of the audit committee to prepare financial statements or engage in the myriad of decisions relating to the preparation of those statements. The committee's job is one of oversight and monitoring. In carrying out this job, it acts in reliance on senior financial management and the outside auditors.

No one expects or wants the audit committee to involve itself in discussions that plainly should be between management and the auditor. That is not oversight. But an audit committee actively engaged and drawing into view the significant judgments involved and any differences in opinion by asking the tough questions is engaged in effective oversight.

¶102

There are baseline situations or judgments that go to the very heart of whether the accounting is sound. And those situations or judgments demand audit committee oversight. If the audit committee cannot have an independent discussion with the auditor on the quality of the accounting, then audit committee oversight is nothing more than a facade. (See remarks of SEC Chairman Levitt at the Audit Committee Symposium, June 29, 1999.)

Thus, it is evident that the role of the audit committee is one of proactive oversight of the financial reporting and disclosure process and the results of that process. After Sarbanes-Oxley, it is also one of managing the outside auditors. The audit committee cannot and should not supplant the day-to-day responsibilities of management to ensure the accuracy of the financial statements.

Rather, the audit committee's function is based, in part, on its ability to carry out the necessary level of due diligence, relying on experts such as the chief financial officer, internal auditor, and independent external auditors. And then, with counsel from its legal advisers, the audit committee should document the processes it followed, the conclusions it reached, and the basis for those conclusions in an appropriate fashion, such as in the committee charter and minutes. (See remarks of SEC Chief Accountant Lynn Turner, Seminar on Corporate Accountability, March 10, 2001.)

Sources of information

In order for audit committees to fulfill their role as watchdogs over the financial reporting process, committee members need to receive important information about the company's business activities and the proper accounting for those activities. One source for this information is management. Managers constitute an important source of information because it is they who receive daily reports and make the daily decisions. But the audit committee should not rely solely on management to meet its information needs. Audit committee members must look to other sources. External auditors can be a valuable source of information. Because of their independence and their familiarity with accounting techniques used by many companies, external auditors offer an important perspective. (See Remarks of former SEC Deputy Chief Accountant John Morrissey, General Audit Management Conference, March 21, 2000.)

Defining its role in charter

A well-functioning audit committee will spend a significant amount of time defining the scope of its oversight duties and how it discharges them. A good audit committee should memorialize its understanding of its role, its duties, and its process in a charter. In focusing its activities on oversight of the entire reporting process, the committee will be more likely to recognize those duties better left to management, including the internal auditor and the outside auditors.

Review of relationships

It is imperative to the integrity and effectiveness of the audit committee oversight process that all parties recognize that the audit committee and full board, as the representatives of the shareholders, are the ultimate entities to which the auditors are accountable. As such, the audit committee should review regularly the relationship between management and the outside and internal auditors.

¶102

Audit committees bring business judgment to bear on the financial matters within their purview. The SEC believes that agency rules facilitate the work of audit committees by establishing clear legal standards that they can use as benchmarks against which to exercise business judgment.

¶ 103 Auditor Disclosure of Fraud

As part of the Private Securities Litigation Reform Act of 1995, Congress added Section 10A to the Exchange Act to require auditors that take certain actions upon discovery of an illegal act. If an auditor learns of an illegal act that may be consequential to the company, Section 10A requires the auditor to inform the appropriate level of management of the illegal act and to assure that the company's audit committee is adequately informed as well. If management fails to act, and the independent accountant determines that the illegal act would have a material effect on the company's financial statements, the accountant must report the information to the board of directors.

A company whose board of directors receives such a report must inform the SEC not later than one business day after receipt of the report and, further, must give the independent accountant making the report a copy of the notice given to the SEC. An accountant who does not receive a copy of the notice before the expiration of the required one business day must either resign from the engagement or give the SEC a copy of its report not later than one business day following the failure to receive notice. An outside auditor electing to resign from the engagement must give the SEC a copy of its report not later than one business day following the company's failure to notify the SEC.

Because Section 10A is triggered regardless of whether an illegal act has a material effect on the company's financial statements, when the illegal act consists of a misstatement in the financial statements, the auditor must report that illegal act to the audit committee irrespective of any netting of the misstatements with other financial statement items. (See Staff Accounting Bulletin No. 99.)

Section 10A provides that no independent public accountant will be liable in a private action for any finding, conclusion or statement in the report. The SEC can, however, impose a civil penalty against an independent accountant that has willfully violated the statute's reporting provisions.

CHAPTER **2**

COMMITTEE'S COMPOSITION AND DUTIES

¶ 201 In General

The Sarbanes-Oxley Act mandates sweeping corporate disclosure and financial reporting reforms to improve the responsibility of public companies for their financial disclosures. Many of these reforms impose substantial new duties and requirements on the audit committee, as discussed throughout this chapter.

Section 2 of the Act defines "audit committee" to mean a committee established by and amongst a company's board of directors for the purpose of overseeing the company's accounting and financial reporting processes and audits of its financial statements. If a company has no such committee, the Act designates the entire board of directors as the company's audit committee. (Sarbanes-Oxley Act Section 2(a)(3).)

¶ 202 Sarbanes-Oxley Directive to SEC

Sarbanes-Oxley Act Section 301 promotes strong, effective audit committees in the performance of their oversight role. By increasing the competence of audit committees, the provisions are designed to further greater accountability and improve the quality of financial disclosure and oversight of the process by qualified and independent audit committees.

In light of corporate scandals such as the Enron failure, Congress determined that vigilant and informed oversight by a strong, effective, and independent audit committee could help to counterbalance pressures to misreport results and impose increased discipline on the process of preparing financial information. Improved oversight may help detect fraudulent financial reporting earlier and perhaps thus deter it or minimize its effects. Congress therefore codified a number of audit committee provisions in the securities laws in order to help rectify auditing misconduct and to enhance the effectiveness of audit committee oversight of public company audits.

Oversight of Independent Auditor

The auditing process may be compromised when auditors view their main responsibility as serving the company's management rather than its full board of directors or its audit committee. For this reason, the Sarbanes-Oxley Act requires audit committees to be directly responsible for the appointment, compensation, and oversight of the work of auditors, and requires auditors to report directly to the audit committee. (Sarbanes-Oxley Act Section 301; Exchange Act Section 10A(m)(2).)

Independence of Audit Committee

The Act mandates that audit committee members be independent and then enhances audit committee independence by barring audit committee members from accepting consulting fees or being affiliated persons of the company or its subsidiaries other than in the member's capacity as a member of the board or any board committee. The SEC is authorized to exempt particular relationships with respect to audit committee members as it determines appropriate in light of the circumstances. (Sarbanes-Oxley Act Section 301; Exchange Act Section 10A(m)(3).)

Procedures to Receive Complaints

The Act contains several additional provisions regarding audit committees. The Act requires audit committees to have in place procedures to receive and address complaints regarding accounting, internal control, or auditing issues. Further, it provides protection for corporate whistle blowers by specifying that audit committees must establish procedures for employees' anonymous submission of concerns regarding accounting or auditing matters. (Sarbanes-Oxley Act Section 301; Exchange Act Section 10A(m)(4).)

Hiring Counsel and Advisers

The Act also requires public companies to provide their audit committees with authority and funding to engage independent counsel and other advisers as they determine necessary in order to carry out their duties. (Sarbanes-Oxley Act Section 301; Exchange Act Section 10A(m)(5).)

Directions to SEC

Exchange Act Section 10A(m)(1), added by Sarbanes-Oxley Act Section 301 (reproduced at ¶ 2006), requires the SEC to direct, by rule, the national securities exchanges and national securities associations to prohibit the listing of any security of an issuer that is not in compliance with the enumerated standards regarding audit committees.

A company may have either a separately designated audit committee composed of members of its board or, if it chooses to do so or if it fails to form a separate committee, the entire board of directors would constitute the audit committee. If the entire board constituted the audit committee, the SEC mandates for the new SRO audit committee rules would apply to the company's board as a whole.

Because the SEC rules impose audit committee requirements that only would apply to issuers listed on a national securities exchange or listed in an automated inter-dealer quotation system of a national securities association, the requirements would apply only to issuers that are so listed. None of the requirements of Sarbanes-Oxley Act Section 301 or the underlying rules apply to other reporting companies under Exchange Act Section 13(a) or 15(d).

¶ 203 Independence of Committee

Sarbanes-Oxley demands that all the members of an audit committee be independent. Section 301 provides that, to be considered independent, an audit committee member cannot accept any consulting, advisory, or other compensatory fee from the company, other than in the member's capacity as a member of the board or any board committee, and cannot be an affiliated person of the company or any of its subsidiaries. (See ¶ 2006.) Thus, as discussed separately below, there are two basic criteria for audit committee independence: (1) not accepting a fee from the company; and (2) not being affiliated with the company

Fee Payment Prohibition

Implementing Sarbanes-Oxley, the SEC rules ban payment of consulting, advisory, or compensatory fees to audit committee members.

If the committee member is also a company shareholder, payments made to all shareholders of that class generally, such as dividends, will not be prohibited by this provision. Also, to conform the application of the compensatory fee prohibition with the affiliate prohibition, SEC rules clarify that the compensatory fee prohibition applies to fees from the company or any subsidiary.

The rules do not, however, specify any limits or restrictions on fees paid for capacity as a member of the board of directors or any board committee.

To prevent evasion of the requirement, disallowed payments to an audit committee member include payments made either directly or indirectly. For example, payments to spouses raise questions regarding independence comparable to those raised by payments to members themselves. In addition, payments for services to law firms, accounting firms, consulting firms, investment banks or financial advisory firms in which audit committee members are partners, members, executive officers or hold similar positions are the kinds of compensatory payments that were intended to be precluded by Sarbanes-Oxley.

The SEC rules, therefore, mandate that indirect acceptance of compensatory payments includes payments to spouses, minor children or stepchildren or children or stepchildren sharing a home with the member.

In addition, indirect acceptance includes payments accepted by an entity in which the audit committee member is a partner, member, officer such as a managing director occupying a comparable position or executive officer, or occupies a similar position, and which provides accounting, consulting, legal, investment banking or financial advisory services to the company or a subsidiary. This prohibition does not include limited partners, non-managing members and those occupying similar positions who, in each case, have no active role in providing services to the entity.

A number of other commercial relationships are not covered by the prohibition. For example, the rules do not prevent non-advisory financial services such as lending, check clearing, maintaining customer accounts, stock brokerage services or custodial and cash management services.

Further, the rules relate only to requirements for audit committee membership. They do not affect the ability of a director associated with an entity that provides such services to a listed issuer from otherwise serving on that company's board of directors, to the extent SRO rules permit such relationships.

The formulation developed by the SEC includes those persons, such as partners or members in professional organizations, regardless of control, whose compensation could be directly affected by the prohibited fees, even if they are not the primary service provider.

Compensation

The SEC rules specify that, unless listing standards provide otherwise, compensatory fees do not include the receipt of fixed amounts of compensation under a retirement plan, including deferred compensation, for prior service with the company so long as the compensation is not contingent in any way on continued service. The requirement that the compensation be fixed precludes retirement payments that are tied to the continued performance of the relevant entity. The requirement that the compensation be fixed, however, does not preclude customary objectively determined adjustment provisions such as cost of living adjustments.

Look-back provisions

The prohibitions apply only to current relationships with the audit committee member and related persons. They do not extend to a "look back" period before appointment to the audit committee, although listing standards usually require such periods. This approach is consistent with the language in Sarbanes-Oxley and the SEC's method of building and relying on SRO independence standards that already include look back periods for a broad variety of relationships.

De minimus exception

Neither the Sarbanes-Oxley Act nor the SEC rules provide a de minimus exception to the fee prohibition. The policies and purposes of Sarbanes-Oxley, particularly the use of the term "any" when describing such fees, weigh against providing such an exception.

Moreover, given the narrow class of services covered by the rules, the SEC feels that the lack of a de minimis exception should be less necessary. In addition, the SEC reasons that, if the level of compensation that the member or associated entity receives is truly de minimis, requiring a company to locate another provider so that the member can remain qualified for audit committee service should not be overly burdensome.

Affiliated Person Prohibition

The second basic criterion for determining independence is that an audit committee member cannot be an affiliated person of the company or any subsidiary. Consistent with other definitions of these terms under the securities laws, the SEC defines "affiliate" of, or a person "affiliated" with, a specified person, to mean a person that directly, or indirectly, controls, or is controlled by, or is under common control with, the person specified. "Control," in turn, means the possession of the power to direct or cause the direction of the management and policies of a person, whether through the ownership of voting securities, by contract, or otherwise.

Executive officers, directors that are also employees of an affiliate, general partners and managing members of an affiliate will be deemed to be affiliates. The limitation on directors will exclude outside directors of an affiliate from the automatic designation. Passive, non-control positions, such as limited partners, and those that do not have policy making functions, are not covered.

The formulation for being deemed to be an affiliate is narrower than the formulation of covered positions for the indirect acceptance aspect of the no compensation prong of the definition of independence due to their different purposes. A wider formulation for the no compensation prong was meant to capture those whose compensation is more directly linked to fees from the prohibited services but who otherwise do not hold executive positions.

Third-party representative

Consistent with historical SEC interpretations of the term "affiliate," an affiliate could not evade the prohibitions in the rule simply by designating a third-party representative or agent that it directs to act in its place.

Safe harbor

The definition of "affiliated person" requires a factual determination based on a consideration of all relevant facts and circumstances. In order to facilitate this analysis, the SEC adopted a safe harbor under which a person who is not an executive officer or a shareholder owning 10% or more of any class of voting equity securities will be deemed not to control. Note that the ownership prong should be based on ownership of any class of voting equity securities, instead of any class of equity securities.

Those persons that cannot rely on the safe harbor would not be deemed to be or presumed to be affiliates. They would need to conduct a facts and circumstances analysis of control.

The SEC cautioned that the 10% shareholder prong in the safe harbor should not be viewed as an upper ownership limit for non-affiliate status. While SROs in their listing rules could establish an upper ownership limit that would preclude independence, the SEC safe harbor does not establish such a limit.

The safe harbor is designed to identify a group of those that are not affiliates so as to provide comfort to those persons that no additional facts and circumstances analysis is necessary. It only creates a safe harbor position for non-affiliate status. Failing to meet the 10% ownership threshold has no bearing on whether a particular person is an affiliate based on an evaluation of all facts and circumstances. A director who is not an executive officer but beneficially owns more than 10% of company stock could be determined to be not an affiliate under a facts and circumstances analysis of control.

The safe harbor does not in any way specify or imply that a certain level of share ownership automatically presumes that a person is an affiliate. To prevent further misconceptions, the SEC added an explicit paragraph to the final rules to reinforce these points.

The rules clarify that the safe harbor is available not just for determinations with respect to the company, but to any specified person. Thus, the safe harbor is also available for determinations concerning the company's subsidiaries, which are also covered by the affiliate prohibition.

Beneficial ownership must be determined for purposes of the safe harbor, as well as for other aspects of the rule, such as the multiple-listing exception (see below), consistent with Exchange Act Rule 13d-3.

Exemption for New Issuers

Sarbanes-Oxley authorizes the SEC to exempt from the independence requirements particular relationships with respect to audit committee members, if appropriate in light of the circumstances. The SEC has exercised this exemptive power with regard to companies coming to market for the first time because these companies may face particular difficulty in recruiting members that meet the independence requirements. The Commission also believes that the audit committee of a new public company may function more effectively if it can maintain historical knowledge and experience during the transition to public company status.

Thus, new issuers must have:

- at least one fully independent member at the time of an their initial listing,
- a majority of independent members within 90 days, and
- a fully independent committee within one year.

Overlapping Board Memberships

Many companies, particularly financial institutions with a holding company structure, operate or obtain financing through subsidiaries. For these companies, the composition of the boards of the parent company and the subsidiary are sometimes similar given the control structure between the parent and the subsidiary. If an audit committee member of the parent is otherwise independent, merely serving also on the board of a controlled subsidiary should not adversely affect the board member's independence, assuming that the board member also would be considered independent of the subsidiary except for the member's seat on the parent's board.

With this dynamic in mind, the SEC granted an exemption from the affiliated person requirement for a committee member that sits on the board of directors of both a company and any affiliate so long as, except for being a director on each such board of directors, the member otherwise meets the independence requirements for each entity, including the receipt of only ordinary-course compensation for serving as a member of the board, audit committee, or any other board committee of each entity.

Audit committee members will still be required to be independent of the company and its affiliate, but the exemption will apply regardless of the source of control. Thus, the exemption is not conditioned on the subsidiary being both consolidated and majority-owned. Some companies may possess the requisite ownership to establish control, but may not consolidate the subsidiary due to particular accounting situations, while others may have the requisite control to consolidate by means other than ownership.

Foreign Private Issuers

The SEC has granted an accommodation to foreign private issuers operating under a dual holding company structure. Typically, in this situation, each holding company is a foreign private issuer organized in a different national jurisdiction. The holding companies together collectively own and supervise the management of one or more businesses conducted as a single economic enterprise.

The boards of directors of these dual holding companies may have all, some or no members in common. The dual holding companies may have established a joint audit committee for the group consisting of directors from each dual holding company. The audit committee members of such entities would otherwise meet the independence requirements for the overall group, but could technically be considered affiliates, or as persons who are not directors, because of the particular structural form of the dual holding companies.

¶203

In recognition of the dual structure, the SEC rules provide that, when an issuer is one of two dual holding companies, those companies may designate one audit committee for both companies so long as each audit committee member is a member of the board of directors of at least one of the dual holding companies.

In addition, dual holding companies will not be deemed to be affiliates of each other by virtue of their dual holding company arrangements with each other, including where directors of one dual holding company are also directors of the other dual holding company, or where directors of one or both dual holding companies are also directors of the businesses jointly controlled, directly or indirectly, by the dual holding companies, and in each case receive only ordinary-course compensation for serving as a member of the board of directors, audit committee or any other board committee of the dual holding companies.

Exemptive Requests and No-Action Letters

Given the purposes behind the Sarbanes-Oxley Act, the SEC will not entertain exemptions or waivers for particular relationships on a case-by-case basis. Similarly, Commission staff will not entertain no-action letter or exemption requests in this area. The SEC does, however, have the exemptive authority to respond to, and will remain sensitive to, evolving standards of corporate governance, including changes in U.S. or foreign law, to address any new conflicts not anticipated at the time of the rules' initial adoption.

NYSE and Nasdaq Listing Requirements

Through their corporate governance listing standards, the self-regulatory organizations play an important role in assuring that their listed companies establish good governance practices and maintain effective oversight of the reliability of corporate financial information. The Sarbanes-Oxley Act has had a significant impact on these listing standards, particularly when it comes to audit committees and their independence from company management.

In response to a directive of the Sarbanes-Oxley Act, the SEC adopted Rule 10A-3 under the Exchange Act. Rule 10A-3 requires the rules of the national securities exchanges or national securities associations to prohibit the listing of any security of a company that is not in compliance with the rule's requirements regarding audit committees.

As a result of these Commission and Congressional initiatives, the NYSE and Nasdaq adopted rule changes intended to assure that a listed company's board of directors and key committees are comprised in a manner that is designed to provide an objective oversight role and that directors and management adhere to high standards of conduct. In addition, the standards strengthened the independence of audit committees. The SEC approved the changes in November of 2003, (See Release No. 34-48745).

Both the NYSE and Nasdaq listing standards require a company to have a minimum three-person audit committee composed entirely of independent directors. The standards also require each member of the audit committee to meet financial literacy requirements and that at least one audit committee member have increased financial sophistication. Regarding the latter requirement, the standards provide that a director who qualifies as an audit committee financial expert under SEC rules is presumed to qualify for the increased sophistication requirements.

In commentary to its listing standards, the NYSE said that each member of the audit committee must be financially literate, as such qualification is interpreted by the board in its business judgment, or must become financially literate within a reasonable period of time after his or her appointment to the audit committee. Further, at least one member of the audit committee is required to have accounting or related financial management expertise, as the company's board interprets such qualification in its business judgment.

Both the NYSE and Nasdaq adopted the cure period provided in SEC Rule 10A-3(a)(3) for audit committee members who cease to be independent for reasons outside the company's reasonable control. Under the cure provision of the SEC rule, a company is given a chance to cure any defects that would be the basis for a prohibition. Thus, if a member of an audit committee ceases to be independent for reasons outside the company's reasonable control, that person may remain an audit committee member until the earlier of the next annual shareholders meeting or one year from the occurrence of the event that caused the member to be no longer independent.

The NYSE requires a special board determination and disclosure in certain instances if an audit committee member simultaneously serves on the audit committee of more than three public companies.

In commentary to the listing standards, the NYSE cautioned that, because of the audit committee's demanding responsibilities, and the time commitment attendant to committee membership, each prospective audit committee member should evaluate carefully the existing demands on his or her time before accepting the assignment. Additionally, if an audit committee member simultaneously serves on the audit committees of more than three public companies, and the listed company does not limit the number of audit committees on which its audit committee members serve, then in each case, the board must determine that such simultaneous service would not impair the ability of the member to effectively serve on the audit committee and disclose such determination in the company's proxy statement.

The NASD rules provide that, under exceptional and limited circumstances, the board may appoint one audit committee member who is not independent and who is not a current officer or employee of the company or a family member of such person if the board determines that membership on the committee by the individual is required by the best interests of the company and its shareholders. Further, the board must disclose, in the next annual proxy statement subsequent to such determination, the nature of the relationship and the reasons for that determination. A member appointed under this exception would not be permitted to serve longer than two years and would not be permitted to chair the audit committee.

Both the NYSE and Nasdaq require that the audit committee have a written charter addressing the committee's purpose and responsibilities. The SEC believes that requiring companies to specify the enhanced audit committee duties in their formal written charters, and to delineate how the committee carries out those duties, will help assure that the audit committee, management, investors, and the company's auditors recognize the function of the audit committee and the relationship among the parties.

Moreover, the NYSE and Nasdaq explicitly require the audit committee to have the duties specified in SEC Rule 10A-3, including direct responsibility for the appointment, compensation, retention and oversight of the company's outside auditor; the ability to engage outside advisors; the ability to obtain funding for the audit committee and its outside advisors; and the responsibility to establish procedures for the receipt, retention and treatment of complaints regarding accounting, internal accounting controls or auditing matters, including procedures for the confidential, anonymous submission of employee complaints.

The NYSE audit committee charter provision provides details as to the duties and responsibilities of the audit committee that must be addressed. These include:

- the responsibility to annually obtain and review a report by the independent auditor;
- discuss the company's financial statements with management and the independent auditor;
- discuss the company's earnings press releases, as well as financial information and earnings guidance provided to analysts and rating agencies;
- discuss policies with respect to risk assessment and risk management;
- meet separately and periodically with management, and with the external and internal auditors;
- review with the independent auditors any audit problems or difficulties and management's response;
- set clear hiring policies for employees or former employees of the independent auditors;
- report regularly to the board

In its regular report to the board, the audit committee should review any issues that arise with respect to the quality or integrity of the company's financial statements, the company's compliance with legal or regulatory requirements, the performance and independence of the company's independent auditors, or the performance of the internal audit function. (See NYSE commentary to Section 303A(7), NYSE Listed Company Manual).

Annual Review of Auditor

After reviewing the independent auditor's report and its work throughout the year, the audit committee will be in a position to evaluate the auditor's qualifications, performance and independence. According to the NYSE, this evaluation should include the review and evaluation of the lead partner of the independent auditor.

In making its evaluation, the audit committee should take into account the opinions of management and the company's internal auditors. In addition to assuring the regular rotation of the lead audit partner as required by law, the audit committee should further consider whether, in order to assure continuing auditor independence, there should be regular rotation of the audit firm itself. The audit committee should present its conclusions with respect to the independent auditor to the full board. (See NYSE commentary to Section 303A(7), NYSE Listed Company Manual).

Discussion of Earnings Releases

The NYSE has assured that the audit committee's duty to discuss earnings releases, as well as financial information and earnings guidance, may be done generally. For example, they may discuss the types of information to be disclosed and the type of presentation to be made. Further, the audit committee need not discuss in advance each earnings release or each instance in which a company may provide earnings guidance. (See NYSE commentary to Section 303A(7), NYSE Listed Company Manual).

Risk Management Discussion

It is ultimately the duty of senior management to manage the company's exposure to risk. But the audit committee must discuss guidelines and policies to govern the process by which this is handled. The audit committee should discuss the company's major financial risk exposures and the steps management has taken to monitor and control such exposures. Many financial companies manage their risk through mechanisms other than the audit committee. The processes these companies have in place should be reviewed in a general manner by the audit committee, but they need not be replaced by the audit committee. (See NYSE commentary to Section 303A(7), NYSE Listed Company Manual).

Sessions with Management and Review of Auditor

To perform its oversight functions most effectively, the audit committee must have the benefit of separate sessions with management, the independent auditors and those responsible for the internal audit function. And the standards require all listed companies to have an internal audit function. In the NYSE's view, these separate sessions may be more productive than joint sessions in surfacing issues warranting committee attention. (See NYSE commentary to Section 303A(7), NYSE Listed Company Manual).

It is similarly important that the audit committee regularly review with the independent auditor any difficulties it encountered in the course of the audit work, including any restrictions on scope or on access to requested information, as well as any significant disagreements with management. Among the items the audit committee may want to review with the auditor are:

- any accounting adjustments that were noted or proposed by the auditor but were passed as immaterial or otherwise;

- any communications between the audit team and the audit firm's national office respecting auditing or accounting issues presented by the engagement;

- any management or internal control letter issued, or proposed to be issued, by the audit firm to the company.

- any discussion of the responsibilities, budget and staffing of the company's internal audit function.

Accurate Financial Statements

While the fundamental responsibility for the company's financial statements and disclosures rests with management and the independent auditor, the NYSE generally expects the audit committee to review:

- major issues on accounting principles and financial statement presentations, including significant changes in the company's application of accounting principles;

- major issues as to the adequacy of the company's internal controls and any special audit steps adopted in light of material control deficiencies;

¶203

- analyses prepared by management or the independent auditor setting forth significant financial reporting issues and judgments made in connection with the preparation of the financial statements, including analyses of the effects of alternative GAAP methods;

- the effect of regulatory and accounting initiatives, as well as off-balance sheet structures, on the financial statements; and

- the type and presentation of information to be included in earnings press releases, particularly the use of pro forma information, as well as any earnings guidance.

It is important to note that the NYSE considers the specified audit committee functions to be the sole responsibility of the audit committee; and, as such, they may not be allocated to a different committee.

¶ 204 Oversight of Outside Auditor

Sarbanes-Oxley reinforces the concept that one of the audit committee's primary functions is to enhance the independence of the audit function, thereby furthering the objectivity of financial reporting. Moreover, the SEC has long recognized the importance of an auditor's independence in the audit process.

The auditing process may be compromised when a company's outside auditors view their main responsibility as serving the company's management rather than its full board of directors or its audit committee. This may occur if the auditor views management as its employer with hiring, firing and compensatory powers. Under these conditions, the auditor may not have the appropriate incentive to raise concerns and conduct an objective review. Further, if the auditor does not appear independent to the public, then investor confidence is undermined and one purpose of the audit is frustrated.

To promote auditor independence, the auditor should be hired, evaluated and, if necessary, terminated by the audit committee. This would help align the auditor's interests with those of shareholders.

In furtherance of these goals, SEC rules provide that the audit committee is directly responsible for the appointment, compensation, retention and oversight of the work of any public accounting firm engaged to prepare or issue an audit report or performing other audit, review or attest services for the company. This oversight would include the resolution of disagreements between management and the auditor regarding financial reporting.

The independent auditor will report directly to the audit committee.

The audit committee can retain the outside auditor, which includes the power to terminate the outside auditor. In addition, in connection with these oversight duties, the audit committee has ultimate authority to approve all audit engagement fees and terms. The SEC has provided these duties as examples. They are not intended to be an exclusive list of responsibilities.

The rules embody the concept that specific decisions regarding the execution of the audit committee's oversight duties, as well as decisions on the extent of desired involvement by the audit committee, are best left to the discretion of the audit committee of the individual company in assessing individual corporate circumstances.

The scope of the services included in the requirement, including "audit, review or attest services," encompass the same services covered in the "Audit

Fees" category in a company's disclosure of fees paid to its independent public accountants. As discussed in the SEC release revising the auditor independence requirements, this category includes services that normally would be provided by the accountant in connection with statutory and regulatory filings or engagements.

In addition to services necessary to perform an audit or review in accordance with generally accepted auditing standards, this category also may include services that generally only the independent accountant reasonably can provide, such as comfort letters, statutory audits, attest services, consents and assistance with and review of documents filed with the Commission.

This approach does not affect the operation of other SEC rules regarding permissible services; or preclude the audit committee from oversight or other involvement in the provision of audit-related or other permissible services.

The SEC has decided not to extend the audit committee's duties to the appointment, compensation, retention and oversight of a company's internal auditor.

Instructions to the rules clarify that the audit committee requirements neither conflict with nor affect the application of any requirement or ability under a company's governing law or documents or other home country legal or listing provisions that require or permit shareholders to ultimately vote on, approve or ratify such requirements. In addition, if such responsibilities are vested with shareholders, and the company provides a recommendation or nomination regarding such matters to its shareholders, the audit committee must be responsible for making the recommendation or nomination.

The instructions also provide that the audit committee requirements do not conflict with requirements in a company's home jurisdiction prohibiting the full board of directors from delegating such responsibilities, such a auditor selection, to the audit committee or limit the degree of such delegation. In that case, the audit committee must be granted such responsibilities, which can include advisory powers, with respect to such matters to the extent permitted by law, including submitting nominations or recommendations to the full board.

Foreign Private Issuers

In certain jurisdictions, the government must select the outside auditor for some foreign private issuers. Instructions clarify that the requirements in SEC rules do not conflict with any requirement in a company's home jurisdiction vesting such responsibilities with government. Similar to the other instructions, in such an instance the audit committee should be granted such responsibilities, which can include advisory powers, with respect to such matters to the extent permitted by law.

¶ 205 Procedures for Handling Complaints

The audit committee must place some reliance on management for information about the company's financial reporting process. Since the audit committee is dependent to a degree on the information provided to it by management and internal and outside auditors, it is imperative for the committee to cultivate open and effective channels of information.

Management may not have the appropriate incentives to self-report all questionable practices. A company employee or other individual may be reticent to report concerns regarding questionable accounting or other matters for fear of management reprisal.

The establishment of formal procedures for receiving and handling complaints should serve to facilitate disclosures, encourage proper individual conduct and alert the audit committee to potential problems before they have serious consequences.

Thus, implementing a Sarbanes-Oxley mandate, SEC rules require audit committees to establish procedures for:

- The receipt, retention and treatment of complaints received by the company regarding accounting, internal accounting controls or auditing matters; and
- The confidential, anonymous submission by company employees of concerns regarding questionable accounting or auditing matters.

The SEC did not mandate specific procedures that the audit committee must establish. Instead, it preferred to leave flexibility to the audit committee to develop appropriate procedures in light of a company's individual circumstances, so long as the required parameters are met.

Given the variety of listed companies, audit committees should be provided with flexibility to develop and utilize procedures appropriate for their circumstances. The procedures that will be most effective to meet the requirements for a small company with few employees could be quite different from the processes and systems that would need to be in place for large, multinational corporations with thousands of employees in many different jurisdictions. Thus, a "one-size-fits-all" approach is not appropriate.

The SEC expects each audit committee to develop procedures that work best consistent with its company's individual circumstances to meet the requirements.

Although the scope of the requirements generally includes complaints received by a company regardless of source, Exchange Act Section 10A(m)(4)(B) and the relevant portion of the rules referring to confidential, anonymous submission of concerns are directed to employees of the company. But note that the requirement is not limited to only employees in the financial reporting area.

Investment Companies

Investment companies rarely have direct employees. Thus, some have suggested that, for investment companies, the confidential, anonymous submission requirements should extend to employees of entities engaged by an investment company to prepare or assist in preparing its financial statements.

The SEC encourages the SROs to consider the appropriate scope of the requirement with regard to investment companies, taking account of the fact that most services are rendered to an investment company by employees of third parties, such as the investment adviser, rather than by the investment company's own employees.

¶ 206 Authority to Engage Advisors

To be effective, an audit committee must have the necessary resources and authority to fulfill its function. Since the audit committee likely is not equipped to self-advise on all accounting, financial reporting or legal matters, effective performance of its role dictates that the committee have the authority to engage its own outside advisors, including experts in particular areas of accounting, as it determines necessary.

Cautionary Note: This authority should be apart from counsel or advisors hired by management, especially when potential conflicts of interest with management may be apparent.

The advice of outside advisors may be necessary to identify potential conflicts of interest and assess the company's disclosure and other compliance obligations with an independent and critical eye. Often, outside advisors can draw on their experience and knowledge to identify best practices of other companies that might be appropriate. The assistance of outside advisors also may be needed to independently investigate questions that may arise regarding financial reporting and compliance with the securities laws.

Thus, the SEC rules specifically authorize the audit committee to engage outside advisors, including counsel, as it determines necessary to carry out its duties. The rules do not preclude, however, access to, or advice from, the company's internal counsel or regular outside counsel. They also do not require an audit committee to retain independent counsel.

¶ 207 Funding

The SEC rules mandate that the company must provide funding to the audit committee in three distinct areas:

- To compensate any public accounting firm engaged for the purpose of preparing or issuing an audit report or performing other audit, review or attest services for the company

- To pay any advisors employed by the audit committee.

- To fund ordinary administrative expenses of the audit committee that are necessary or appropriate in carrying out its duties.

The appropriate funding will be determined by the audit committee in its capacity as a committee of the board of directors. The rules do not set funding limits. There is a belief, and the SEC seems to share it, that audit committee members' own fiduciary duties to the company, coupled with natural oversight by the board of directors as a whole, will address any possible funding abuses.

In general, the reasoning behind the independent funding is that an audit committee's effectiveness may be compromised if it is dependent on management to compensate the independent auditor or the advisors that it employs, especially when potential conflicts of interest with management may be apparent.

Independent funding will also further the standard relating to the audit committee's responsibility to appoint, compensate, retain and oversee the outside auditor. Similarly, it will add meaning to the standard relating to the audit committee's authority to engage independent advisors.

Not only could an audit committee be hindered in its ability to perform its duties objectively by not having control over the ability to compensate these advisors, but the role of the advisors also could be compromised if they have to rely on management for compensation. Thus, absent such a provision, both the audit committee and the advisors could be less willing to address disagreements or other issues with management.

¶ 208 Exemptions

Sarbanes-Oxley made no distinction when it prohibited the listing of any security of an issuer that does not meet the new standards for audit committees. Accordingly, the SEC rules apply not just to voting equity securities, but to any listed security, regardless of its type, including debt securities and derivative securities.

Investors in all securities, whether common equity or fixed income, will benefit from the increased financial oversight of a company resulting from a strong and effective audit committee.

To avoid undue burdens, however, the SEC adopted several exemptions consistent with the purposes and policies of Sarbanes-Oxley, such as the overlapping board exemption and the multiple-listing exemption.

Multiple Listings

Many companies today issue multiple classes of securities through various ownership structures on various markets. For example, a company may have a class of common equity securities listed on one market, several classes of debt listed on one or more other markets, and derivative securities listed on yet another market. If an issuer already was subject to the audit committee requirements as a result of one listing, there would be little or no additional benefit from having the requirements imposed on the issuer due to an additional listing.

In addition, companies often issue non-equity securities through controlled subsidiaries for various reasons. Requiring these subsidiaries, which often have no purpose other than to issue or guarantee the securities, to be subject to the audit committee requirements would add little additional benefit if the subsidiary is closely controlled or consolidated by a parent issuer that is subject to the requirements. Instead, imposing the requirements on these subsidiaries could create an onerous burden on the parent to recruit and maintain an audit committee meeting the requirements for each specific subsidiary.

With this in mind, the SEC granted an exemption from the requirements for listings of additional classes of securities of an issuer at any time it is subject to the requirements as a result of the listing of a class of common equity or similar securities. The additional listings could be on the same market or on different markets. The exemption for additional classes of a listed issuer will apply if any class of the issuer's securities is listed on a national securities exchange or national securities association subject to these rules.

But note that, just as an SRO may adopt standards for audit committees that are stricter than those provided in Sarbanes-Oxley, they also may apply their listing standards to classes of securities where Sarbanes-Oxley would not require it. For example, in the case of an issuer with a class of debt securities listed on an SRO subject to these rules, another SRO may condition listing by that issuer of its common equity securities on full compliance with that second SRO's listing standards regarding the new audit committee requirements.

Moreover, since the SEC rules do not embody a first in time principle, once the class of common equity securities was listed on the second SRO subject to SEC requirements, unless SRO rules provide otherwise, the multiple-listing exemption could be applied in respect of the debt securities listed on the first SRO.

The exemption was also extended to listings of non-equity securities by subsidiaries of a parent company so long as the parent is subject to the requirements as a result of the listing of a class of equity securities. This exemption is conditioned on ensuring that the parent company's audit committee is in the appropriate position to provide oversight for the subsidiary's financial reporting.

This is most likely to be the case if the parent consolidates the subsidiary into its own financial statements. Nevertheless, the SEC understands that a parent may possess the requisite ownership threshold, but may not consolidate the subsidiary due to particular accounting situations. Similarly, 50% owned joint ventures may not be consolidated by the two parents that exercise joint control.

Thus, the exemption includes listings of non-equity securities by a direct or indirect subsidiary that is consolidated or at least 50% beneficially owned by a parent company, if the parent company is subject to the requirements as a result of the listing of a class of its equity securities. However, if the subsidiary were to list its own equity securities (other than non-convertible, non-participating preferred securities), the subsidiary must meet the requirements to protect its own shareholders.

The multiple-listing exemption is available to U.S. subsidiaries if the parent is a foreign private issuer, even if the foreign parent is relying on one of the special exemptions for foreign private issuers. However, the special exemptions available to the foreign parent are not available to its U.S. subsidiary.

Security Futures Products

The SEC has bestowed an exemption from the audit committee requirements for the listing of a security futures product cleared by a clearing agency that is registered under Exchange Act Section 17A or exempt from registration under Section 17A(b)(7). A similar exemption was provided for the listing of standardized options issued by a clearing agency registered under Exchange Act Section 17A.

The exemptions are based on the fact that the role of the clearing agency for security futures products and standardized options is fundamentally different from a conventional issuer of securities. For example, the purchaser of these products does not, except in the most formal sense, make an investment decision regarding the clearing agency. As a result, information about the clearing agency's business, its officers and directors and its financial statements is less relevant to investors in these products than to investors in the underlying security.

Similarly, the investment risk in these products is determined by the market performance of the underlying security rather than the performance of the clearing agency. Moreover, the clearing agencies are self-regulatory organizations subject to regulatory oversight. Furthermore, unlike a conventional issuer, the clearing agency does not receive the proceeds from sales of security futures products or standardized options.

¶ 209 Foreign Issuers

Sarbanes-Oxley makes no distinction between domestic and foreign issuers. With the growing globalization of the capital markets, the importance of maintaining effective oversight of the financial reporting process is relevant for listed securities of any issuer, regardless of its domicile. Many foreign private issuers already maintain audit committees, and the global trend appears to be toward establishing audit committees. Thus, the SEC rules apply to listings by foreign private issuers as well as domestic issuers.

The Commission is aware, however, that its requirements may conflict with legal requirements, corporate governance standards and the methods for providing auditor oversight in the home jurisdictions of some foreign issuers. Thus, the SEC has attempted to address concerns regarding the specific areas in which foreign corporate governance arrangements differ significantly from general practices among U.S. corporations.

Supervisory Boards

Some countries, such as Germany, require that non-management employees, who would not be viewed as independent under SEC regulations, serve on the supervisory board or audit committee. Having such employees serve on the board or audit committee can provide an independent check on management, which itself is one of the purposes of the independence requirements under the Sarbanes-Oxley Act. Thus, the SEC has provided a limited exemption from the independence requirements to address this concern, so long as the employees are not executive officers, as defined by Exchange Act Rule 3b-7.

Rule 3b-7 defines executive officer to be a company president, any vice president in charge of a principal business unit, division or function (such as sales, administration or finance), any other officer who performs a policy-making function or any other person who performs similar policy-making functions. Executive officers of subsidiaries may be deemed executive officers of the company if they perform such policy-making functions

Some foreign private issuers have a two-tier board system, with one tier designated as the management board and the other tier designated as the supervisory or non-management board. In this circumstance, the SEC believes that the supervisory board is the body within the company best equipped to comply with the requirements.

In the case of foreign private issuers with two-tier board systems, the term "board of directors" means the supervisory or non-management board for purposes of Sarbanes-Oxley. As such, the supervisory board can either form a separate audit committee or, if the entire board is independent, the entire board can be designated as the audit committee.

Controlling Shareholders

Controlling shareholders are more prevalent among foreign issuers than in the U.S., and they have traditionally played a more prominent role in corporate governance. In jurisdictions providing for audit committees, representation of controlling shareholders on these committees is common. The SEC believes that a limited exception from the independence requirements can accommodate this practice without undercutting the fundamental purposes of the rules.

Thus, SEC rules provide that one member of the audit committee can be a controlling shareholder representative so long as the "no compensation" prong of the independence requirements is satisfied, the member has only observer non-voting status, is not the chair of the audit committee, and is not an executive officer of the company.

This limited exception is designed to address foreign practices, assure independent membership and an independent chair of the audit committee,

¶209

and still exclude management from the committee. Since the exemption is designed to provide only a limited accommodation for the practices of some foreign private issuers, it was not extended to domestic issuers.

Foreign Governments

Foreign governments may have significant shareholdings in some foreign private issuers or may own special shares that entitle the government to exercise certain rights relating to these issuers. However, due to their shareholdings or other rights, these representatives may not be considered independent under SEC rules.

To address foreign practices, any audit committee member can be a representative of a foreign government or foreign governmental entity so long as the "no compensation" prong of the independence requirement is satisfied and the member is not an executive officer of the company. Further, the exemption applies regardless of the manner in which the foreign government owns its interest. Thus, it may hold shares directly, or through various branches or agencies, or through an institution organized under public law. The legal form of the entity that holds the governmental shareholdings is not determinative.

Boards of Auditors

Although there is a trend toward having audit committees in foreign jurisdictions, several foreign jurisdictions require or provide for auditor oversight through a board of auditors or similar body, or groups of statutory auditors, that are in whole or in part separate from the board of directors. These boards of auditors or statutory auditors are intended to be independent of management, although their members may not in all cases meet all of the independence requirements set forth in Sarbanes-Oxley. In addition, although these bodies provide independent oversight of outside auditors, they may not have all of the responsibilities set forth in the SEC rules.

The establishment of an audit committee in addition to these bodies, with duplicative functions, might not only be costly and inefficient, but it also could generate possible conflicts of powers and duties. Thus, the SEC provides that the listing of securities of a foreign private issuer will be exempt from all of the audit committee requirements if the issuer meets the following requirements:

- The foreign private issuer has a board of auditors or similar body, or has statutory auditors, established and selected pursuant to home country legal or listing provisions expressly requiring or permitting such a board or similar body;

- The board of auditors must be either separate from the board of directors, or composed of one or more members of the board of directors and one or more members that are not also members of the board of directors;

- The board of auditors are not elected by management and no executive officer is a member;

- Home country legal or listing provisions set forth or provide for standards for the independence of the board of auditors from the company or its management;

- The board of auditors, in accordance with any applicable home country legal or listing requirements or the company's governing documents, is responsible for the appointment, retention and oversight of the work of any public accounting firm engaged (including, the resolution of disagreements between management and the auditor regarding financial reporting) for the purpose of preparing or issuing an audit report or performing other audit, review or attest services for the company; and

- The remaining requirements in the rule, such as the complaint procedures requirement, advisors requirement and funding requirement, apply to the board of auditors, to the extent permitted by law.

This formulation attempts to address the jurisdictions that provide for boards of auditors or similar structures. In all instances, the requirements in the exemption are to apply consistent with home country requirements.

The SEC recognizes that these bodies, although designed to provide independent oversight of outside auditors, may not meet all of the same requirements or have all of the responsibilities set forth in the rules. The Commission, however, reasons that this approach is still a preferable method of implementing the Sarbanes-Oxley Act protections against the backdrop of this particular category of conflicting home country governance framework.

Cautionary Note: There is no requirement that the issuer must also be listed on a market outside the U.S. In addition, the relief was not extended to foreign private issuers that have audit committees.

¶ 210 Passive Issuers

Asset-backed issuers are subject to substantially different reporting requirements. Most significantly, they generally need not file the types of financial statements that other companies must file. Also, such entities typically are passive pools of assets, without a board of directors or persons acting in a similar capacity. Thus, the audit committee rules exclude asset-backed issuers.

Similarly, the SEC rules allow SROs to exclude issuers that are organized as trusts or other unincorporated associations that do not have a board of directors or persons acting in a similar capacity and whose activities are limited to passively owning or holding securities, rights, collateral or other assets on behalf of, or for the benefit of, the holders of the listed securities. Structures such as royalty trusts are included in the exemption because they are mere conduits though which proceeds on the underlying assets are distributed to shareholders.

The exemption does not, however, extend to structures that hold, in addition to the royalty interest, an interest in the operating company that actually owns the oil and gas properties, such as structures commonly known as Canadian income trusts. In these situations, the trustee often also delegates significant management decisions to an operating company, which in turn may delegate those decisions to a manager. The operating company often has a board of directors that is appointed by both the manager and the trust unit holders. Such structures should be treated in a manner similar to limited partnerships.

¶ 211 Compliance Procedures

Sarbanes-Oxley does not establish specific mechanisms for an exchange or securities association to ensure that companies comply with the audit committee standards on an ongoing basis. SROs must comply with statutory provisions and SEC rules and must enforce their own rules, including rules that govern listing requirements and affect their listed issuers.

In addition, the SEC rules direct the SROs to require a listed issuer to notify the applicable SRO promptly after a company executive officer becomes aware of any material noncompliance with the audit committee requirements. In addition, the SEC encouraged, but did not require, SROs to impose a similar requirement for noncompliance with other SRO listing standards that pertain to corporate governance standards apart from the audit committee requirements.

Curing Defects

Sarbanes-Oxley specifies that there must be appropriate procedures for a company to have an opportunity to cure any defects that would be the basis for a prohibition of its securities as a result of its failure to meet the audit committee standards, before imposition of such a prohibition. To effectuate this mandate, the SEC rules require SROs to establish such procedures before they prohibit the listing of or delist any security.

The SEC believes that existing continued listing or maintenance standards and delisting procedures of the SROs generally will suffice as procedures for a firm to have an opportunity to cure any defects on an ongoing basis. These procedures already provide for notice and opportunity for a hearing, an opportunity for an appeal and an opportunity to cure any defects before securities are delisted. The SEC cautioned, however, that these procedures cannot include an extended exemption or waiver of the requirements apart from those provided for in the rules.

The SEC decided not to mandate specific time periods for an opportunity to cure defects. But the Commission expects that the rules of each SRO will provide for definite procedures and time periods for compliance to the extent they do not already do so.

Loss of Independence

There are rare situations when audit committee members cease to be independent for reasons outside their reasonable control. For example, an audit committee member could be a partner in a law firm that provides no services to the listed issuer on which the member sits, but the listed issuer could acquire another company that is one of the law firm's clients. Without an opportunity to cure such a defect, the audit committee member would cease to be independent.

Additional time may be necessary to cure such defects, such as ceasing the company's relationship with the audit committee member's firm or replacing the audit committee member.

Thus, the SEC allows SRO implementing rules to provide that audit committee members who cease to be independent for reasons outside their reasonable control may, with notice by the issuer to the applicable exchange or securities association, remain an audit committee member until the earlier of the next annual company meeting or one year from the occurrence of the event that caused the member to no longer be independent.

¶ 212 Disclosure of Section 301 Requirements

The SEC believes it is important for investors to know if a company is availing itself of one of the exemptions from the audit committee rules. Thus, companies must disclose their reliance on an exemption and their assessment of whether, and if so, how, such reliance will materially adversely affect the ability of their audit committee to act independently and to satisfy the other requirements of the rules.

This disclosure should appear in, or be incorporated by reference into, annual reports filed with the Commission. The disclosure should also appear in proxy statements or information statements subject to the proxy rules for shareholders' meetings at which elections for directors are held.

The purpose of the disclosure is not to single out particular companies or to imply that a particular listed company's home country regime is somehow less effective. Instead, the disclosure is designed to provide additional transparency to investors regarding the audit committee arrangements and the company's assessment of the effectiveness of those arrangements.

The disclosure is to be included in Part III of annual reports on Form 10-K and 10-KSB through an addition to Item 401 of Regulations S-K and S-B. Consequently, companies subject to the proxy rules will be able to incorporate the required disclosure from a proxy or information statement that involves the election of directors into the annual report, if the company filed such proxy or information statement within 120 days after the end of the fiscal year covered by the report. (See General Instruction G.(3) of Form 10-K and General Instruction E.3 of Form 10-KSB.)

For foreign private issuers that file their annual reports on Form 20-F, the disclosure requirement will appear in new Item 16D. For foreign private issuers that file their annual reports on Form 40-F, the disclosure requirement will appear in paragraph (14) to General Instruction B.

For registered investment companies, the disclosure will appear in Item 5(b) of Form N-CSR and Item 22(b)(14) of Schedule 14A.

Unit Investment Trusts

Unit investment trusts are excluded from the disclosure requirements relating to their use of the general exemption for UITs. As a passive investment vehicle, a UIT has no board of directors, and there is little reason why investors would expect a UIT to have an audit committee.

Multiple-Listing Exemption

Similarly excluded are companies availing themselves of the multiple-listing exemption. These companies, or their controlling parents, will be required to comply with the audit committee requirements as a result of a separate listing. Thus, disclosure of the use of that exemption will not serve the purpose of highlighting for investors those issuers that are different from most other listed issuers.

Other Exemptions

Finally, the SEC also excluded from the exemption disclosure requirement those companies that rely on the exemptions for overlapping boards, security futures products, standardized options, securities issued by foreign governments and securities issued by asset-backed issuers and similar passive issuers.

For overlapping boards, issuers relying on that exemption will still be required to have independent directors, so disclosure of the exemption would not serve to highlight those issuers that are different from most issuers.

Regarding security futures products, standardized options, foreign governments and asset-backed issuers and similar passive issuers, like unit investment trusts, there would be little reason to believe that they would have audit committees.

SEC proxy rules currently require companies to disclose in their proxy statement or information statement, if action is to be taken with respect to the election of directors, whether the company has a standing audit committee, the names of each committee member, the number of committee meetings held by the audit committee during the last fiscal year and the functions performed by the committee. (See Item 7(d)(1) of Schedule 14A.) Identical information is required with respect to nominating and compensation committees of the board of directors

The SEC believes it important for investors to be able to readily determine basic information about the composition of the audit committee. To foster greater availability of this basic information, the SEC also requires that disclosure of the members of the audit committee be included or incorporated by reference in the annual report. Also, because the Exchange Act now provides that in the absence of an audit committee the entire board of directors will be considered to be the audit committee, a company that has not separately designated an audit committee must disclose that the entire board of directors is acting as the audit committee.

Similarly, the SEC rules require foreign private issuers that file their annual reports on Form 40-F to disclose members of the audit committee. Foreign private issuers that file their annual reports on Form 20-F already must identify the members of their audit committee in their annual reports. The SEC also requires these issuers to disclose if the entire board of directors is acting as the audit committee.

If the company is relying on the exemption in Exchange Act Rule 10A-3(c)(3) because it has a board of auditors or similar body, the disclosure required by that item with regard to the company's audit committee can be provided with respect to the company's board of auditors, or similar body. (See instruction to Item 6.C in Form 20-F.)

The rules are similar for registered management investment companies. (See Item 22(b)(14) of Schedule 14A and Item 5 of Form N-CSR.)

Listed issuers that do not have to disclose their reliance on one of the rule's exemptions, such as a subsidiary relying on the multiple-listing exemption, a foreign government issuer or an asset-backed issuer or similar issuer, are excluded from the requirement to disclose whether or not they have a separate audit committee. Because these listed issuers need not disclose that they are availing themselves of an exemption to the audit committee requirements, it would be anomalous to require them to disclose whether or not they have an audit committee.

Similarly, unit investment trusts need not disclose their use of the exemption under Exchange Act Rule 10A-3(c)(6)(ii). (See Exchange Act Rule 10A-3(d).) UITs are not subject to any requirement that they disclose whether or not they have a separate audit committee, since UITs do not file proxy or information statements where action must be taken with respect to election of directors, or Form N-CSR, where such disclosure would be made.

¶212

Chapter 3

Internal Controls

¶ 301 In General

To improve the quality of reporting and increase investor confidence, the Sarbanes-Oxley Act requires management to assess the company's internal controls. Specifically, Section 404 (reproduced at ¶ 2007) requires that annual reports filed with the SEC be accompanied by a statement by company management that management is responsible for creating and maintaining adequate internal controls. Management must also present its assessment of the effectiveness of those controls. Section 404 is modeled on a similar requirement enacted in 1991 and imposed on depository institutions through Section 36 of the Federal Deposit Insurance Act.

In addition, the company's auditor must report on and attest to management's assessment of the company's internal controls. In requiring the registered public accounting firm preparing the audit report to attest to and report on management's assessment of internal controls, Congress does not intend that the auditor's evaluation be the subject of a separate engagement or the basis for increased charges or fees.

High quality audits typically incorporate extensive internal control testing. Congress intends that the auditor's assessment of the company's system of internal controls should be considered to be a core responsibility of the auditor and an integral part of the audit report.

A key aspect of management's responsibility for the preparation of financial information is its responsibility to establish and maintain an internal control system.

In 1992, the Committee of Sponsoring Organizations of the Treadway Commission (COSO) undertook an extensive study of internal control. COSO defined internal control as "a process, effected by an entity's board of directors, management and other personnel, designed to provide reasonable assurance regarding the achievement of objectives" in three categories: (1) effectiveness and efficiency of operations; (2) reliability of financial reporting, and (3) compliance with applicable laws and regulations.

COSO further stated that internal control over each of these objectives consisted of the control environment, risk assessment, control activities, information and communication, and monitoring. In 1995, the AICPA's Auditing

Standards Board in Statement on Auditing Standards No. 78 codified this definition of internal controls.

The SEC believes that the purpose of internal controls and procedures for financial reporting is to ensure that companies have processes designed to provide reasonable assurance that the company's:

- transactions are properly authorized;
- assets are safeguarded against unauthorized or improper use; and
- transactions are properly recorded and reported.

All of the above are designed to permit the preparation of the financial statements in conformity with generally accepted accounting principles.

Implementing the Sarbanes-Oxley Act Section 302 certification requirements, the SEC required a company's principal executive and financial officers to certify the information in their companies' quarterly and annual reports. Specifically, these officers have to certify that they have disclosed to company's auditors and to the audit committee all significant deficiencies in the design or operation of internal controls that could adversely affect the company's ability to record, process, summarize and report financial data and have identified for the auditors any material weaknesses in internal controls; and any fraud, whether or not material, that involves management or other employees who have a significant role in the internal controls.

The senior officers must also certify that they have indicated in the report whether or not there were significant changes in internal controls or in other factors that could significantly affect internal controls subsequent to the date of their evaluation, including any corrective actions with regard to significant deficiencies and material weaknesses.

Impact on Audit Committees

Audit committees will be impacted by the new internal controls. Although internal auditors are not specifically mentioned in the Sarbanes-Oxley Act, they have within their purview of internal control the responsibility to examine and evaluate all of a company's systems, processes, operations, functions, and activities. Thus, they are subject to a number of challenges in the Sarbanes-Oxley era.

The audit committee has a role to play in ensuring that the company has robust internal and reporting controls. The new regulatory regime helps the committee in this regard by requiring that officers assess the company's controls, and certify that they have disclosed any significant deficiencies to the audit committee. To foster additional support for internal auditors and to help meet the requirements of the Act for handling complaints relating to internal controls, it is advisable for the head of internal audit to have a direct line of communication to the audit committee. (See remarks of SEC Commissioner Cynthia Glassman to the American Society of Corporate Secretaries, Sept. 22, 2002.)

The internal control structure, and the internal audit team that tests and reinforces that structure, is crucial to the success of a company in stemming fraud and abuse, and in the preparation of accurate financial statements. As such, the importance of the audit committees' understanding of the companies' internal control structure and their assessment of internal audit's effectiveness is crucial in ensuring this important link in the chain is solid. (See remarks of

SEC Chief Accountant Robert K. Herdman at the Tulane Corporate Law Institute, March 7, 2002.)

The Sarbanes-Oxley Act requires the audit committee to be directly responsible for the appointment, compensation, and oversight of the work of the external independent auditors. The Act also requires the auditor to report on and attest to management's assessment of the company's internal controls.

Thus, internal auditors must help corporate risk officers and managers reinvigorate the risk assessment and control process over financial reporting and now, under Sarbanes-Oxley, other public disclosures. In turn, in order to be effective, internal auditors should report directly to the audit committee, in the view of some regulators, who reason that the company's entire quality assurance and monitoring program will be tainted if the internal auditors are not accountable to the audit committee. (Remarks by Federal Reserve Board Governor Susan Schmidt Bies, Institute of Internal Auditors Conference, May 7, 2003.)

In addition, the COSO Report states that the composition of a company's board and audit committee, and how the directors fulfill their duties related to the financial reporting process, are key aspects of the company's control environment. An important element of the company's internal control over financial reporting is the involvement of the board or audit committee in overseeing the financial reporting process, including assessing the reasonableness of management's accounting judgments and estimates and reviewing key filings with regulatory agencies.

Best Practice: The audit committee should actively engage the internal auditor to ensure that risk assessment and control process over financial reporting are vigorous.

Independence of Internal Auditor

The issue of internal auditor independence directly involves the audit committee. The internal auditor should demonstrate independence from management and loyalty to the audit committee, and not just the appearance of independence. In turn, the audit committee should require the highest possible level of independence for the internal audit process and eliminate any threats to this independence, such as the tendency for some internal auditors to act as management consultants within the organization.

Internal auditors add value by being effective independent assessors of the quality of the internal control framework and processes. Auditors lose their independence when they perform management consulting roles for which they later will have to render an opinion. (Remarks by Federal Reserve Board Governor Susan Schmidt Bies, Institute of Internal Auditors Conference, May 7, 2003.)

Internal auditors can play a valuable role as the independent eyes and ears of the audit committee around the organization. As they work throughout the organization, they know which managers and which projects are likely to entail greater weaknesses in controls. Prompt reporting to the audit committee and timely resolution of audit findings will build credibility with the committee.

If an audit committee asks an internal auditor for recommendations on how to improve independence, the typical response should be that the test for any recommended change is whether it makes management more accountable for the ongoing effectiveness of internal controls and makes the internal audit function more effective in monitoring and process validation. (Remarks by Federal Reserve Board Governor Susan Schmidt Bies, Institute of Internal Auditors Conference, May 7, 2003.)

Audit Committee Oversight

The question of how granular audit committee oversight over the internal control process should be is inherently difficult. Beyond the strict regulatory requirements, the clear thrust of the rules is that audit committee members need to be inquisitive, which means they should put their financial literacy to good use.

This does not mean, however, that audit committee members have to re-audit the financial statements or re-design internal controls. It does mean that they should have a healthy skepticism and pursue issues until they are satisfied they have received adequate information to make an informed judgment. This is especially true with respect to instances that involve real or potential conflicts of interest for management or auditors. (See remarks of SEC Commissioner Cynthia Glassman to the American Society of Corporate Secretaries, Sept. 22, 2002.)

Best Practice: Risk-focused audit programs should be reviewed regularly to ensure audit resources are focused on the higher-risk areas as the company grows and produces and processes change. As lower-risk areas come up for review, auditors should do enough transaction testing to be confident in their risk rating. Audit committees should receive reports on all breaks in internal controls to determine where the auditing process can be strengthened. (See remarks of Federal Reserve Board Governor Susan Schmidt Bies, Institute of Internal Auditors Conference, May 7, 2003.)

In a broad sense, there is the belief that audit committees must pave the way for quality assurance over the internal audit and provide for the utmost independence, objectivity, and professionalism of the internal audit process. The audit committee sets the tone for the internal audit. (See remarks of Federal Reserve Board Governor Susan Schmidt Bies at the Conference of State Bank Supervisors, May 30, 2003.)

With all this in mind, it is instructive to discuss the SEC's internal control rules adopted to implement the Sarbanes-Oxley provisions on internal control.

Taking control of internal audit

The internal audit is one of the few corporate functions with both the ability and the duty to look across all of the management silos within the company and make sure that the system of internal controls has no gaps. As such, internal auditors are in the unique position to understand the evolution of all forms of risks and controls across the organization. Because of this, internal auditors are the eyes and ears of the audit committee around the organization. They can only be such, however, when the internal audit function is independent of all control processes because when an auditor becomes part of the management process the independent view is lost. (See remarks of Federal Reserve Board Governor Susan Schmidt Bies before the Institute of Internal Auditors, May 19, 2004).

For example, internal auditors lose their independence when they perform management consulting roles for which they later will have to render an opinion. Thus, audit committees are advised to demand the highest possible level of independence for the internal audit process and eliminate any threats to this independence, such as the tendency of some internal auditors to act as management consultants within the organization. (See remarks of Governor Susan Schmidt Bies before the Bank Administration Institute's Fiduciary Risk Management seminar, April 26, 2004).

More broadly, former SEC Chairman Roderick Hills has advised audit committees to take firm control over internal auditors, which means selecting their own candidates for these jobs by interviewing multiple candidates. They cannot leave the job to management. In particular, audit committees must pay more attention to the role of internal auditors. If they do not take responsibility for the selection, retention and compensation of the internal auditor, Hills noted, they can hardly complain if the internal auditor is reluctant to criticize management. He believes that audit committees assuring themselves of the support of external and internal auditors will be alerted to the subtle problems of the audit process. Their job then is to take whatever time is necessary to deal with those problems. (See testimony of former SEC Chairman Roderick Hills before the House Financial Services Committee, July 22. 2004).

Hills attached to his written testimony a report by a panel composed of senior former and current regulators that said audit committees, in addition to managing the outside auditor, must be in charge of the internal audit function. The report was issued as part of the 103rd American Assembly on the future of the accounting profession. Participants in the assembly also included former Federal Reserve Board Chairman Paul Volcker, former SEC Chairmen David Ruder, Roderick Hills, and Harold Williams, and current SEC Chairman William Donaldson, as well as PCAOB Chairman William McDonough. Although they participated in the assembly, the current regulators did not vote on the report.

The panel emphasized that audit committees must continue to assert their central role in corporate governance. In particular, they must seek out their auditors and make clear to them that the committee is the client and will support the auditors, even in the case of a conflict between auditors and management. While the chief internal auditor may report for administrative purposes to the CEO or CFO, the panel recommends that the audit committees supervise the decisions to hire, compensate and retain the personnel engaged in the internal audit function. The committee must determine bonuses and protect the career paths of the internal auditors who, the panel reasoned, can undertake their duties effectively only if the audit committee assures them that they need not fear reprisals from those whom they audit.

Similarly, the Breeden Report recommended that the audit committee provide continuous oversight and review of the internal accounting and finance functions, and the company's internal audit program, including regular review of the long range plan of work and risk assessments prepared by the internal auditors. The audit committee should also review with senior management the staffing levels of the internal audit department and the overall competence of the personnel. (a report to the U.S. District Court for the SDNY on corporate governance for the future of MCI, Inc., commonly referred to as the Breeden Report, contained a number of best practices for audit committees. The report, issued in August of 2003, was the work of former SEC chairman Richard C. Breeden).

According to the Breeden Report, the internal audit department should report for administrative purposes to the CFO, including matters such as budget, staffing levels, promotions and advancement, training activities and location of resources. But the audit committee should provide review and oversight and be responsible for insuring the independence, competence and experience of the department. The CFO should be able to request specific projects, but approval of internal audit's work plan should come from the audit committee.

The U.K. Combined Code on Corporate Governance also directs the audit committee to monitor and review the effectiveness of the company's internal audit function and ensure that internal audit has the necessary resources and access to information. The audit committee should also approve the appointment or termination of the head of internal audit.

According to the U.K. code, in reviewing the work of internal auditors, the audit committee should:

- ensure that the internal auditor has direct access to the board chair and to the audit committee and is accountable to the committee;

- review and assess the annual internal audit work plan;

- receive periodic reports on the results of the internal auditors' work;

- monitor management's responsiveness to the internal auditor's findings and recommendations;

- meet annually with the head of internal audit without management present; and

- assess the role and effectiveness of internal audit in the overall context of the company's risk management system.

¶ 302 SEC Rules

Implementing Sarbanes-Oxley Act Section 404, the SEC adopted rules requiring management's annual internal control report to contain the following:

- a statement of management's responsibility for establishing and maintaining adequate internal control over corporate financial reporting;

- a statement identifying the framework used by management to evaluate the effectiveness of this internal control;

- management's assessment of the effectiveness of this internal control as of the end of the company's most recent fiscal year; and

- a statement that its auditor has issued an attestation report on management's assessment. (See Item 308(a), Regulation S-K.)

Under the rules, management must disclose any material weakness and will be unable to conclude that the company's internal control over financial reporting is effective if there are one or more material weaknesses in such control. Further, the framework on which management's evaluation is based will have to be a suitable, recognized control framework that is established by a body or group that has followed due process procedures, including the broad distribution of the framework for public comment.

Note that management must state whether or not the company's internal control over financial reporting is effective. According to the SEC, a negative assurance statement indicating that nothing has come to management's attention to suggest that the company's internal control over financial reporting is not effective will not be acceptable.

Auditor Attestation

The SEC rules also require a company to file, as part of its annual report, the attestation report of the registered public accounting firm that audited the company's financial statements. (See Item 308(b), Regulation S-K.)

Control Framework

The SEC rules specify that management must base its evaluation of the effectiveness of the company's internal control over financial reporting on a suitable, recognized control framework that is established by a body or group that has followed due process procedures, including the broad distribution of the framework for public comment.

The Commission believes that the use of standard measures will enhance the quality of the internal control report and promote the comparability of the internal control reports of different companies. The rules require management's report to identify the evaluation framework employed to assess the effectiveness of the company's internal control over financial reporting. In the SEC's view, a suitable framework must:

- be free from bias;

- permit reasonably consistent qualitative and quantitative measurements of a company's internal control;

- be sufficiently complete so that those relevant factors that would alter a conclusion about the effectiveness of a company's internal controls are not omitted; and

- be relevant to an evaluation of internal control over financial reporting.

The rules do not, however, mandate use of a particular framework. The SEC has indicated that the COSO Framework satisfies its criteria and may be used as an evaluation framework for purposes of management's annual internal control evaluation and disclosure requirements. The Guidance on Assessing Control published by the Canadian Institute of Chartered Accountants and the Turnbull Report published by the Institute of Chartered Accountants in England & Wales are examples of other suitable frameworks.

The rules require management's report to identify the evaluation framework used by management to assess the effectiveness of the company's internal control over financial reporting.

The SEC is aware that some of the evaluation frameworks used to assess a foreign company's internal controls in its home country do not require a statement regarding whether the company's system of internal control has been effective. Under the rules, management of a foreign reporting company who relies on such an evaluation framework used in its home country is nevertheless under an obligation to state affirmatively whether its company's internal controls are effective.

¶ 303 Auditor Independence Issues

The SEC recognizes that, because the independent auditor must attest to management's assessment of internal control over financial reporting, management and the auditors will need to coordinate their processes of documenting and testing the internal controls.

But companies and their auditors must remember that SEC rules on auditor independence prohibit an auditor from providing certain nonaudit services to an audit client. Auditors may assist management in documenting internal controls, but when the auditor is engaged to assist management in documenting internal controls, management must be actively involved in the process.

Cautionary Note: While understanding of the need for coordination between management and the auditor, the SEC cautions that management cannot delegate its responsibility to assess its internal controls over financial reporting to the auditor. Management's acceptance of responsibility for the documentation and testing performed by the auditor does not satisfy the auditor independence rules.

¶ 304 Material Weakness and Significant Deficiency

In assessing the effectiveness of the company's internal controls, management must include disclosure of any identified material weaknesses in the company's internal control over financial reporting. According to the SEC, management is not permitted to conclude that the company's internal controls are effective if there are one or more material weaknesses in the company's internal control over financial reporting.

The SEC rules thus provide a threshold for concluding that a company's internal controls are effective in that management is precluded from determining that a company's internal controls are effective if it identifies one or more material weaknesses in them.

The rules also specify that management's report must include disclosure of any material weakness in the company's internal control identified by management in the course of its evaluation.

The terms material weakness and significant deficiency both represent deficiencies in the design or operation of internal control that could adversely affect a company's ability to record, process, summarize and report financial data consistent with the assertions of management in the company's financial statements, with a material weakness constituting a greater deficiency than a significant deficiency (see definitions below). In the SEC's view, an aggregation of significant deficiencies could constitute a material weakness in a company's internal controls.

While all material weaknesses must be identified and disclosed, management is not obligated to disclose the existence or nature of identified significant deficiencies. However, if management identifies a significant deficiency that, when combined with other significant deficiencies, is determined to be a material weakness, management must disclose the material weakness and, to the extent material to an understanding of the disclosure, the nature of the significant deficiencies. (See FAQ of June 23, 2004, Q. 11).

In addition, if a material change is made to either disclosure controls and procedures or to internal controls in response to a significant deficiency, the company must disclose the change and should consider whether it is necessary to discuss further the nature of the significant deficiency in order to render the disclosure not misleading. (See FAQ of June 23, 2004, Q. 11).

Definitions of Material Weakness and Significant Deficiency

In its adopting release (34-47986, Fed. Sec. L. Rep., 2003 CCH Dec., ¶ 86,923) for the rules implementing Section 404 of Sarbanes-Oxley, the Commission expressed an intention to incorporate the definitions of "significant deficiency" and "material weakness" as they exist in the standards used by auditors of public companies. Looking to the definitions adopted by the PCAOB is consistent with this intention and, accordingly, the SEC staff will apply the PCAOB definitions in interpreting the Commission rules in this area. (See FAQ of June 23, 2004, Q. 13).

In Auditing Standard No. 2, the PCAOB defines a "significant deficiency" as a control deficiency, or combination of control deficiencies, that adversely affects the company's ability to initiate, authorize, record, process, or report external financial data reliably in accordance with generally accepted accounting principles such that there is more than a remote likelihood that a misstatement of the company's annual or interim financial statements that is more than inconsequential will not be prevented or detected. (Auditing Standard No. 2, Paragraph 9;see Release No. 34-49544 (SEC 2004), Fed. Sec. L. Rep. ¶ 87,203.)

The Board defines a "material weakness" as a significant deficiency, or combination of significant deficiencies, that results in more than a remote likelihood that a material misstatement of the annual or interim financial statements will not be prevented or detected. (Auditing Standard No. 2, Paragraph 10;see Release No. 34-49544 (SEC 2004), Fed. Sec. L. Rep. ¶ 87,203.)

The PCAOB's Accounting Standard No. 2 on internal control over financial reporting identifies a number of circumstances that, because of their likely significant negative effect on internal control over financial reporting, are significant deficiencies as well as strong indicators that a material weakness exists.

One of these circumstances is the audit committee's ineffective oversight of the company's external financial reporting and internal control over financial reporting. The Board explained the inclusion of this circumstance by stating that effective oversight by the audit committee is essential to the company's achievement of its objectives and is an integral part of the monitoring of internal control.

The standard requires the auditor to evaluate factors related to the effectiveness of the audit committee's oversight, including whether committee members act independently from management. As part of the evaluation of the independence of committee members, auditors evaluate how audit committee members are nominated and selected.

Other factors used in judging the effectiveness of the audit committee are the clarity with which the committee's responsibilities are articulated and how well the audit committee and management understand those responsibilities. In addition, the level of involvement and interaction with the independent auditor is considered, as well as the level of involvement and interaction with internal audit, including the committee's line of authority and role in appointing and compensating employees in the internal audit function.

In addition, the amount of time that the audit committee devotes to control issues and the amount of time that committee members are able to devote to committee activity is part of the mix.

This aspect of the standard, however, has proved controversial. The specter of auditors evaluating the effectiveness of the audit committee troubles a number of people. The Sarbanes-Oxley Act makes the audit committee directly responsible for the appointment, compensation, and oversight of the work of the auditor. With this in mind, commenters have generally suggested that the requirement that auditors evaluate the audit committee's effectiveness places auditors and audit committee in an untenable conflict since no auditor would dare criticize the committee that must approve the outside auditors.

Some commenters even believe that the standard is contrary to the objectives of the Sarbanes-Oxley Act to strengthen the role of the audit committee. They believe that the audit committee's authority can be diluted if it could be questioned and evaluated by the outside auditor it can hire and fire. Also, some of the standards auditors would use to judge audit committee effectiveness are subjective, such as how well the committee and management understand audit committee duties. More broadly, others feared that the adoption of the standard would lead to a wary relationship between the parties rather than the positive, open communications that are needed and that were envisioned by Congress.

But the PCAOB has defended the standard by pointing out the positive aspects of auditor evaluation of audit committees. While conceding that legitimate questions can be raised about whether auditors should be expected to assess the effectiveness of the committee that has the power to hire or fire them, PCAOB member Daniel Goelzer said that more fundamentally the standard illustrates that auditors are well-positioned to evaluate and monitor the governance processes related to the financial reporting of their public company clients. He emphasized that auditors may be uniquely positioned to help audit committees as they struggle with the new duties thrust upon them by Sarbanes-Oxley.

The major auditing firms deal with hundreds of audit committees, he reasoned, and therefore have an ability few others share to compare and contrast performance and to develop expertise concerning best practices. In his view, the Board's standard builds on this idea. He predicted that clients and auditors will begin to more clearly realize this expertise and look to auditors for their recommendations, just as they have with respect to the more traditional aspects of internal control.

Member Goelzer does not believe that this requirement is particularly burdensome since, in his view, most auditors already have a good sense of which clients have dysfunctional audit committees. Communicating that judgment may often be more difficult than making it. (See remarks of PCAOB Member Dan Goelzer before the Association of the Bar of the City of New York, Dec, 13, 2004).

Similarly, PCAOB Chairman William McDonough believes that the standard will empower both auditors and audit committees, who should welcome an assessment by the auditor it hired. At the same time, the auditor should feel comfortable giving a report card on the directors in charge of the appointment.

Informing the Audit Committee

Audit committees will need to have a working understanding of what constitutes a material weakness and a significant deficiency because Auditing Standard No. 2 requires the auditor to inform the audit committee in writing of all significant deficiencies and material weaknesses in internal control. The standard further provides that, when timely communication is important, the auditor should communicate significant deficiencies and material weaknesses during the course of the audit rather than at the end of the engagement. The committee will then have an obligation to consider that information and act on it as necessary.

Board Member Goelzer has advised audit committees to probe the auditor to understand why it characterized each deficiency as it did and to compare management's evaluation of deficiencies with the auditor's. Committees will also need to understand management's remedial plan for the material weakness. (See remarks of PCAOB Member Dan Goelzer before the Association of the Bar of the City of New York, Dec, 13, 2004).

This is important because Auditing Standard No. 2 provides that a significant deficiency that remains uncorrected after a reasonable period of time is a strong indicator of a material weakness. Thus, left unaddressed, significant deficiencies can evolve into material weaknesses.

The Board designed the communication mandate with several objectives in mind. First, communicating all significant deficiencies and material weaknesses that the auditor believes exist as of year-end enables management and the audit committee to understand whether the auditor has reached conclusions similar to management's regarding the severity of the deficiencies. Second, communicating any significant deficiencies and material weaknesses as of an interim date allows management and the audit committee to take corrective action as soon as possible. In this manner, management might be able to correct a significant deficiency or material weakness identified by the auditor in advance of the date of its annual Section 404 assessment.

It can be seen that Auditing Standard No. 2 imposes important new obligations on audit committees. For example, it requires detailed audit committee involvement in the retention of the auditor to provide any internal control-related services, such as assisting in documenting controls. The effect of this requirement is that the standard prohibits category-based audit committee approval of non-audit services related to internal control. Any engagement to provide internal control-related services for an audit client must be specifically pre-approved by the audit committee. (See remarks of PCAOB Member Dan Goelzer before the Association of the Bar of the City of New York, Dec, 13, 2004).

¶ 305 Evaluation Methods

Since the methods of conducting evaluations of internal control over financial reporting will vary from company to company, the SEC does not specify the method or procedures to be performed in an evaluation. In conducting an evaluation and developing an assessment of the effectiveness of internal controls, however, a company must maintain evidential matter, including documentation, to provide reasonable support for management's assessment of the effectiveness of the company's internal controls. The SEC considers developing and maintaining such evidential matter to be an inherent element of effective internal controls and the rules remind companies to maintain such evidential matter.

The assessment of a company's internal control over financial reporting must be based on procedures sufficient both to evaluate its design and to test its operating effectiveness. Controls subject to such assessment include, but are not limited to:

- controls over initiating, recording, processing and reconciling account balances, classes of transactions and disclosure and related assertions included in the financial statements;

- controls related to the initiation and processing of non-routine and non-systematic transactions;

- controls related to the selection and application of appropriate accounting policies;

- and controls related to the prevention, identification, and detection of fraud.

The nature of a company's testing activities will largely depend on the circumstances of the company and the significance of the control.

But note that inquiry alone generally will not provide an adequate basis for management's assessment. This does not mean that management personally must conduct the necessary activities to evaluate the design and test the operating effectiveness of the company's internal controls. Activities, including those necessary to provide management with the information on which it bases its assessment, may be conducted by non-management personnel acting under the supervision of management.

¶ 306 Location of Management's Report

Although the SEC rules do not specify where management's internal control report must appear in the company's annual report, the Commission said the report should be in close proximity to the corresponding attestation report issued by the company's public accounting firm. The SEC expects that many companies will choose to place the internal control report and attestation report near the companies' MD&A disclosure or in a portion of the document immediately preceding the financial statements.

¶ 307 Quarterly Evaluations

As a general principle, the SEC believes that each company should have the flexibility to design its system of internal controls to fit its particular circumstances. The management of each company should perform evaluations of the design and operation of the company's entire system of internal control over financial reporting over a period of time that is adequate for it to determine whether, as of the end of the company's fiscal year, the design and operation of the company's internal control over financial reporting are effective

With this in mind, the SEC dropped its demand for quarterly evaluations of internal controls as extensive as the annual evaluation. Instead, the Commission requires a company's management, with the participation of the principal executive and financial officers, to evaluate any change in the company's internal controls that occurred during a fiscal quarter that has materially affected, or is reasonably likely to materially affect, the company's internal control over financial reporting.

A company must disclose any change in its internal control over financial reporting that occurred during the fiscal quarter covered by the quarterly report, or the last fiscal quarter in the case of an annual report, that has materially affected, or is reasonably likely to materially affect, the company's internal controls.

Although the rules do not expressly require the company to disclose the reasons for any change that occurred during a fiscal quarter, or to otherwise elaborate about the change, a company will have to determine, on a facts and circumstances basis, whether the reasons for the change, or other information about the circumstances surrounding the change, constitute material information necessary to make the disclosure about the change not misleading under the antifraud rule.

Foreign Private Issuers

The management of a foreign private issuer that has Exchange Act reporting obligations must also, like its domestic counterparts, report any material changes to the company's internal controls. However, because foreign private issuers need not file quarterly reports, SEC rules clarify that a foreign private issuer's management need only disclose in the annual report the material changes to its internal control over financial reporting that have occurred in the period covered by the annual report.

The management of a foreign private issuer must disclose in its annual report filed on Form 20-F or 40-F any change in its internal control over financial reporting that occurred during the period covered by the annual report and that materially affected, or is reasonably likely to affect, this internal control.

Disclosure Controls and Procedures

While an evaluation of the effectiveness of disclosure controls and procedures must be undertaken quarterly, the SEC expects that for purposes of disclosure by domestic companies, the traditional relationship between disclosure in annual reports on Form 10-K and intervening quarterly reports on Form 10-Q will continue. Disclosure in an annual report that continues to be accurate need not be repeated. Rather, disclosure in quarterly reports may make appropriate reference to disclosures in the most recent annual report, and where appropriate intervening quarterly reports, and disclose subsequent developments required to be disclosed in the quarterly report.

¶ 308 Disclosure to Audit Committee

The SEC expects that as certifying officers become aware of a significant deficiency, material weakness or fraud requiring disclosure outside of the formal evaluation process, or after management's most recent evaluation of internal control over financial reporting, they will disclose it to the company's auditors and to the audit committee.

Similarly, under PCAOB Auditing Standard No.2, the independent auditor must communicate in writing to management and the audit committee all significant deficiencies and material weaknesses identified during the audit. The written communication should be made prior to the issuance of the auditor's report on internal control over financial reporting and distinguish between those matters considered to be significant deficiencies and those considered to be material weaknesses. (Auditing Standard No. 2, Paragraph 207, see Release No. 34-49544 (SEC 2004), Fed. Sec. L. Rep. ¶ 87,203.)

¶ 309 Auditor Attestation of Management's Assessment

Section 404(b) requires every registered public accounting firm that prepares or issues an audit report for a company to attest to, and report on, the assessment made by company the management. The attestation and report required by Section 404(b) must be made in accordance with standards for attestation engagements issued by the Public Company Accounting Oversight Board.

Section 103 of Sarbanes-Oxley directs the Public Company Accounting Oversight Board to adopt auditing standards requiring registered public accounting firms to present in each audit report or in a separate report: (1) the scope of the auditor's testing of the internal control structure and procedures of the issuer; (2) the findings of the auditor from such testing; (3) the auditor's evaluation of whether such internal control structure and procedures include maintenance of records that in reasonable detail accurately and fairly reflect the transactions and dispositions of the assets of the issuer, provide reasonable assurance that transactions are recorded as necessary to permit preparation of financial statements in accordance with generally accepted accounting principles, and that receipts and expenditures of the issuer are being made only in accordance with authorizations of management and directors of the issuer; and (4) a description, at a minimum, of material weaknesses in such internal controls, and of any material noncompliance found on the basis of such testing.

Auditing Standard No. 2

Complying with Sarbanes-Oxley, the PCAOB adopted Auditing Standard No. 2. (See Release No. 34-49544 (SEC 2004), Fed. Sec. L. Rep.¶ 87,203.) Under the standard, the auditor's objective in an audit of internal control over financial reporting is to express an opinion on management's assessment of the effectiveness of the company's internal control over financial reporting.

To render such an opinion, the standard requires the auditor to obtain reasonable assurance about whether the company maintained, in all material respects, effective internal control over financial reporting as of the date specified in management's report. To obtain reasonable assurance, the auditor is required to evaluate both management's process for making its assessment and the effectiveness of internal control over financial reporting. In order to provide the type of report at the level of assurance demanded by Sarbanes-Oxley, reasoned the Board, the auditor must evaluate both management's assessment process and the effectiveness of internal control over financial reporting. (Paragraph E12; see Release No. 34-49544 (SEC 2004), Fed. Sec. L. Rep. ¶ 87,203.)

For these reasons the standard refers to the attestation required by Section 404(b) as the audit of internal control over financial reporting instead of an attestation of management's assessment. The standard takes this approach both because the auditor's objective is to express an opinion on management's assessment of the effectiveness of internal control over financial reporting, just as the auditor's objective in an audit of the financial statements is to express an opinion on the fair presentation of the financials, and because the level of assurance obtained by the auditor is the same in both cases. (Paragraph E20; see Release No. 34-49544 (SEC 2004), Fed. Sec. L. Rep. ¶ 87,203.) Furthermore, the standard describes an integrated audit of the financial statements and internal control over financial reporting and allows the auditor to express his or her opinions on the financial statements and on the effectiveness of internal control in separate reports or in a single, combined report.

Thus, the PCAOB believes that the expression of two opinions in all reports on management's assessment and on the effectiveness of internal control over financial reporting is a superior approach that balances the concerns of many different interested parties. This approach is consistent with the scope of the audit, results in more consistent reporting in differing circumstances, and makes the reports more easily understood by report users.

Use of Work of Others

Auditing Standard No. 2 allows the independent auditor to use the work of others, such as the internal auditors, but also creates an overall boundary on the use of the work of others by requiring that the auditor's own work provide the principal evidence for the audit opinion. The standard describes an evaluation process, focusing on the nature of the controls subject to the work of others and the competence and objectivity of the persons who performed the work, that the auditor should use in determining the extent to which he or she may use the work of others.

For example, based on the nature of the controls in the control environment, auditors should not use the work of others to reduce the amount of work they perform on the control environment. Similarly, auditors must perform walkthroughs themselves. On the other hand, the auditor could use the work of others to test controls over the period-end financial reporting process.

However, given the nature of these controls, auditors would normally determine that they should perform more of these tests themselves, and that for any of the work of others the auditors used, the degree of competence and objectivity of the individuals performing the work should be high. Therefore, the auditor might use the work of internal auditors in this area to some degree but not the work of others within the company. Because of the importance of these decisions, Auditing Standard No. 2 provides additional direction.

As mentioned, Auditing Standard No. 2 requires that, on an overall basis, the auditor's own work must provide the principal evidence for the audit opinion. Because the amount of work related to obtaining sufficient evidence to support an opinion about the effectiveness of controls is not susceptible to precise measurement, the auditor's judgment as to whether he or she has obtained the principal evidence for the opinion will be qualitative as well as quantitative.

For example, the auditor might give more weight to work performed on pervasive controls and in areas such as the control environment than on other controls such as controls over routine, low-risk transactions. Also, the work the auditor performs in the control environment and walkthroughs provide an important part of the principal evidence the auditor needs to obtain.

These principles interact to provide the auditor with considerable flexibility in using the work of others and also prevent inappropriate over-reliance on the work of others. Although Auditing Standard No. 2 requires that the auditor reperform some of the tests performed by others in order to use their work, it does not set any specific requirement on the extent of the reperformance. For example, the standard does not require that the auditor reperform tests of controls over all significant accounts for which the auditor uses the work of others. Rather, Auditing Standard No. 2 relies on the auditor's judgment, such that the re-testing is sufficient to enable the auditor to evaluate the quality and effectiveness of the work.

The Board believes that this considerable flexibility in using the work of others should translate into a strong encouragement for companies to develop high-quality internal audit, compliance, and other such functions. The more highly competent and objective these functions are, and the more thorough their testing, the more the auditor will be able to use their work.

¶309

Evaluating Test Results

Both management and the auditor may identify deficiencies in internal control over financial reporting. A control deficiency exists when the design or operation of a control does not allow the company's management or employees, in the normal course of performing their assigned functions, to prevent or detect misstatements on a timely basis.

Auditing Standard No. 2 requires the auditor to evaluate the severity of all identified control deficiencies because such deficiencies can have an effect on the auditor's overall conclusion about whether internal control is effective. The auditor also has a responsibility to make sure that certain parties, such as the audit committee, are aware of control deficiencies that rise to a certain level of severity.

Under the standard, a control deficiency (or a combination of internal control deficiencies) should be classified as a significant deficiency if, by itself or in combination with other control deficiencies, it results in more than a remote likelihood that a misstatement in the company's annual or interim financial statements that is more than inconsequential will not be prevented or detected. A significant deficiency should be classified as a material weakness if, by itself or in combination with other control deficiencies, it results in more than a remote likelihood that a material misstatement in the company's annual or interim financial statements will not be prevented or detected.

The definitions of significant deficiency and material weakness focus on likelihood and magnitude as the framework for evaluating deficiencies. The Board anticipates that this framework will bring increased consistency to these evaluations yet preserve an appropriate degree of judgment. Additionally, Auditing Standard No. 2 includes examples of how these definitions would be applied in several different scenarios.

Significant Deficiencies

Auditing Standard No. 2 identifies a number of circumstances that, because of their likely significant negative effect on internal control over financial reporting, are significant deficiencies as well as strong indicators that a material weakness exists. The audit of internal control over financial reporting and the audit of the company's financial statements are an integrated activity and are required by Sarbanes-Oxley to be a single engagement. The results of the work performed in a financial statement audit provide evidence to support the auditor's conclusions on the effectiveness of internal control, and vice-versa.

Therefore, if the auditor discovers a material misstatement in the financial statements as a part of the audit of the financial statements, the auditor should consider whether internal control over financial reporting is effective. That the company's internal controls did not first detect the misstatement is, therefore, a strong indicator that the company's internal control over financial reporting is ineffective.

Timing might be a concern for some companies, particularly as it relates to making preliminary drafts of the financial statements available to the auditor. However, changes to the financial statement preparation process that increase the likelihood that the financial information is correct prior to providing it to the auditors likely will result in an improved control environment.

The auditor also must exercise judgment when performing this evaluation. For example, if the auditor initially identified a material misstatement in the financial statements but, given the circumstances, determined that management would have found the misstatement on a timely basis before the financial statements were made publicly available, the auditor might appropriately determine that the circumstance was a significant deficiency but not a material weakness. Yet another circumstance indicating significant deficiencies as well as strong indicators that a material weakness exists is that significant deficiencies communicated to management and the audit committee have remained uncorrected after reasonable periods of time.

Significant deficiencies in internal control that are not also determined to be material weaknesses are not so severe as to require the auditor to conclude that internal control is ineffective. However, these deficiencies are, nonetheless, significant, and the auditor should expect the company to correct them.

Management's failure to correct significant deficiencies within a reasonable period of time reflects poorly on tone-at-the-top, and directly on the control environment as a whole. Additionally, the significance of the deficiency can change over time. For example, major changes in sales volume or added complexity in sales transaction structures might increase the severity of a significant deficiency affecting sales.

Forming an Opinion and Reporting

Auditing Standard No. 2 permits the auditor to express an unqualified opinion if the auditor has identified no material weaknesses in internal control after having performed all of the procedures that the auditor considers necessary in the circumstances. In the event that the auditor cannot perform all of the procedures that the auditor considers necessary in the circumstances, Auditing Standard No. 2 permits the auditor to either qualify or disclaim an opinion. If an overall opinion cannot be expressed, Auditing Standard No. 2 requires the auditor to explain why.

Auditor's Report

The auditor's report must include two opinions as a result of the audit of internal control over financial reporting: one on management's assessment and one on the effectiveness of internal control over financial reporting. The Board decided that two opinions will most clearly communicate to report readers the nature and results of the work performed and most closely track with the requirements of Sarbanes-Oxley.

The auditor's report must follow the same disclosure model as management's assessment. The SEC's final rules implementing Section 404(a) require management's assessment to disclose only material weaknesses, not significant deficiencies. Therefore, because management's assessment will disclose only material weaknesses, the auditor's report may disclose only material weaknesses. It should be noted, however, that the SEC rules indicated that an aggregation of significant deficiencies may constitute a material weakness in a company's internal control over financial reporting, in which case disclosure would be required.

The SEC's final rules implementing Section 404(a) state that management is not permitted to conclude that the company's internal control over financial reporting is effective if there are one or more material weaknesses in the internal control over financial reporting. In other words, in such a case, management must conclude that internal control is not effective. A qualified or except for conclusion is not allowed.

Similar to the reporting of significant deficiencies, the reporting model for the auditor must follow the required reporting model for management. Therefore, because management must express an adverse conclusion if a material weakness exists, the auditor's opinion on the effectiveness of internal control over financial reporting must also be adverse. Auditing Standard No. 2 does not permit a qualified opinion in the event of a material weakness. However, Auditing Standard No. 2 also requires an opinion on management's assessment in every audit report.

In the event of a material weakness, the auditor could express an unqualified opinion on management's assessment, so long as management properly identified the material weakness and concluded in their assessment that internal control was not effective. If the auditor and management disagree about whether a material weakness exists, for example the auditor concludes a material weakness exists but management does not and therefore makes the conclusion in its assessment that internal control is effective, and then the auditor would render an adverse opinion on management's assessment.

Testing Controls on Fraud

Strong internal controls provide better opportunities to detect and deter fraud.For example, many frauds resulting in financial statement restatement relied on management's ability to exploit weaknesses in internal control. To the extent that the internal control reporting required by Section 404 can help restore investor confidence by improving the effectiveness of internal controls and reducing the incidence of fraud, the auditing standard on performing the audit of internal control over financial reporting should emphasize controls that prevent or detect errors as well as fraud.

For this reason, Auditing Standard No. 2 specifically addresses and emphasizes the importance of controls over possible fraud and requires the auditor to test controls specifically intended to prevent or detect fraud that is reasonably possible to result in material misstatement of the financial statements. In the Board's view, an attestation engagement to examine management's assessment of internal control requires the same level of work as an audit of internal control over financial reporting.

The objective of an audit of internal control over financial reporting is to form an opinion on whether management's assessment of the effectiveness of the company's internal control over financial reporting is fairly stated in all material respects. The Sarbanes-Oxley Act requires the auditor's report to present an evaluation of whether the internal control structure provides reasonable assurance that transactions are recorded as necessary, among other requirements. (See Section 103(a)(2)(A)(iii).) Importantly, the auditor's conclusion will pertain directly to whether the auditor can agree with management that internal control is effective, not just to the adequacy of management's process for determining whether internal control is effective.

In the Board's view, an auditing process restricted to evaluating what management has done would not provide the auditor with a sufficiently high level of assurance that management's conclusion is correct. The auditor needs to evaluate management's assessment process to be satisfied that management has an appropriate basis for its conclusion.

The auditor, however, also needs to test the effectiveness of internal control to be satisfied that management's conclusion is correct and, therefore, fairly stated. Indeed, investors expect the independent auditor to test whether the company's internal control over financial reporting is effective, and Auditing Standard No. 2 requires the auditor to do so.

Integrated Audit

Auditing Standard No. 2 embodies an integrated standard that both:(1) addresses the work required to audit internal control over financial reporting and the relationship of that audit to the audit of the financial statements; and (2) refers to the attestation of management's assessment of the effectiveness of the internal control as the audit of internal control over financial reporting. The Board decided that these audits should be integrated for two reasons.

First, the objectives of, and work involved in performing, an audit of internal control over financial reporting and an audit of the financial statements are closely related. Second, Sarbanes-Oxley Act Section 404(b) provides that the auditor's attestation of management's assessment of internal control cannot be the subject of a separate engagement.

In addition, each audit provides the auditor with information relevant to the auditor's evaluation of the results of the other audit. For example, the auditor's discovery of misstatements in the financial statements while performing financial statement auditing procedures indicates that there may be weaknesses in the company's internal control over financial reporting. Because of the significance of this interrelationship, the Board clarified that, in order to conduct and report on the results of an audit of internal control over financial reporting pursuant to Auditing Standard No. 2, the auditor also must audit the company's financial statements.

¶ 310 Investment Companies

The internal control assessment and attestation requirements of Sarbanes-Oxley Act Section 404 do not apply to registered investment companies, and the SEC has not extended any of the requirements that would implement Section 404 to investment companies.

The certification requirements implementing Sarbanes-Oxley Act Section 302, however, do not exempt investment companies. Thus, under the SEC rules, investment companies must maintain internal control over financial reporting. Signing officers must state that they are responsible for establishing and maintaining internal control over financial reporting, and that they have designed such internal controls, or caused them to be designed under their supervision, in order to provide reasonable assurance regarding the reliability of financial reporting and the preparation of financial statements for external purposes in accordance with generally accepted accounting principles.

The SEC also requires disclosure of any change in the investment company's internal control over financial reporting that occurred during the most recent fiscal half-year that has materially affected, or is reasonably likely to materially affect, the company's internal controls.

Signing officers must state that they have disclosed to the investment company's auditors and the audit committee all significant deficiencies and material weaknesses in the design or operation of internal control over financial reporting that are reasonably likely to adversely affect the investment company's ability to record, process, summarize, and report financial information.

¶ 311 Disclosure Controls/Internal Controls Compared

There has been some confusion as to the differences between a company's disclosure controls and procedures and a company's internal control over financial reporting. Exchange Act Rule 13a-15(d) defines "disclosure controls and procedures" to mean controls and procedures designed to ensure that information required to be disclosed by the company in the reports that it files or submits under the Exchange Act is recorded, processed, summarized and reported, within SEC-specified time periods.

The definition further states that disclosure controls and procedures include controls and procedures designed to ensure that the information required to be disclosed by a company in the reports that it files or submits is accumulated and communicated to the company's management, including its principal executive and principal financial officers, as appropriate to allow timely decisions regarding required disclosure.

Although there is substantial overlap between a company's disclosure controls and procedures and its internal controls, the SEC has admitted, there are some elements of disclosure controls and procedures that are not subsumed by internal controls and some elements of internal controls that are not subsumed by the definition of disclosure controls and procedures.

The broad COSO description of internal controls, which includes the efficiency and effectiveness of a company's operations and the company's compliance with laws and regulations (not restricted to the federal securities laws), would not be wholly subsumed within the definition of disclosure controls and procedures.

Some components of internal control over financial reporting will be included in disclosure controls and procedures for all companies. In particular, disclosure controls and procedures will include those components of internal control that provide reasonable assurances that transactions are recorded as necessary to permit preparation of financial statements in accordance with generally accepted accounting principles. However, in designing their disclosure controls and procedures, companies can be expected to make judgments regarding the processes on which they will rely to meet applicable requirements.

In doing so, some companies might design their disclosure controls and procedures so that certain components of internal control over financial reporting pertaining to the accurate recording of transactions and disposition of assets or to the safeguarding of assets are not included. For example, a company might have developed internal controls that include as a component of safeguarding of assets dual signature requirements or limitations on signature authority on checks. That company could nonetheless determine that this component is not part of disclosure controls and procedures.

The SEC believes that, while there is substantial overlap between internal controls and disclosure controls and procedures, many companies will design their disclosure controls and procedures so that they do not include all components of internal control over financial reporting.

Since August 2002, SEC rules have required quarterly evaluations of disclosure controls and procedures and disclosure of the conclusions regarding effectiveness of disclosure controls and procedures. These evaluation and disclosure requirements will continue to apply to disclosure controls and procedures, including the elements of internal control over financial reporting that are subsumed within disclosure controls and procedures.

The SEC rules require quarterly evaluation of the effectiveness of disclosure controls and procedures. While the evaluation is of effectiveness overall, a company's management has the ability to make judgments that evaluations, particularly quarterly evaluations, should focus on developments since the most recent evaluation, areas of weakness or continuing concern or other aspects of disclosure controls and procedures that merit attention.

Finally, the nature of the quarterly evaluations of those components of internal control over financial reporting that are subsumed within disclosure controls and procedures should be informed by the purposes of disclosure controls and procedures.

For example, where a component of internal control over financial reporting is subsumed within disclosure controls and procedures, even where systems testing of that component would clearly be required as part of the annual evaluation of internal controls, management could make a different determination of the appropriate nature of the evaluation of that component for purposes of a quarterly evaluation of disclosure controls and procedures.

Foreign Private Issuers

SEC rules require the management of a foreign private issuer to evaluate and disclose conclusions regarding the effectiveness of the its disclosure controls and procedures only in the annual report and not on a quarterly basis. The primary reason for this treatment is because foreign private issuers are not subject to mandated quarterly reporting requirements under the Exchange Act.

¶ 312 Internal Control Over Financial Reporting

On a broad level, a key aspect of management's responsibility for the preparation of financial information has been its responsibility to establish and maintain an internal control system over financial reporting. Effective internal control over financial reporting is a process designed to provide reasonable assurance regarding the reliability of financial reporting. But, since we do not live in a perfect world, effective internal control over financial reporting cannot, and does not, provide absolute assurance of achieving financial reporting objectives. (PCAOB staff interpretation of June 23, 2004).

Over the years there has been some confusion over the exact meaning and scope of the term internal control. From the outset, it was recognized that internal control is a broad concept that extends beyond the accounting functions of a company. Early attempts to define the term focused primarily on clarifying the portion of a company's internal control that an auditor should consider when planning and performing an audit of a company's financial statements. However, this did not improve the level of understanding of the term, nor satisfactorily provide the guidance sought by auditors.

In 1977, based on SEC recommendations, Congress enacted the Foreign Corrupt Practices Act, which codified the accounting control provisions contained in Statement of Auditing Standards No. 1 (codified as 320 in the Codification of Statements on Auditing Standards). Under the FCPA, companies that have a class of securities registered under Section 12 of the Exchange Act, or that are required to file reports under Section 15(d) of the Exchange Act, are required to devise and maintain a system of internal accounting controls sufficient to provide reasonable assurances that: transactions are executed in accordance with management's authorization; transactions are recorded as necessary to permit preparation of financial statements in conformity with GAAP; access to assets is permitted only in accordance with management's authorization; and the recorded accountability for assets is compared with the existing assets at reasonable intervals and appropriate action is taken with respect to any differences. (See Exchange Act Section 13(b)(2).)

In 1985, a private-sector initiative known as the National Commission on Fraudulent Financial Reporting, also known as the Treadway Commission, was formed to study the financial reporting system in the United States. In 1987, the Treadway Commission issued a report recommending that its sponsoring organizations work together to integrate the various internal control concepts and definitions and to develop a common reference point. In response, the Committee of Sponsoring Organizations of the Treadway Commission (COSO) undertook an extensive study of internal control to establish a common definition that would serve the needs of companies, independent public accountants, legislators and regulatory agencies, and to provide a broad framework of criteria against which companies could evaluate the effectiveness of their internal control systems.

The Treadway Commission was sponsored by the AICPA, the American Accounting Association, the Financial Executives International (formerly Financial Executives Institute), the Institute of Internal Auditors and the Institute of Management Accountants (formerly the National Association of Accountants).

In 1992, COSO published its Internal Control Integrated Framework. The COSO Framework defined internal control as "a process, effected by an entity's board of directors, management and other personnel, designed to provide reasonable assurance regarding the achievement of objectives" in three categories: 1)effectiveness and efficiency of operations; 2) reliability of financial reporting; and 3)compliance with applicable laws and regulations. COSO further stated that internal control consists of: the control environment; risk assessment; control activities; information and communication; and monitoring. In 1996, COSO issued a supplement to its original framework to address the application of internal control over financial derivative activities.

Internal Control Over Financial Reporting/SEC-PCAOB Efforts

The SEC rules and PCAOB Auditing Standard No. 2 contain essentially the same definition for "internal control over financial reporting." The SEC defines the term to mean a process designed by, or under the supervision of, the principal executive and principal financial officers, or persons performing similar functions, and effected by the board of directors, management and other personnel, to provide reasonable assurance regarding the reliability of financial reporting and the preparation of financial statements for external purposes in accordance with generally accepted accounting principles and includes those policies and procedures that:

- pertain to the maintenance of records that in reasonable detail accurately and fairly reflect the company's transactions and dispositions of assets;

- pertain to the maintenance of records that in reasonable detail accurately and fairly reflect the company's transactions and dispositions of assets;

- provide reasonable assurance regarding prevention or timely detection of unauthorized acquisition, use or disposition of corporate assets that could have a material effect on the financial statements.

According to the SEC, the scope of the term "preparation of financial statements in accordance with generally accepted accounting principles" used in the definition encompasses financial statements prepared for regulatory reporting purposes. The two elements of the definition dealing with maintenance of records and providing assurance that transactions are recorded were included to make clear that the assessment of management in its internal control report to which the company's public accounting firm will be required to attest and report specifically covers the matters referenced in Section 103 of Sarbanes-Oxley.

It can be seen that the concept of "reasonable assurance" has been built into the Sarbanes-Oxley Act and into the definition of "internal control over financial reporting" and is also integral to the auditor's opinion. In addition, management's assessment of the effectiveness of internal control over financial reporting is expressed at the level of reasonable assurance. Reasonable assurance includes the understanding that there is a remote likelihood that material misstatements will not be prevented or detected on a timely basis. Although not absolute assurance, reasonable assurance is, nevertheless, a high level of assurance. (Paragraph 17 of Auditing Standard No. 2; see Release No. 34-49544 (SEC 2004), Fed. Sec. L. Rep. ¶ 87,203.)

That said, regulators recognize that there are limitations on the amount of assurance the auditor can obtain as a result of performing the audit of internal control over financial reporting. Such limitations arise because an audit is conducted on a test basis and requires the exercise of professional judgment. Nevertheless, the audit of internal control over financial reporting includes obtaining an understanding of the internal controls, testing and evaluating their design and operating effectiveness, and performing such other procedures as the auditor considers necessary to obtain reasonable assurance about whether the internal controls are effective. Paragraph 18 of Auditing Standard No. 2; see Release No. 34-49544 (SEC 2004), Fed. Sec. L. Rep. ¶ 87,203.) But note that the auditor's report on internal control over financial reporting does not relieve management of its responsibility for assuring users of its financial reports about the effectiveness of internal control over financial reporting.

Finally, it should be remembered that there is no difference in the level of work performed or assurance obtained by the auditor when expressing an opinion on management's assessment of effectiveness or when expressing an opinion directly on the effectiveness of internal control over financial reporting. In either case, auditors must obtain sufficient evidence to provide a reasonable basis for their opinion and the use and evaluation of management's assessment is inherent in expressing either opinion. Paragraph 19 of Auditing Standard No. 2; see Release No. 34-49544 (SEC 2004), Fed. Sec. L. Rep. ¶ 87,203.)

Another element of the definition makes explicit reference to assurances regarding use or disposition of the company's assets. This provision was included to make clear that the safeguarding of assets is one of the elements of internal control over financial reporting. Safeguarding of assets had long been a primary objective of internal accounting control.

CHAPTER **4**

AUDIT COMMITTEE FINANCIAL EXPERT

¶ 401 In General

The Sarbanes-Oxley Act directed the SEC to adopt rules requiring disclosure of whether a company has at least one financial expert on its audit committee, and if not, the reasons why. Section 407 (reproduced at ¶ 2008) lists four attributes that the SEC must consider in defining financial expert:

- An understanding of generally accepted accounting principles and financial statements;

- Experience in (a) the preparation or auditing of financial statements of generally comparable issuers, and (b) the application of such principles in connection with the accounting for estimates, accruals, and reserves;

- Experience with internal accounting controls; and

- An understanding of audit committee functions.

Implementing the statutory mandate, the SEC adopted rules requiring companies to disclose whether they have at least one audit committee financial expert serving on their audit committee, and if so, the name of the expert and whether the expert is independent of management. A company that does not have an audit committee financial expert must disclose this fact and explain why it has no such expert. (See Item 401(h), Regulation S-K.)

Background and Purpose

Congress intended the Sarbanes-Oxley Act to enhance corporate responsibility by effecting significant change. Therefore, although many companies likely will be able to determine that they already have a financial expert serving on their audit committees, the SEC believes that the fact that some companies will not be able to draw this conclusion unless they are able to attract a new director with the requisite qualifications is consistent with the Act.

The primary benefit of having financial experts on audit committees is that they have a greater level of financial sophistication or expertise that will allow them to serve as a resource for the committee in carrying out its important corporate governance functions.

The disclosure about the financial expert is designed to increase transparency regarding key aspects of corporate conduct and thereby improve the quality of information available to investors. Greater transparency should also assist the market in properly valuing securities, which in turn should lead to more efficient capital allocation. Investors should benefit from this disclosure by being able to consider it when reviewing currently required disclosure about all directors' past business experience and making voting decisions.

Compliance Transition Period

The SEC provided a limited transition period for compliance. Companies must comply with the audit committee financial expert disclosure requirements in their annual reports for fiscal years ending on or after July 15, 2003. Recognizing that smaller businesses may have the greatest difficulty attracting qualified audit committee financial experts, the SEC allows small business issuers to comply in their annual reports for fiscal years ending on or after December 15, 2003.

¶ 402 Financial Expertise

Note that the SEC decided to use the term "audit committee financial expert" in rules implementing Section 407 instead of the more basic term "financial expert" used in Sarbanes-Oxley. The SEC believes that "audit committee financial expert" suggests more pointedly that the designated person has characteristics that are particularly relevant to the audit committee's functions, such as:

- A thorough understanding of the audit committee's oversight role,

- Expertise in accounting matters as well as an understanding of financial statements, and

- The ability to ask the right questions to determine whether the company's financial statements are complete and accurate. (See Release No. 33-8177 (SEC 2003), 2000 CCH Dec. ¶ 86,818.)

Identification of Expert

Although Sarbanes-Oxley does not specifically require disclosure of the name of the audit committee financial expert, the SEC deemed it appropriate to require such information. Disclosure of the name of the company's financial expert will assist investors in evaluating the company's annual report and proxy or information statement disclosure describing the background and business experience of the company's directors.

Independence

Similarly, Sarbanes-Oxley does not require disclosure of whether the financial expert is independent. However, believing that such disclosure may be important to investors, the SEC does require companies to tell investors if the financial expert is independent. Investors may be interested to know, for example, if the only financial expert on the audit committee is the company's chief financial officer or another individual who is responsible for, or partici- pates in, the preparation of the company's financial statements.

If the board determines that the company has more than one audit committee financial expert serving on its audit committee, the company may, but need not, disclose the names of those additional persons. If the company chooses to identify such persons, it must also disclose if they are independent.

Two-Part Definition

Generally tracking Section 407, the SEC adopted a two-part definition of "audit committee financial expert." The first part details the attributes that an audit committee financial expert must possess, while the second part discusses the means by which a person must acquire the necessary attributes. (See Item 401(h)(2) and (3), Regulation S-K.)

¶402

First, to be an audit committee financial expert, a person must have the following attributes:

- An understanding of generally accepted accounting principles and financial statements;

- The ability to assess the general application of such principles in connection with the accounting for estimates, accruals and reserves;

- Experience preparing, auditing, analyzing or evaluating financial statements that present a breadth and level of complexity of accounting issues that are generally comparable to the breadth and complexity of issues that can reasonably be expected to be raised by the company's financial statements, or experience actively supervising one or more persons engaged in such activities;

- An understanding of internal controls and procedures for financial reporting; and

- An understanding of audit committee functions.

Second, a person must have acquired these attributes through certain means. Specifically, the person must have gained financial expertise through any one or more of the following:

- Education and experience as a principal financial officer, principal accounting officer, controller, public accountant or auditor or experience in one or more positions that involve the performance of similar functions;

- Experience actively supervising a principal financial officer, principal accounting officer, controller, public accountant, auditor or person performing similar functions;

- Experience overseeing or assessing the performance of companies or public accountants with respect to the preparation, auditing or evaluation of financial statements; or

- Other relevant experience

Collective Possession of Attributes

An audit committee financial expert must possess all five required attributes. The fact that the audit committee as a whole possesses the five requisite attributes does not satisfy the requirement. Although Congress did not explicitly require the SEC to incorporate all of the attributes listed in Section 407, it also did not limit the Commission to consideration of those attributes.

Sarbanes-Oxley did not contemplate that a company could disclose that it has an audit committee financial expert by virtue of the fact that the audit committee members collectively possess all of the attributes of an expert. The statute directs the SEC to issue rules requiring a company to disclose whether its audit committee is comprised of "at least one member" who is a financial expert. Due to the statute's use of this specific language, there is no doubt that Congress had in mind individual experts and did not contemplate a "collective" expert.

The SEC finds it appropriate under the rules, however, for a company disclosing that it does not have an audit committee financial expert to explain the aspects of the definition that various members of the committee satisfy.

¶402

Attribute of Assessing GAAP

Note that the audit committee financial expert must have the ability to assess the general application of generally accepted accounting principles in connection with the accounting for estimates, accruals and reserves, and need not have experience applying these principles.

The SEC dropped its proposal to require such experience to satisfy better the congressional intent and to reflect more accurately the role to be played by audit committees. The Commission also recognized that the pool of persons possessing the highly specialized technical knowledge that some thought the proposal necessitated may be so small that a substantial percentage of companies in certain industries would be compelled to disclose that they could not retain an expert without recruiting a person associated with a competitor.

The Commission does not intend for the new requirements to lead to such a result. An audit committee financial expert must be able to assess the general application of generally accepted accounting principles in connection with accounting for estimates, accruals and reserves. This general attribute provides the necessary background for an audit committee when addressing more detailed industry-specific standards or other particular topics. Experience with such detailed standards or topics is not a necessary attribute of audit committee financial expertise.

Attribute of Experience with Financial Statements

Sarbanes-Oxley clearly intends that an audit committee financial expert must have experience actually working directly and closely with financial statements in a way that provides familiarity with the contents of the statements and the processes behind them. The SEC recognizes that many people actively engaged in industries such as investment banking and venture capital investment have had significant direct and close exposure to, and experience with, financial statements and related processes. Similarly, professional financial analysts closely and regularly scrutinize financial statements.

These types of individuals often hold positions requiring them to inspect financial statements with a healthy dose of skepticism. They therefore would be well prepared to diligently and zealously question both management and the company's auditor about the financial statements.

Effective audit committee members must have both the ability and the determination to ask the right questions. Therefore, the attribute broadly includes persons with experience performing extensive financial statement analysis or evaluation.

Potential audit committee financial experts should also be considered to possess this attribute by virtue of their experience actively supervising a person who prepares, audits, analyzes or evaluates financial statements. The term "active supervision" means more than the mere existence of a traditional hierarchical reporting relationship between a supervisor and those being supervised.

Rather, it means that a person engaged in active supervision participates in, and contributes to, the process of addressing, albeit at a supervisory level, the same general types of issues regarding preparation, auditing, analysis or evaluation of financial statements as those addressed by those being supervised. It also means that the supervisor should have experience that has contributed to the general expertise necessary to prepare, audit, analyze or

¶402

evaluate financial statements that is at least comparable to the general expertise of those being supervised. A principle executive officer should not be presumed to qualify.

A principal executive officer with considerable operations involvement, but little financial or accounting involvement, likely would not be exercising the necessary active supervision. Active participation in, and contribution to, the process of addressing financial and accounting issues that demonstrates a general expertise in the area would be necessary.

Another component of the attribute is that an audit committee financial expert have experience with financial statements that present accounting issues that are "generally comparable" to those raised by the company's financial statements.

This phrase does not imply that a person must have previous experience in the same industry as the company that is evaluating the person as a potential audit committee financial expert, or that the person's experience must have been with a company subject to Exchange Act reporting requirements.

The requirement focuses on the breadth and level of complexity of the accounting issues with which the person has had experience. A company's board of directors will make the necessary assessment based on particular facts and circumstances.

In making its assessment, the board should focus on a variety of factors such as the size of the company with which the person has experience, the scope of that company's operations and the complexity of its financial statements and accounting. Familiarity with particular financial reporting or accounting issues, or any other narrow area of experience, should not be dispositive.

Attribute of Understanding Internal Controls

The audit committee financial expert must understand the purpose, and be able to evaluate the effectiveness, of a company's internal controls and procedures for financial reporting. It is important that the audit committee financial expert understand why the internal controls and procedures for financial reporting exist, how they were developed, and how they operate. Previous experience establishing or evaluating a company's internal controls and procedures for financial reporting can contribute to a person's understanding of these matters, but the attribute does not require experience with internal controls.

Acquiring the Attributes Through Experience

The SEC dropped the proposed requirement that an audit committee financial expert must have gained the relevant experience with a company that, at the time the person held such position, was required to file Exchange Act reports. This move was a recognition that many private companies are contractually required to prepare audited financial statements that comply with generally accepted accounting principles. Similarly, a potential expert may have gained relevant experience at a foreign company that is publicly traded in its home market but is not registered under the Exchange Act.

Experience overseeing or assessing the performance of companies or public accountants with respect to the preparation, auditing or evaluation of financial statements can provide a person with in-depth knowledge and experience of accounting and financial issues. For example, individuals serving in governmental, self-regulatory and private-sector bodies overseeing the banking, insurance and securities industries work on issues related to financial statements on a regular basis. Such experience can constitute a useful background for an audit committee financial expert.

Other Relevant Experience

, The SEC rules state simply that a person may acquire the necessary attributes of an audit committee financial expert through other relevant experience. The rules do not require the company to disclose the basis for the board's determination that a person has similar expertise and experience. A reference to the board's judgment with respect to this provision would be redundant because the board must make all determinations as to whether a person qualifies as an expert.

Allowing a person to have "other relevant experience" recognizes that an audit committee financial expert can acquire the requisite attributes of an expert in many different ways. The SEC believes that this expertise should be the product of experience and not, for example, merely education.

Cautionary Note: Under the rules, if a person qualifies as an expert by virtue of possessing other relevant experience, the company's disclosure must briefly list that person's experience.

List of Factors

The proposed definition included a non-exclusive list of qualitative factors for a company's board to consider in assessing audit committee financial expert candidates. The SEC decided not to include the list in the final definition of audit committee financial expert because it did not want the list to be used as a mechanical checklist. However, the SEC said the list can still serve as guidance to be used in considering a person's knowledge and experience as a whole.

The factors on the list focused on the breadth and level of a potential audit committee financial expert's experience, understanding and involvement in relevant activities, including the person's length of experience in relevant positions, and the types of duties held by such person in those positions. The SEC believes that the board should consider all the available facts and circumstances, including but not limited to, qualitative factors of the type identified in the proposal. The factors are:

- The level of the person's accounting or financial education, including whether the person has earned an advanced degree in finance or accounting;

- Whether the person is a certified public accountant, or the equivalent, in good standing, and the length of time that the person actively has practiced as a certified public accountant, or the equivalent;

- Whether the person is certified or otherwise identified as having accounting or financial experience by a recognized private body that establishes and administers standards in respect of such expertise, whether that person is in good standing with the recognized private body, and the length of time that the person has been actively certified or identified as having this expertise;

- Whether the person has served as a principal financial officer, controller or principal accounting officer of a company that, at the time the person held such position, was required to file reports pursuant to Exchange Act Section 13(a) or 15(d), and if so, for how long;

¶402

- The person's specific duties while serving as a public accountant, auditor, principal financial officer, controller, principal accounting officer or position involving the performance of similar functions;

- The person's level of familiarity and experience with all applicable laws and regulations regarding the preparation of financial statements that must be included in reports filed under Exchange Act Section 13(a) or 15(d);

- The level and amount of the person's direct experience reviewing, preparing, auditing or analyzing financial statements that must be included in reports filed under Exchange Act Section 13(a) or 15(d);

- The person's past or current membership on one or more audit committees of companies that, at the time the person held such membership, were required to file reports pursuant to Exchange Act Section 13(a) or 15(d);

- The person's level of familiarity and experience with the use and analysis of financial statements of public companies; and

- Whether the person has any other relevant qualifications or experience that would assist him or her in understanding and evaluating the registrant's financial statements and other financial information and to make knowledgeable and thorough inquiries whether:

- The financial statements fairly present the financial condition, results of operations and cash flows of the company in accordance with generally accepted accounting principles; and

- The financial statements and other financial information, taken together, fairly present the financial condition, results of operations and cash flows of the company.

In the case of a foreign private issuer, the board also should consider the person's experience with public companies in the foreign private issuer's home country, generally accepted accounting principles used by the issuer, and the reconciliation of financial statements with U.S. generally accepted accounting principles.

Qualifications

The fact that a person previously has served on an audit committee does not, by itself, justify the board of directors in grandfathering that person as an audit committee financial expert. Similarly, the fact that a person has experience as a public accountant or auditor, or a principal financial officer, controller or principal accounting officer or experience in a similar position does not, by itself, justify the board of directors in deeming the person to be an audit committee financial expert.

In addition to determining that a person possesses an appropriate degree of knowledge and experience, the board must ensure that it names an audit committee financial expert who embodies the highest standards of personal and professional integrity. In this regard, a board should consider any disciplinary actions to which a potential expert is, or has been, subject in determining whether that person would be a suitable audit committee financial expert.

Because of the significant role the audit committee plays in the filing of financial statements, including the preparation and filing of their own report, it is hard to believe that an accountant serving as a financial expert on an audit committee would not be practicing before the Commission. Therefore, any accountant, while suspended or barred from practice under Rule 102(e) of the Commission's Rules of Practice, generally would not be eligible to serve as a financial expert.

Foreign Private Issuers

With respect to foreign private issuers, the audit committee financial expert's understanding must be of the generally accepted accounting principles (GAAP) used by the foreign private issuer in preparing its primary financial statements filed with the SEC.

SEC rules require foreign private issuers that do not prepare their primary financial statements in accordance with U.S. GAAP to include a reconciliation to those principles in their filed financial statements. Although an understanding of reconciliation to U.S. GAAP would be helpful, the SEC believes that the proper focus of audit committee financial expertise is on the principles used to prepare the primary financial statement.

The SEC is also sensitive to the fact that requiring an audit committee financial expert to possess expertise relating to U.S. GAAP could burden foreign private issuers who use home country accounting principles or international accounting standards to prepare their primary financial statements.

The question of how foreign private issuers with boards of auditors or similar bodies or statutory auditors should comply with the audit committee financial expert disclosure requirements was troubling. One commenter suggested that the audit committee financial expert's expertise should be related to home country GAAP even if the issuer's primary financial statements are filed with the Commission in conformity with U.S. GAAP.

Because Congress intended Sarbanes-Oxley Act Section 407 to strengthen audit committee oversight of the preparation and audit of financial statements presented to U.S. investors, the SEC believes that the audit committee financial expert's expertise should be related to the body of GAAP used in the company's primary financial statements filed with the Commission.

The SEC does, however, acknowledge the differing regulatory structures of foreign jurisdictions. Therefore, the SEC added a sentence to the instructions to the audit committee financial expert disclosure provisions to clarify that, for purposes of those provisions, the term "audit committee" means the board of auditors or similar bodies or statutory auditors, if the issuer meets the criteria specified in new Rule 10A-3(c)(3).

¶ 403 Safe Harbor

Unlike other provisions of Sarbanes-Oxley that impose substantive mandates, the requirements contemplated by Section 407 are entirely disclosure-based. The mere designation of the audit committee financial expert would not impose a higher degree of individual responsibility on that person, nor would the designation decrease the duties of other audit committee members or the board of directors.

The SEC concluded that it would adversely affect the audit committee's operation and its vital role in the financial reporting system, and systems of corporate governance more generally, if courts were to conclude that the designation of an audit committee financial expert affected that person's duties or liability as an audit committee member or board member. It would be adverse to the interests of investors and to the operation of markets if the designation affected the duties or liabilities to which any member of the company's audit committee or board is subject. The SEC codified this position by including a safe harbor in the new audit committee disclosure item to clarify that:

- A person who is determined to be an audit committee financial expert will not be deemed an "expert" for any purpose, including for purposes of Securities Act Section 11, as a result of being designated as an audit committee financial expert.

- The designation of persons as audit committee financial experts does not impose on them any duties or liability that are greater than the duties and liability imposed on them as a member of the audit committee and board of directors in the absence of such designation.

- The designation of a person as an audit committee financial expert does not affect the duties or liability of any other member of the audit committee or the board.

Although other audit committee members may look to the audit committee financial expert as a resource on issues, audit committee members should work together to perform the committee's responsibilities. The safe harbor provides that other audit committee members may not abdicate their responsibilities.

This safe harbor clarifies that any information in a registration statement reviewed by audit committee financial experts is not "expertised" unless they are acting in the capacity of some other type of traditionally recognized expert. Similarly, because audit committee financial experts are not experts for purposes of Securities Act Section 11, they are not subject to a higher level of due diligence with respect to any portion of the registration statement.

Section 11 imposes liability for material misstatements and omissions in a registration statement, but provides a defense to liability for those who perform adequate due diligence. The level of due diligence required depends on the position held by a defendant and the type of information at issue. The type of information can be categorized as either "expertised," which means information that is prepared or certified by an expert who is named in the registration statement, or "non-expertised."

The role of the financial expert is to assist the audit committee in overseeing the audit process, not to audit the company. A conclusion that a financial expert is an "expert" for purposes of Section 11 might suggest a higher level of due diligence than is consistent with the audit committee's oversight duties.

In adopting the safe harbor, the SEC emphasized that all directors bear significant responsibility. State law generally imposes a fiduciary duty upon directors to protect the interests of shareholders, requiring directors to inform themselves of relevant facts and to use a critical eye in assessing information prior to acting on a matter. The SEC rules provide that the status of an audit committee financial expert does not alter duties under either federal or state law.

¶ 404 Board Determination

The Sarbanes-Oxley Act does not explicitly state who at the company should determine whether a person qualifies as an audit committee financial expert. The SEC believes that the board of directors in its entirety, as the most broad-based body within the company, is best-equipped to make the determination, subject to state law principles such as the business judgment rule.

Some foreign private issuers have a two-tier board, with one tier designated as the management board and the other tier designated as the supervisory or non- management board. In this circumstance, the supervisory board would be best-equipped to determine if a person qualifies as an audit committee financial expert.

¶ 405 Placement of Disclosure

The SEC rules require companies to include the new disclosure in their annual reports. A company may choose to include the audit committee financial expert disclosure in its proxy or information statement if the company incorporates such information by reference into its annual report.

Like a domestic issuer, a foreign private issuer will have to disclose whether it has an audit committee financial expert in its Exchange Act annual report. Because foreign private issuers are not subject to Regulation S-K, however, Forms 20-F and 40-F require the audit committee financial expert disclosure.

¶ 406 Investment Companies

The SEC applied substantially identical rules requiring investment companies to disclose annually that its board of directors has determined that the company either has at least one audit committee financial expert serving on its audit committee, and if so, the name of the expert and whether the expert is independent. An investment company disclosing that it does not have an audit committee financial expert must explain why it does not have such an expert. The disclosure requirements apply to all registered management investment companies, regardless of whether they have to file reports under Exchange Act Section 13(a) or 15(d).

Registered management investment companies must provide the audit committee financial expert disclosure in Item 3 of Form N-CSR. Small business investment companies must provide this disclosure in an exhibit to Form N-SAR.

As with an operating company, the board of an investment company must ensure that it names an audit committee financial expert who embodies the highest standards of personal and professional integrity. In this regard, the SEC advises the board to consider any disciplinary actions to which a potential expert is, or has been, subject in determining whether that person would be a suitable audit committee financial expert.

The SEC has adopted a test for whether an audit committee financial expert may be considered independent that differs from the test for operating companies. The definition of independence adopted for operating companies refers to the definition of independent used in Item 7(d)(3)(iv) of Schedule 14A, which generally is not applicable to investment companies.

To be considered independent, members of an investment company's audit committee may not, other than in their capacity as members of the audit committee, the board of directors, or any other board committee, accept directly or indirectly any consulting, advisory, or other compensatory fee from the issuer or be an "interested person" of the investment company, as defined in Investment Company Act Section 2(a)(19).

¶ 407 Asset-Backed Issuers

Due to their special nature, the SEC has exempted asset-backed issuers from the Section 407 disclosure provisions. The Commission reasoned that asset-backed issuers generally need not file the financial statements that other companies must file. Moreover, they are typically passive pools of assets, without an audit committee or board of directors or persons acting in a similar capacity.

CHAPTER 5

REPORT, CHARTER AND PROXY DISCLOSURE

¶ 501 Background

Since the early 1940s, the SEC has shown a continuing interest in promoting effective and independent audit committees. The SEC has often stressed the importance of audit committees to enable boards of directors to better fulfill their oversight responsibilities with regard to a company's accounting, financial reporting, and control obligations.

Beginning in the 1970s, in a number of SEC actions, companies consented to the establishment of audit committees as part of settling the actions. In *SEC v. Mattel* (D DofC 1974), 1974-1975 CCH Dec. ¶ 94,754, a court ordered the company to establish a financial controls and audit committee of four directors to review accounting procedures and controls, financial reports, and press releases. (See also *SEC v. Intercontinenal Diversified Corp.* (D DofC 1978),1977-1978 CCH Dec ¶ 96,271, in settling SEC enforcement action the company agreed to establish an audit committee consisting of independent members of its board of directors.)

As part of settling SEC enforcement actions, companies have also agreed to allow their existing audit committees to undertake additional duties. For example, in *SEC v. Litton Industries, Inc.* (D DofC 1981), 1981 CCH Dec. ¶ 97,891, a company charged with failure to adequately disclose the deferral of excess costs incurred in connection with military shipbuilding agreed to allow its audit committee to review cost deferral and revenue recognition determinations relating to some military procurements.

"Numbers Game" Speech

In a seminal speech in 1998, former SEC Chairman Arthur Levitt said that qualified, committed, independent and tough-minded audit committees represent the most reliable guardians of the public interest. The Chairman decried the type of audit committee whose members lack expertise in the basic principles of financial reporting as well as the mandate to ask probing questions. He had heard of an audit committee that convened only twice a year before the regular board meeting for fifteen minutes and whose duties were limited to a perfunctory presentation.

In contrast, Mr. Levitt sketched a better scenario in which audit committees meet twelve times a year before each board meeting; where every member has a financial background; where there are no personal ties to the chairman or the company; where they have their own advisers; where they ask tough questions of management and outside auditors; and where, ultimately, the interest of investors is being served. (Remarks by Arthur Levitt on the "Numbers Game" at the NYU Center for Law and Business, Sept 28, 1998.)

Blue Ribbon Committee

After Chairman Levitt's "Numbers Game" speech, the Blue Ribbon Committee on Improving the Effectiveness of Corporate Audit Committees was organized. This committee consisted of a group of investors, business executives, CEOs in the accounting profession, and leading legal experts. The blue ribbon panel was headed by John Whitehead, former Deputy Secretary of State and retired senior partner of Goldman, Sachs, and Ira Millstein, a lawyer and noted corporate governance expert.

In its report, the committee produced a number of recommendations. Since the report was issued, the New York Stock Exchange, the American Stock Exchange and the National Association of Securities Dealers have voted to modify their listing requirements to implement certain of these recommendations. At the SEC, the Commission adopted rules to implement some of the committee's recommendations.

SEC Disclosure Requirements

The SEC does not mandate that companies have an audit committee. But the listing standards of the primary U.S. securities exchanges do mandate that companies have an audit committee.

The increased scrutiny of audit committees coincides with significant changes in the financial markets, such as technological developments and increasing pressure on companies to meet earnings expectations. In turn, it is more important than ever for the financial reporting process to remain disciplined and credible. In this climate, it is reasonable to conclude that additional disclosures about a company's audit committee and its interaction with the company's auditors and management will promote investor confidence in the integrity of the financial reporting process.

The audit committee has a crucial role to play in assuring high quality financial reporting. By actively overseeing the financial reporting process, on a regular and in-depth manner, audit committees can reduce the incidence of earnings management. (Remarks by former SEC Deputy Chief Accountant John Morrissey, General Audit Management Conference, New Orleans, Louisiana, March 21, 2000.)

It was against this backdrop that the SEC acted to impose disclosure duties with regard to audit committees. Late in 1999, the Commission adopted rules to improve disclosure relating to the functioning of corporate audit committees and to enhance the reliability and credibility of public company financial statements. (Release No. 34-42266 (SEC 1999), 1999-2000 CCH Dec. ¶ 86,230.) Discussion of these disclosure requirements follows below.

¶ 502 Audit Committee Report

The rules require that companies include reports of their audit committees in their proxy statements. As discussed below, the report must state whether the audit committee, among other things, reviewed and discussed the audited financial statements with management, discussed with certain matters with the auditors, and recommended that the board include the audited financial statements in the company's annual report.

Background and Purpose

The SEC believes that disclosure will promote investor confidence in the markets by informing investors about the important role that audit committees play in the financial reporting process and will also enhance the reliability and credibility of corporate financial statements. A driving force behind the audit disclosure rules is a fear that inappropriate earnings management is distorting the true financial performance of many companies.

Given the changes in the financial markets, the SEC believes it is vitally important for investors to remain confident that they are receiving the highest quality financial reporting. The demand for reliable financial information is at an all time high, as technology makes information available to more people more quickly. The new dynamics of the capital markets have presented companies with an increasingly complex set of challenges. One challenge is that companies are under increasing pressure to meet earnings expectations.

In the SEC's view, the market changes and the increased pressures on companies to maintain positive earnings trends have highlighted the importance of strong and effective audit committees. The effective oversight of the financial reporting process is fundamental to preserving the integrity of the reporting system by overseeing and monitoring the participation of company management and the independent auditors in the financial reporting process. Audit committees are the corporate participant best able to perform that oversight function.

Generally, the SEC rules are intended to facilitate discussions among managers, outside auditors, and an independent, financially literate, audit committee.

The required disclosure is designed to help inform shareholders of the audit committee's oversight with respect to financial reporting and underscore the importance of that role. The SEC believes that, under state corporation law, the more informed the audit committee becomes through its discussions with management and the auditors, the more likely that the business judgment rule will apply and provide broad protection. Those discussions should serve to strengthen the information and reporting system that should be in place.

Contents of Report

As mentioned above, the SEC rules require that companies include reports of their audit committees in their proxy statements. The audit committee report must appear over the printed names of each member of the committee. This requirement is designed to emphasize for shareholders the importance of the audit committee's oversight role in the financial reporting process. Audit committee members do not, however, have to provide individual signatures.

In the report, the audit committee must state whether it has:

- Reviewed and discussed the audited financial statements with management;

- Discussed with the independent auditors the matters required to be discussed by Statement on Auditing Standards No. 61 (discussed below);

- Received from the auditors disclosures regarding the auditors' independence required by Independence Standards Board Standard No. 1 (discussed below) and discussed with the auditors their independence;

- Recommended, based on the review and discussions noted above, to the board of directors that the audited financial statements be included in the company's annual report for the last fiscal year for filing with the SEC.

¶502

The audit committee must disclose whether the review and discussions took place and whether the disclosures were received. The rules do not require the audit committee to perform the review and have the discussions, nor do they require it to take specific actions or adopt specific procedures. Similarly, the SEC does not require disclosure of the details of deliberations between or among the audit committee members, independent auditors, and management.

Statement on Accounting Standards No. 61

SAS 61 requires independent auditors to communicate certain matters related to the conduct of an audit to those who have responsibility for oversight of the financial reporting process, specifically the audit committee. Among the matters to be communicated to the audit committee are:

- methods used to account for significant unusual transactions;

- the impact of significant accounting policies in controversial or emerging areas for which there is a lack of authoritative guidance or consensus;

- the process used by management in formulating particularly sensitive accounting estimates and the basis for the auditor's conclusions regarding the reasonableness of those estimates; and

- disagreements with management over the application of accounting principles, the basis for management's accounting estimates, and the disclosures in the financial statements.

ISB Standard No. 1

This standard requires each auditor to disclose in writing to its client's audit committee all relationships between the auditor and the company that, in the auditor's judgment, reasonably may be thought to bear on independence and to discuss the auditor's independence with the audit committee.

In connection with an auditor's ISB-mandated discussion, audit committee members should request details of any matters that may affect the auditor's independence as well as the role and status of any individual at the audit firm whose independence may be in question. (See remarks of John Morrissey, former SEC Deputy Chief Accountant, at the General Audit Management Conference, March 21, 2000.)

¶ 503 Audit Committee Charter

The SEC believes that audit committees that have their responsibilities specified in a written charter are more likely to play an effective role in overseeing the company's financial reports. The charter should reflect the reasoned judgment of the board of directors regarding the role the company expects the audit committee to play. The Commission does not, however, require companies to adopt audit committee charters, nor does it dictate the content of the charter if one is adopted.

The Commission does not require companies to prepare audit committee charters. SEC rules, however, do require that companies disclose in their proxy statements whether their boards of directors have adopted a written charter for the audit committee and, if so, include a copy of the charter as an appendix to the proxy statement at least once every three years.

Concern had been expressed that the requirement to attach the charter would result in boilerplate charters. But the SEC believes that it is useful for shareholders to know about the duties of audit committees. While the Commission recognizes the inevitability that some of the same provisions will appear in charters of different audit committees, companies are encouraged to tailor the charters to their specific circumstances. (A sample audit committee charter, reproduced with permission from Financial Executives International (FEI), appears in the Appendix.)

The Blue Ribbon Committee on Improving the Effectiveness of Corporate Audit Committees had recommended that the audit committee state whether it has satisfied its responsibilities during the prior year in compliance with its charter. The SEC was concerned, however, that requiring a statement about compliance with the charter could have the undesired effect of encouraging skimpy, broadly-worded and vague committee charters to minimize the audit committee members' exposure to liability. Accordingly, the SEC does not require any statements about whether the audit committee has complied with the charter

As part of settling an SEC action, a company agreed to adopt an updated charter for its audit committee consistent with the blue ribbon committee's recommendations and the Commission's recently adopted audit committee rules. (*In re Microstrategy, Inc.* Release No. 34-43724, December 14, 2000.) The settlement required the charter to include provisions relating to:

- The independence of audit committee members;

- The oversight responsibilities of the audit committee, including those with respect to the positions and functions of the chief financial officer and director of internal audit; and

- The reporting obligations of the audit committee under Item 306 of Regulation S-K and Item 7(d)(3) of Schedule 14(a).

Best Practices

The following is a checklist of best practices in developing a charter for the audit committee. The charter should:

- Be written and tailored to the company environment,

- Clearly indicate committee duties and responsibilities.

- Be carefully reviewed and approved by the board of directors and periodically challenged and updated by the committee or board or both.

- Define the background and experience requirements for committee members.

- Define the committee's authority and specific responsibilities, particularly those relative to business and financial risk identification and related controls, compliance with laws and regulations, and oversight of internal and external audit activities.

- Set guidelines for the committee's relationships/meetings with members of the management team, internal/external auditors, and others, as appropriate.

- Set the frequency and general timing of meetings, allowing adequate time for preparation of substantive reporting to the full board.

- Define the committee's accountability and reporting requirements to the board and to the shareholders.

- Provide the authority for access to internal and external resources as the committee may require.

- Be reviewed, with input from appropriate members of management, auditors, and counsel.[1]

Proxy Statement

According to the SEC, the mandated disclosures in the rules must appear in the company's proxy statement because they could have a direct bearing on shareholders' voting decisions and because the proxy statement is actually delivered to shareholders and is accessible on the SEC's website. Companies must provide the disclosure only in a proxy statement relating to an annual meeting of shareholders at which directors are to be elected (or special meeting or written consents in lieu of such meeting). The disclosure needs to be provided only one time during the year (e.g., in a proxy statement for an annual meeting at which directors are to be elected, but not in proxy solicitation material used in a subsequent election contest during that same year).

¶ 504 Liability and Safe Harbors

The SEC does not believe that improved disclosure about the audit committee and increased involvement by the audit committee should result in increased exposure to liability. Because the language focuses on the annual audited financial statements and the filing of those financial statements with the Commission, the agency believes that this requirement will provide investors with a better understanding of the audit committee's oversight role in the financial reporting process. The committee's recommendation that the financial statements be used in SEC filings already is implicit in and consistent with board members signing the company's annual report, the SEC reasoned.

In addition, in performing its oversight function, the audit committee likely will be relying on advice and information that it receives in its discussions with management and the independent auditors. Accordingly, the text of the new requirement acknowledges that the audit committee had such discussions with management and the auditors, and, based on those discussions, made decisions about the financial statements and the filing of the company's annual report.

This approach is consistent with state corporation law that allows board members to rely, when reaching business judgments, on the representations of management and the opinions of experts retained by the corporation when reaching business judgments. In addition, the blue ribbon committee noted the impracticability of having the audit committee do more than rely upon the information it receives, questions, and assesses in making this disclosure.

Compliance with the disclosure requirement is mandatory, but there is no mandatory retention period for the information disclosed. Further, the audit committee will have to disclose whether it had certain discussions with management and the company's independent auditors. The substance of the discussions would not, however, have to be disclosed.

Some companies may seek the help of outside experts, particularly outside legal counsel, in formulating responses to the new requirements. In some circumstances, for instance, the audit committee may seek the advice of legal counsel before making the required disclosure about the audited financial statements.

Safe Harbors

The SEC rules provide safe harbors for the new proxy statement disclosures to protect companies and their directors from certain liabilities under the federal securities laws. In order to allay fears of liability on the part of audit committee members, the safe harbors would track the treatment of compensation committee reports under Item 402 of Regulation S-K.

Under the safe harbors, the additional disclosure would not be considered soliciting material, filed with the Commission, subject to Regulation 14A or 14C (and, therefore, not subject to the antifraud provisions of Rules 14a-9 or 14c-6) or to the liabilities of Exchange Act Section 18, except to the extent that the company specifically requests that it be treated as soliciting material, or specifically incorporates it by reference into a document filed under the Securities Act or the Exchange Act.

Although urged to do so, the Commission declined to provide a safe harbor from private litigation. In mandating disclosure by and about audit committees, the SEC did not intend to subject companies or their directors to increased exposure to liability under the federal securities laws, or to create new standards for directors to fulfill their duties under state corporation law. The Commission does not believe that the disclosure requirements will result in increased exposure to liability or create new standards.

To the extent the disclosure requirements would result in more clearly defined procedures for, and disclosure of, the operation of the audit committee, liability claims alleging breach of fiduciary duties under state law actually may be reduced. Accordingly, the agency believes that the safe harbors adopted are appropriate and sufficient.

According to former Chairman Levitt, if Delaware corporate law and the SEC's own administrative actions stand for a single proposition, it is that an active, involved and educated committee or board can rest more easily at night than a board composed of directors who merely go through the motions and watch the clock. In Mr. Levitt's view, greater disclosure, transparency, and oversight will not create greater legal exposure. Nor will a clear and necessary delineation of basic responsibilities create greater legal exposure. (Speech by SEC Chairman at the Audit Committee Symposium, New York, N.Y. June 29, 1999.)

¶ 505 Mutual Funds and Foreign Private Issuers

The SEC generally exempts mutual funds from the proxy disclosure statement requirements. However, closed-end funds are not similarly excluded since the SEC believes that application of the disclosure requirements to closed-end funds is warranted because of the critical role that audit committees play in overseeing the financial reporting process.

Foreign private issuers with a class of securities registered under Exchange Act Section 12 or that file reports under Exchange Act Section 15(d) are excluded from the audit committee disclosure mandates. Foreign private issuers currently are exempt from the proxy rules, need not file quarterly reports and are subject to different corporate governance regimes in their home countries. Accordingly, the SEC said it is not appropriate to extend the new requirements to foreign private issuers at this time.

¶ 506 Proxy Statement Disclosure

SEC proxy rules have for many years required certain proxy statement disclosures concerning audit committees. Specifically, if action is to be taken with respect to the election of directors, companies must disclose in their proxy statement or information statement: whether the company has a standing audit committee; the names of each committee member; the number of committee meetings held by the audit committee during the last fiscal year; and the functions performed by the committee. (See Item 7(d)(1) of Schedule 14A.) Identical information is required with respect to nominating and compensation committees of the board of directors

The SEC concluded that investors should be able to determine basic information about the audit committee's composition. To foster greater availability of this basic information, the Commission also requires that disclosure of the members of the audit committee be included or incorporated by reference in the annual report. In addition, because the Exchange Act now provides that, in the absence of an audit committee, the entire board of directors will be treated as the audit committee, a company that has not separately designated an audit committee must disclose that the entire board of directors is acting as the audit committee.

Similarly, the SEC rules require foreign private issuers that file their annual reports on Form 40-F to disclose members of the audit committee. Foreign private issuers that file their annual reports on Form 20-F already must identify the members of their audit committee in their annual reports. The Commission also requires these issuers to disclose if the entire board of directors is acting as the audit committee.

Although the Commission recognized that the adoption of this disclosure requirement could indirectly stimulate the establishment of audit committees, the Commission believes that disclosure of the nonexistence of an audit committee serves a valid informational purpose. In particular, whether or not a company has an audit committee and, if so, information concerning its functioning, helps the shareholders assess the effectiveness of the board's oversight of the company's accounting functions.

In light of the importance of strong committee systems and their impact on the oversight capabilities of the board of directors, shareholders who are being asked to make voting decisions with respect to the election of directors are entitled to know whether or not these important committees exist.

Agreeing with the SEC's assessment, one court held that a proxy statement regarding the existence of an audit committee of the company's board of directors was materially false and misleading since the audit committee never met or functioned. The proxy statement falsely conveyed to shareholders the impression that effective oversight of their company's accounting functions was being exercised by the board of directors. *SEC v. Falstaff* (CA DofC 1980), 1980 CCH Dec. ¶ 97,505. The court reasoned that the audit committee's existence implies a structured investigation and analysis of a company's fiscal welfare. Informal procedures may be adequate, but formal entities such as committees create at least the impression of great care and precision through detailed review and oversight. Stating that an audit committee, with its implication of careful oversight, existed when it did not is thus misleading.

¶506

Change in Accountants

The SEC believes that one of the principal duties of an audit committee should be that of recommending or approving the engagement or discharge of the company's independent accountants. Thus, the Commission requires disclosure in proxy statements and reports on Form 8-K of whether changes in accountants were recommended or approved by the board of directors or the audit committee. Companies that have audit committees must affirmatively state whether the committee reviewed the change. The SEC reasons that these disclosures should be useful to investors in better understanding and evaluating the company's relationship with its independent accountants. (See Section 604.04, Codification of Financial Reporting Policies.)

CHAPTER 6

REPORT TO AUDIT COMMITTEE

¶ 601 Introduction

Congress believes that it is important for the audit committee to be aware of key assumptions underlying a company's financial statements and of disagreements that the auditor has with management. The audit committee should be informed in a timely manner of such disagreements so that it can independently review them and intervene if necessary to assure the audit's integrity,

Thus, Sarbanes-Oxley Act Section 204 (reproduced at ¶ 2004) requires an accounting firm performing an audit to report in a timely manner to the company's audit committee:

- The critical accounting policies and practices to be used;

- All alternative treatments of financial information within GAAP that have been discussed with management;

- Any accounting disagreements between the auditor and management; and

- Other material written communications between the auditor and management.

Congressional Intent

The requirement is based on a belief that communication with the audit committee about such policies facilitate the audit committee's oversight of the financial reporting process. Moreover, investors should benefit by the audit committee being better informed and being in a position to challenge nontypical, aggressive, or improper applications of GAAP used by management to enhance or manipulate reports of the company's financial results or financial condition.

In addition, the requirement that auditors discuss specific accounting issues with the company's audit committee will not only increase the understanding of the company's board of directors, but also prevent directors from later claiming they were not informed about the company's accounting practices. (See remarks of Sen. Carl Levin, Cong. Rec., July 10, 2002, p. S6565.)

SEC Rules

Tracking Sarbanes-Oxley, SEC rules require a public accounting firm that audits a company's financial statements to report specified information to the audit committee, including:

- All critical accounting policies and practices used by the company;

- All material alternative accounting treatments within GAAP that have been discussed with management;

- Other material written communications between the accounting firm and management, such as any management letter or schedule of unadjusted differences; and

- In the case of investment companies, all non-audit services provided to entities in the investment company complex that were not pre-approved by the investment company's audit committee. (See 17 CFR 210.2-07.)

¶ 602 Critical Accounting Policies

The independent auditor must communicate to the audit committee all critical accounting policies and practices. In cautionary guidance set forth almost eight months before passage of Sarbanes-Oxley, the SEC said that critical accounting policies are those that are both most important to the portrayal of the company's financial condition and results and also require management's most difficult, subjective or complex judgments, often as a result of the need to make estimates about the effect of matters that are inherently uncertain. (See Release No. 33-8040 (SEC 2001), 2001-2002 CCH Dec. ¶ 86,609.)

As part of that cautionary advice, the SEC said that, prior to finalizing and filing annual reports, audit committees should review the selection, application and disclosure of critical accounting policies. Consistent with auditing standards, audit committees should be apprised of the evaluative criteria used by management in their selection of the accounting principles and methods. Proactive discussions between the audit committee and the company's senior management and auditor about critical accounting policies are appropriate.

The SEC advises accountants and companies to read and refer to the December 2001 Cautionary Guidance (Release No. 33-8040) to determine the types of matters that should be communicated to the audit committee. The Commission does not require that those discussions follow a specific form or manner, but does minimally expect that the discussion of critical accounting estimates and the selection of initial accounting policies will include the reasons why estimates or policies meeting the criteria in the cautionary guidance are or are not considered critical and how current and anticipated future events impact those determinations.

In addition, the SEC anticipates that the communications regarding critical accounting policies will include an assessment of management's disclosures along with any significant proposed modifications by the accountants that were not included.

¶ 603 Alternative Accounting Treatments

The SEC rules require communication by accountants to audit committees of all alternative treatments within GAAP for policies and practices related to material items that have been discussed with management, including the ramifications of the use of such alternative treatments and disclosures and the treatment preferred by the accounting firm. The rules are intended to cover recognition, measurement, and disclosure considerations related to the accounting for specific transactions as well as general accounting policies.

The communications regarding specific transactions should identify, at a minimum, the underlying facts, financial statement accounts impacted, and applicability of existing corporate accounting policies to the transaction. In addition, if the accounting treatment proposed does not comply with existing corporate accounting policies, or if an existing corporate accounting policy is not applicable, then an explanation of why the existing policy was not appropriate or applicable and the basis for the selection of the alternative policy should be discussed.

Regardless of whether the accounting policy selected preexists or is new, the entire range of alternatives available under GAAP that were discussed by management and the accountants should be communicated along with the reasons for not selecting those alternatives. If the accounting treatment selected is not, in the accountant's view, the preferred method, the SEC expects that the reasons why the accountant's preferred method was not selected by management also will be discussed.

Communications regarding general accounting policies should focus on the initial selection of and changes in significant accounting policies, as required by GAAS, and should include the impact of management's judgments and accounting estimates, as well as the accountant's judgments about the quality of the entity's accounting principles.

The discussion of general accounting policies should include the range of alternatives available under GAAP that were discussed by management and the accountants along with the reasons for selecting the chosen policy.

If an existing accounting policy is being modified, the reasons for the change should also be communicated. If the accounting policy selected is not the accountant's preferred policy, the discussion should include the reasons why the accountant considered one policy to be preferred but that policy was not selected by management.

The separate discussion of critical accounting policies and practices is not considered a substitute for communications regarding general accounting policies, since the discussion about critical accounting policies and practices might not encompass any new or changed general accounting policies and practices.

Likewise, the discussion of general accounting policies and practices is not intended to dilute the communications related to critical accounting policies and practices, since the issues affecting critical accounting policies and practices, such as sensitivities of assumptions and others, may be tailored specifically to events in the current year, and the selection of general accounting policies and practices should consider a broad range of transactions over time.

¶ 604 Other Material Written Communications

In Section 204 (see ¶ 2004), Sarbanes-Oxley specifically cites the management letter and schedules of unadjusted differences as examples of material written communications to be provided to audit committees. Examples of additional written communications that the SEC expects will be considered material to a company include:

- Management representation letter;
- Reports on observations and recommendations on internal controls;
- Schedule of unadjusted audit differences, and a listing of adjustments and reclassifications not recorded, if any;
- Engagement letter; and

- Independence letter.

The SEC does not consider these examples exhaustive, and encourages accountants to critically consider what additional written communications should be provided to audit committees.

¶ 605 Form and Timeliness

Neither Sarbanes-Oxley nor the SEC rules require that the communications between the audit committee and the independent accountant be in writing. The SEC expects, however, that such communications would be documented by the accountant and the audit committee.

Sarbanes-Oxley requires that the outside auditor's report to the audit committee be timely. SEC rules specify that the communications between the auditor and the audit committee must occur before filing the audit report with the Commission pursuant to applicable securities laws.

As a result, these discussions will occur, at a minimum, during the annual audit, but the SEC expects that they could occur as frequently as quarterly or more often on a real-time basis. The Commission is confident that the rules ensure that these communications will occur prior to filing of annual reports and proxy statements, as well as before registration statements and other periodic or current reports when audit reports are included.

¶ 606 Investment Companies

The SEC rules require the accountant to communicate to the audit committee of an investment company annually, and if the annual communication is not within 90 days prior to the filing, provide an update in the 90-day period prior to the filing, of any changes to the previously reported information. Also required would be communication of a description of all non-audit services provided, including fees associated with the services, to the investment company complex that were not subject to the pre-approval requirements for investment companies.

In effect, the rules would require an accountant of an investment company complex where the individual funds have different fiscal year ends to communicate the required information no more frequently than four times during a calendar year. In the SEC's view, this should not place an undue burden on investment company audit committees because many of the boards of directors for investment companies meet on a quarterly basis.

Similarly, the accountant only would need to disclose those non-audit services provided to the investment company complex that they were engaged to perform during the intervening period since their last communication, but for which pre-approval by the investment company's audit committee was not required.

CHAPTER 7

AUDITOR INDEPENDENCE

¶ 701 Introduction and Role of Audit Committee

The independent audit of corporate financial statements is a unique franchise of the accounting profession. For their part, companies have strong incentives to promote auditor independence since it is their financial statements that an auditor examines. Companies have the legal responsibility to file the financial information with the SEC as a condition of accessing the public securities markets, and it is their filings that are legally deficient if auditors who are not independent certify their financial statements.

Thus, independent auditors of company financial statements serve a critical public function. In recognition of its public responsibilities, the auditing profession has long held itself to a standard mandating that auditors must be independent of their corporate clients.

The auditor independence requirement is also embodied in the federal securities laws. The requirement serves two related, but distinct, public policy goals. One goal is to foster high quality audits by minimizing the possibility that any external factors will influence an auditor's judgments. The other related goal is to promote investor confidence in the financial statements of public companies.

The federal securities laws contemplate that investors are more likely to be assured that the financial statements are reliable if they know that the financial information has been subjected to rigorous examination by competent and independent auditors. More to the point, because objectivity rarely can be observed directly, investor confidence in auditor independence rests in large measure on investor perception of such independence.

Former SEC Chairman Arthur Levitt has emphasized that trust in the judgment of the public accountant, which underlies the capital markets, is dependent on the fact and appearance of the auditor's independence from the client. Without confidence in the auditor's objectivity and fairness, reasoned the former chairman, an investor cannot know whether to trust the numbers and, in turn, the financial markets cannot work without access to strong, high-quality financial reporting. (Interview with Gary Stern, President of the Minneapolis Federal Reserve Bank, Sept. 2000).

Under the federal securities laws, public companies must file with the SEC financial statements audited by a public accountant that is independent of the company preparing the financial statements. To implement these requirements, the SEC has promulgated rules defining what it means for an auditor to be independent of his or her audit client.

Prior to November 2000, the SEC auditor independence rules did not explicitly address many of the non-audit services that auditors were performing for audit clients that could imperil their independence. In November 2000, after the first detailed review of the rules in twenty years, the SEC amended its auditor independence rules and significantly revised the types of non-audit services that auditors could provide to their audit clients.

In that release, the SEC enunciated four oft-repeated basic principles of auditor independence: 1) there must not be a mutual or conflicting interest between the accountant and the audit client; 2) the auditor must not be placed in the position of auditing his or her own work; 3) the auditor must not act as management or employee of the audit client; and) 4) the auditor must not be an advocate for the audit client. These four principles are codified in the preliminary note to Section 210.2-01 of Regulation S-K.

Following the financial reporting scandals related to Enron, WorldCom, and other widely owned companies, the Sarbanes-Oxley Act of 2002 was passed. The Act placed auditor independence at the core of its efforts to restore trust and integrity to the financial markets. Moreover, the Act placed the audit committee at the very center of auditor independence.

In addition to prohibiting eight non-audit services, the Act provides that the audit committee must pre-approve all audit services and all non-audit services not already expressly prohibited. As directed by Sarbanes-Oxley, the SEC adopted new auditor independence rules to implement these provisions of the Act. These rules, which generally took effect in May 2003, address key aspects of auditor independence with special emphasis on the provision of non-audit services.

The rules reflect the fact that a conflict of interest arises from the provision of virtually any kind of non-audit service performed by an external auditor for an audit client company. Former SEC Commissioner Bevis Longstreth explained that this conflict derives from the fact that in performing these two kinds of services, audit and non-audit, the audit firm is really serving two different sets of clients. 1) the company's management in the case of non-audit services; and 2) the audit committee in the case of the audit. It is an obvious matter of common experience, explained the former commissioner, that in serving these different clients, which it is duty bound to do with undivided loyalty, the audit firm will be regularly subject to conflicts of interest that will tear at the heart of independence. (See testimony of former SEC Commissioner Bevis Longstreth before the SEC, Sept. 13, 2000).

PCAOB Inspections and Audit Committees

The Sarbanes-Oxley Act also created the Public Company Accounting Oversight Board to regulate auditors of public companies. The Act authorized the PCAOB to establish standards relating to auditor independence, including the power to add to the Act's eight categories of prohibited non-audit services.

Audit committees should understand that the PCAOB conducts regular inspections of audit firms annually or triennially depending on the size of the firm's audit practice and may also conduct special inspections of firms at any time. Board inspectors identify and examine the audits that carry the most risk, and sample what should be simpler, more routine audits. Inspectors also interview the chairs of the audit committees at audited companies to find out how well the auditor is communicating with the committee, which is now responsible to shareholders for hiring and firing the auditor.

¶701

The Board has spoken to audit committee chairs about a number of auditing issues, including the frequency of the committee's discussions with the company's external auditor. While the Board cannot compel the audit committee chairs to talk, most of them do. The interviews are usually conducted by telephone. Other issues discussed during the interviews are the critical accounting judgments raised by the auditor and the committee's philosophy on how it approves non-audit services performed by the auditor.

When an inspection report on an auditor is issued, the Board encourages the audit committee to ask the auditor what the Board concluded and how the findings might affect the audit. The audit committee should also ask if the Board found weaknesses, and if so, how those weaknesses will be corrected, as well as how they affected the company. (See remarks of Board member Dan Goelzer at Business Journal of Milwaukee seminar, Nov. 2004)

¶ 702 Sarbanes-Oxley Requirements

Sarbanes-Oxley Act Section 201 (reproduced at ¶ 2001) prohibits the auditor of the company's financial statements from providing certain non-audit services for the company and permits other non-audit services to be performed only if the service is pre-approved by the audit committee. Section 202 of the Act (reproduced at ¶ 2002) describes the pre-approval process.

The issue of auditor independence is at the center of the legislation. Public confidence in the integrity of financial statements of public companies is based on belief in the independence of the auditor from the audit client. Each of the federal securities laws requires comprehensive financial statements that must be prepared by an independent public or certified accountant.

The statutory independent audit requirement has two sides. It grants a franchise to the nation's public accountants since their services and certification must be secured before an issuer of securities can go to market, have the securities listed on the nation's stock exchanges, or comply with the reporting requirements of the securities laws. This is a source of significant private benefit to public accountants.

But the franchise is conditional. It comes in return for the CPA's assumption of a public duty and obligation. The U.S. Supreme Court has noted that, in certifying the public reports that collectively depict a company's financial status, the independent auditor assumes a public responsibility. That auditor owes ultimate allegiance to the company's creditors and stockholders, as well as to the investing public. This public watchdog function demands that the accountant maintain total independence from the client at all times and requires complete fidelity to the public trust. (*United States v. Arthur Young & Co.* (US Sup. Ct. 1984), 1983-84 CCH Dec. 99,721.)

Congress believes that there is arguably an inherent conflict in the fact that an auditor is paid by the company for which the audit is being performed. That conflict is implicit in the relationship between the auditor and the audit client. In the last fifteen years, however, the rapid growth in management consulting services offered by the major accounting firms has created a second and more substantial conflict that has eroded the independence that the auditor must bring to the audit function.

The Sarbanes-Oxley Act defines "non-audit services" to mean any professional services provided to a company by a registered public accounting firm, other than those provided to a company in connection with an audit or a review of the financial statements of an issuer.

The Senate Banking Committee considered adopting a complete prohibition on non-audit services by accounting firms for their audit clients, but instead decided on a somewhat more flexible approach. The Act establishes the serious separation of the auditing function and other consulting functions that accountants can perform. Generally, under the Act, if you are going to be an auditor, you have to be an auditor, not an auditor and consultant. (See remarks of Sen. Jack Reed, Cong. Rec., July 11, 2002, p. S6617-6618.)

Prohibited Services

Under Section 201 (see ¶ 2001), it is unlawful for a public accounting firm registered with the oversight board that performs an audit for a public company to provide, contemporaneously with the audit, the following non-audit services:

- Bookkeeping or other services related to the accounting records or financial statements of the audit client;
- Financial information systems design and implementation;
- Appraisal or valuation services, fairness opinions, or contribution-in-kind reports;
- Actuarial services;
- Internal audit outsourcing services;
- Management functions or human resources;
- Broker or dealer, investment adviser, or investment banking services;
- Legal services and expert services unrelated to the audit; and
- Any other service that the public company accounting oversight board determines, by regulation, is impermissible.

Public Company Accounting Oversight Board

The new Public Company Accounting Oversight Board may, on a case-by-case basis, exempt any person, company, public accounting firm, or transaction from the prohibition on the provision of non-audit services to the extent that such exemption is necessary or appropriate in the public interest and is consistent with the protection of investors. This exemptive power is subject to SEC review.

Tax Services

A registered public accounting firm may engage in any non-audit service, including tax services, that is not on the prohibited list for an audit client only if the activity is approved in advance by the company's audit committee. No limitations are placed on accounting firms in providing non-audit services to public companies that they do not audit or to any non-public companies.

Congressional Intent

While some had argued that standards for auditor independence should be left to the SEC and the new board, the approach adopted by the Act reflects Congress' belief that the issue of auditor independence is so fundamental to the problems currently being experienced in the financial markets that statutory standards are needed to assure the auditor's independence from the audit client. The Act adopts a strong, balanced approach to assure that, in return for the significant private benefits conferred on accounting firms by the securities laws, they maintain their independence from the companies they audit and fulfill their public trust.

The intention of this provision is to draw a clear line around a limited list of non-audit services that accounting firms may not provide to public company audit clients because their doing so creates a fundamental conflict of interest for the accounting firms. (See remarks of Sen. Paul Sarbanes, Cong. Rec, July 8, 2002, p. S6332.)

The list is based on simple principles. An accounting firm, in order to be independent of its audit client, should not audit its own work, which would be involved in providing bookkeeping services, financial information systems design, appraisal or valuation services, actuarial services, and internal audit outsourcing services to an audit client. The accounting firm should not function as part of management or as an employee of the audit client, which would be required if the accounting firm provides human resources services such as recruiting, hiring, and designing compensation packages for the officers, directors, and managers of an audit client. The accounting firm should not act as an advocate of the audit client, which would be involved in providing legal and expert services to an audit client in legal, administrative, or regulatory proceedings, or serving as a broker-dealer, investment adviser, or investment banker to an audit client, which places the auditor in the role of promoting a client's stock or other interests. (See remarks of Sen. Paul Sarbanes, Cong. Rec., July 8, 2002, p. S6332 and Senate Banking Committee Report No. 107-205.)

The accounting oversight board is given authority to make case-by-case exemptions in instances where the board believes an exemption is in the public interest and consistent with the protection of investors. Further, no limitations are placed on accounting firms in providing non-audit services to public companies that they do not audit or to any private companies. The purpose is to assure the audit's independence, not to put an end to the provision of non-audit services by accounting firms.

As explained by Sen. Sarbanes, if the accounting firm is not the auditor for the company, it can do any of these consulting services it wants. But if it is the auditor, thereby raising a conflict of interest problem, then Congress takes certain services and says those services you cannot do. And the reason is, in order to be independent, the auditor should not audit its own work, as it would do if it did financial information system design or appraisal evaluation services or actuarial services. They are the public company's auditors. They have a carefully defined responsibility as the auditors. The Act does not bar accounting firms from offering consulting services. It simply says that if a firm wants to audit the company, there are certain services it cannot perform. And even in that case, the Act provides the oversight board authority to grant case-by-case exceptions, so if a case could be made why an auditor's performing a consulting service ought to be permitted, there is some flexibility to permit it. (See remarks of Sen. Paul Sarbanes, Cong. Rec., July 8, 2002, p. S6332.)

Pre-Approval by Audit Committee

Section 202 (reproduced at ¶ 2002) requires audit committees to pre-approve audit services, as well as non-audit services other than those proscribed by the Act. Congress believed the protection of investors warrants requiring a company's audit committee to approve in advance the services that the auditor will provide to the company (if those services are not explicitly prohibited under the Act). Thus, the audit committee must pre-approve all of the services, both audit and non-audit, provided to that company by a regis-

¶702

tered accounting firm. Note, however, that a company's audit committee need not to pre-approve non-audit services provided by an accounting firm that is not auditing the issuer.

The audit committee must pre-approve a non-audit service before it commences. The audit committee may pre-approve at any time in advance of the activity. For example, an audit committee may grant pre-approval at its March meeting for a non-audit service that would begin in August. However, the SEC, or the accounting oversight board under its general authority, may specify a maximum period of time in advance of which the approval may not be granted, such as, for example, requiring the pre-approval to be granted no earlier than one year prior to the commencement of the service.

The Act does not limit the number of non-audit services that the audit committee may pre-approve at one meeting or occasion. Congress intends, however, that each non-audit service be specifically identified in order to be approved by the audit committee. Congress does not intend for the statutory requirement to be satisfied by an audit committee voting, for example, to permit any service that management determines appropriate for the auditor to perform or all non-audit services permissible under law.

Congress decided to offer audit committees a delegation option in their administration of the pre-approval requirement. Thus, the Act permits the audit committee to delegate to one or more of its members (who are members of the board of directors) the authority to pre-approve non-audit services. After a delegated member has granted a pre-approval, he or she must report the decision at the next meeting of the full audit committee. This delegation of authority may be useful where, for example, the audit committee is asked to determine whether or not to permit the company's auditor to perform a new non-audit service within a short period of time.

Waiver of Pre-Approval Requirement

Congress has also taken into account the atypical circumstance where an auditor is providing the company with a service that was anticipated to be an audit service within the scope of the engagement, but is later discovered to be a non-audit service. The Act provides that the pre-approval requirement is waived with respect to a non-audit service if:

- The service was not recognized by the company at the time of the audit engagement to be a non-audit service;

- The aggregate amount paid for all services described in (1) is not more than 5 percent of the total amount of revenues paid by the company to the auditor during the fiscal year when the non-audit services are performed;

- The service is promptly brought to the audit committee's attention, and the committee approves the activity prior to the audit's conclusion. This post-approval may be granted by the entire audit committee or by one or more audit committee members (who are members of the board of directors) to whom authority to grant such approvals has been delegated by the audit committee. (See Exchange Act Section 10A(i)(1)(B), at ¶ 2002.)

Audit committee approvals must be disclosed to investors in periodic reports filed with the SEC. (Exchange Act Section 10A(i)(2), at ¶ 2002.)

¶702

The Act specifically notes that audit services may entail providing comfort letters in connection with securities underwriting in order to make clear that providing such a comfort letter is an audit service. In addition, the conference committee inserted language to indicate that an audit of an insurance company required under state law is an auditing service.

Finally, the Act provides that if an audit committee approves an audit service within the scope of the engagement while carrying out its oversight work under new Exchange Act Section 10A(m)(2), the audit service will be deemed to have been pre-approved.

¶ 703 Prohibited Non-Audit Services

Tracking Sarbanes-Oxley, the SEC adopted rules related to the scope of services that independent accountants can provide to their audit clients. The rules clarify the scope of the prohibited services. The prohibited services contained in the rules only apply to non-audit services provided by independent accountants to their audit clients.

These rules do not limit the scope of non-audit services provided by an accounting firm to a non-audit client. Under the Act, the responsibility falls on the audit committee to pre-approve all audit and non-audit services provided by the accountant

Bookkeeping Services

An auditor cannot provide bookkeeping services to the audit client. Auditors cannot audit their own work and maintain their independence. Auditors providing bookkeeping services for their audit clients may be put in the position of later auditing their own work.

In addition, auditors who find errors in the bookkeeping could come under pressure not to raise the issue with the client if doing so could jeopardize the firm's contract with the client for bookkeeping services or result in a heightened litigation risk for the firm. In addition, keeping the books is a management function, which also is prohibited by Sarbanes-Oxley.

The SEC rules provide that all bookkeeping services would cause the auditor to lack independence unless it is reasonable to conclude that the results will not be subject to audit procedures.

The rules utilize the previous definition of bookkeeping or other services in Rule 2-01(c)(4)(i) of Regulation S-X, which focuses on the provision of services involving:

- maintaining or preparing the audit client's accounting records,

- preparing financial statements that are filed with the Commission or the information that forms the basis of financial statements filed with the Commission, or

- preparing or originating source data underlying the audit client's financial statements.

Experience with this definition demonstrates that the concept of bookkeeping and other services is well understood in practice.

Accountants sometimes are asked to prepare statutory financial statements for foreign companies that are not filed with the SEC. Consistent with the Commission's previous rules, an accountant's independence would be impaired when the accountant prepared the statutory financial statements if those statements form the basis of the financial statements that are filed with the SEC.

Under these circumstances, an accounting firm that has prepared the statutory financial statements of an audit client is put in the position of auditing its own work when auditing the resultant U.S. GAAP financial statements.

Financial Information Systems

The SEC rules forbid the auditor to provide any financial information systems design and implementation service, unless it is reasonable to conclude that the results of these services will not be subject to audit procedures during an audit of the audit client's financial statements. Prohibited services specifically precluded include:

- Directly or indirectly operating, or supervising the operation of, the audit client's information system or managing its local area network; or

- Designing or implementing a hardware or software system that aggregates source data underlying the financial statements or generates information that is significant to the audit client's financial statements or other financial information systems taken as a whole.

The rules prohibit the accountant from designing or implementing a hardware or software system that aggregates source data or generates information that is significant to the financial statements taken as a whole. In this context, information would be significant if it is reasonably likely to be material to the financial statements of the audit client.

Since materiality determinations may not be complete before financial statements are generated, the audit client and accounting firm by necessity will need to evaluate the general nature of the information as well as system output during the period of the audit engagement. An accountant, for example, would not be independent of an audit client for which it designed an integrated enterprise resource planning or similar system since the system would serve as the basis for the audit client's financial reporting system.

Designing, implementing, or operating systems affecting the financial statements may place accountants in a management role, or result in the auditing of their own work or attesting to the effectiveness of internal control systems they designed or implemented.

For example, if an auditor designs or installs a computer system that generates the financial records, and that system generates incorrect data, the accountant is placed in a position of having to report on the firms' own work. Investors may perceive that accountants would be unwilling to challenge the integrity and efficacy of the client's financial or accounting information collection systems that they designed or installed.

Note, however, that the prohibition does not preclude the accountant from evaluating the internal controls of a system as it is being designed, implemented or operated either as part of an audit or attest service and making recommendations to management. Likewise, the accountant would not be precluded from making recommendations on internal control matters to management or other service providers in conjunction with the design and installation of a system by another service provider.

Similarly, the rules do not preclude an accounting firm from working on hardware or software systems that are unrelated to the audit client's financial statements or accounting records as long as those services are pre-approved by the audit committee.

Appraisal and Valuation Services

The SEC rules prohibit the accountant from providing any appraisal service, valuation service or any service involving a fairness opinion or contribution-in-kind report for an audit client, unless it is reasonable to conclude that the results of these services will not be subject to audit procedures during an audit of the client's financial statements.

Appraisal and valuation services include any process of valuing assets, both tangible and intangible, or liabilities. They include valuing, among other things, in-process research and development, financial instruments, assets and liabilities acquired in a merger, and real estate. Fairness opinions and contribution-in-kind reports are opinions and reports in which the firm provides its opinion on the adequacy of consideration in a transaction.

To allow the provision of these services would raise the specter that, when it came time to audit the financial statements, auditors would likely be reviewing their own work, including key assumptions or variables that underlie an entry in the financial statements. Also, if the appraisal methodology involves a projection of future results of operations and cash flows, the accountant preparing the projection may be unable to evaluate skeptically and without bias the accuracy of that valuation or appraisal.

The rules do not prohibit an accounting firm from providing such services for non-financial reporting, such as transfer pricing studies, cost segregation studies, and other tax-only valuations purposes.

Also, the rules do not prohibit an accounting firm from utilizing its own valuation specialist to review the work performed by the audit client itself or an independent, third-party specialist employed by the audit client, provided the audit client or the client's specialist, and not the specialist used by the accounting firm, provides the technical expertise that the client uses in determining the required amounts recorded in the client financial statements.

In those instances, accountants would not be auditing their own work because a third party or the audit client is the source of the financial information subject to the audit. Additionally, the quality of the audit may be improved where specialists are utilized in such situations.

Actuarial Services

Auditors providing actuarial services are placed in a position of auditing their own work. In addition, accountants providing these services assume a key management task.

Thus, the SEC rules prohibit an accountant from providing to an audit client any actuarially-oriented advisory service involving the determination of amounts recorded in the financial statements and related accounts for the audit client other than assisting a client in understanding the methods, models, assumptions, and inputs used in computing an amount, unless it is reasonable to conclude that the results of these services will not be subject to audit procedures during an audit of the audit client's financial statements.

It is permitted, however, to advise the client on the appropriate actuarial methods and assumptions that will be used in the actuarial valuations. It is not appropriate for the accountant to provide the actuarial valuations for the audit client.

The rules also provide that accountants may utilize their own actuaries to assist in conducting the audit provided the audit client uses its own actuaries or third-party actuaries to provide management with its actuarial capabilities.

Internal Audit Outsourcing

Historically, a number of companies have outsourced the internal audit function by contracting with an outside source to perform, among other things, all or part of their audits of internal controls.

As emphasized by the Committee of Sponsoring Organizations (COSO), internal auditors play an important role in evaluating and monitoring a company's internal control system. As a result, arguably, internal auditors are, in effect, part of a company's system of internal control.

Before Sarbanes-Oxley, SEC rules allowed a company to outsource part of its internal audit function to the independent audit firm subject to certain exemptions. Sarbanes-Oxley has changed all that. Since external auditors typically will at least partially rely on the existence of an internal audit function and consider its impact on the internal control system when conducting the audit of the financial statements, they may be placed in the position of auditing their firm as part of the internal control system. Further, if the internal audit function is outsourced to an accountant, the accountant assumes a management responsibility and becomes part of the company's control system.

SEC rules now prohibit the outside accountant from providing to the audit client internal audit outsourcing services. This prohibition would include any internal audit service that has been outsourced by the audit client that relates to the client's internal accounting controls, financial systems, or financial statements unless it is reasonable to conclude that the results of these services will not be subject to audit procedures during an audit of the client's financial statements.

During the conduct of the audit in accordance with generally accepted auditing standards, or when providing attest services related to internal controls, the auditor evaluates the company's internal controls and, as a result, may recommend improvements. Doing so is a part of the accountant's responsibilities under GAAS or applicable attestation standards and, therefore, does not constitute an internal audit outsourcing engagement.

Similarly, the prohibition on outsourcing does not preclude engaging the accountant to perform nonrecurring evaluations of discrete items or other programs that are not in substance the outsourcing of the internal audit function.

For example, the company may engage the accountant, subject to the audit committee pre-approval requirements, to conduct agreed-upon procedures engagements related to the company's internal controls, since management takes responsibility for the scope and assertions in those engagements.

The prohibition also does not preclude the accountant from performing operational internal audits unrelated to the internal accounting controls, financial systems, or financial statements.

¶703

Management Functions

The SEC rules prohibit the accountant from acting, even temporarily, as a director, officer, or employee of an audit client, or performing any decision-making, supervisory, or ongoing monitoring function for the client.

However, services in connection with the assessment of internal accounting and risk management controls, as well as providing recommendations for improvements, do not impair an accountant's independence.

Accountants must gain an understanding of their audit clients' systems of internal controls when conducting an audit in accordance with GAAS. With this insight, accountants often become involved in diagnosing, assessing, and recommending to audit committees and management ways in which their audit client's internal controls can be improved or strengthened.

The resulting improvements in the audit client's controls not only result in improved financial reporting but also can facilitate the performance of high quality audits. For these reasons, the SEC will allow accountants to assess the effectiveness of an audit client's internal controls and to recommend improvements in the design and implementation of internal controls and risk management controls.

Designing and implementing internal accounting and risk management controls, a prohibited service under Sarbanes-Oxley, is fundamentally different from obtaining an understanding of the controls and testing the operation of the controls, which is an integral part of any audit of the financial statements of a company.

Similarly, design and implementation of these controls involves decision-making and, therefore, is different from recommending improvements in the internal accounting and risk management controls of an audit client, which is permissible if pre-approved by the audit committee.

For example, management could engage a third-party service provider to design and implement an inventory control system. In the course of that engagement, the third-party service provider might ask the accountant to make recommendations on internal control and accounting system components that have been included in the system being designed. Providing such recommendations to the third-party service provider would not place the independent accountant in the role of management.

Because of this fundamental difference, designing and implementing internal accounting and risk management controls impairs the accountant's independence because it places the accountant in the role of management.

Conversely, obtaining an understanding of, assessing effectiveness of, and recommending improvements to the internal accounting and risk management controls is fundamental to the audit process and does not impair the accountant's independence.

Furthermore, accountants may be engaged by the company, subject to audit committee pre-approval, to conduct an agreed-upon procedures engagement related to the company's internal controls or to provide attest services related to the company's internal controls without impairing their independence.

¶703

Human Resources

The SEC rules provide that an accountant is prohibited from providing human resources functions for audit clients. The accountant's independence is impaired with respect to an audit client when the accountant:

- searches for or seeks out prospective candidates for managerial, executive or director positions;

- acts as negotiator on the audit client's behalf, such as determining position, status, compensation, fringe benefits, or other conditions of employment;

- undertakes reference checks of prospective candidates.

- engages in psychological testing, or other formal testing or evaluation programs, or

- recommends or advises the audit client to hire a specific candidate for a specific job.

Assisting management in human resource selection or development places the accountant in the position of having an interest in the success of the employees that the accountant has selected, tested, or evaluated. Accordingly, observers may perceive that an accountant would be reluctant to suggest the possibility that those employees failed to perform their jobs appropriately, or at least reasonable investors might perceive the accountant to be reluctant, because doing so would require the accountant to acknowledge shortcomings in its human resource service.

The accountant also might have other incentives not to report such employees' ineffectiveness, including that the accountant would identify and be identified with the recruited employees.

Broker-Dealer, Investment Adviser Or Investment Banking Services

Outside accountants are prohibited from performing brokerage or investment advising services for an audit client. Under SEC rules, they cannot:

- Act as a broker-dealer, registered or unregistered, promoter, or underwriter, on behalf of an audit client;

- Make investment decisions on behalf of the client or otherwise have discretionary authority over the client's investments;

- Execute a transaction to buy or sell the client's investment; or

- Have custody of assets of the client, such as taking temporary possession of securities purchased by the client.

Unregistered broker-dealers were included in the prohibition because the nature of the threat to independence is unchanged whether the entity is or is not registered.

Accountants and the companies that employ them should recognize that the key determination required here is a functional one, which is whether the accounting firm or its employee is acting as a broker-dealer.

The failure to register as a broker-dealer does not necessarily mean that the accounting firm is not a broker-dealer. Involvement of accounting personnel as unregistered broker-dealers not only can impair auditor independence, but also would violate Exchange Act Section 15(a).

It is evident that selling an audit client's securities is incompatible with the accountant's duty of assuring the public that the company's financial condition

¶703

is fairly presented. Accountants, in any capacity, recommending to anyone that they buy or sell the securities of an audit client have an interest in whether those recommendations were correct, an interest that could affect the audit of the client whose securities were recommended.

These concepts are echoed in the simple principles included in the legislative history to the Sarbanes-Oxley Act. In such a situation, if an accountant uncovers an accounting error in a client's financial statements, and the accountant, in an investment adviser capacity, had recommended that client's securities to investment clients, the accountant performing the audit may be reluctant to recommend changes to the client's financial statements if the changes could negatively affect the value of the securities recommended by the accountant to its investment adviser clients.

Senator Sarbanes understood this when he said that auditors should not be promoters of the company's stock or other financial interest as they would be if they served as broker, investment adviser, or investment banker for the company since this would place them in a position of serving as an advocate for their audit client. (See 148 Cong. Rec. S7364 (July 25, 2002).)

Brokers often give advice and recommendations on investments and investment strategies, the value of which is measured by the performance of a customer's securities portfolio. When the customer is an audit client, the accountant has an interest in the value of the client's securities portfolio, even as the accountant must determine whether management has properly valued the portfolio as part of an audit. Thus, they would be placed in a position of auditing their own work. Furthermore, the accountant is placed in a position of acting as an advocate on behalf of the client.

But note that the rules do not change the Commission's previous position that an audit firm's broker-dealer division can cover an industry, including industry surveys and analyses, which includes an audit client, when performing analyst functions. However, analysis of a specific audit client's stock places auditors in the position of acting as advocates for the client and would cause them to lose their independence.

Legal Services

Auditors lack independence when they provide legal services to an audit client. Specifically, the SEC rules prohibit an accountant from providing to an audit client any service that, under circumstances in which the service is provided, could be provided only by someone licensed, admitted, or otherwise qualified to practice law in the jurisdiction in which the service is provided.

This prohibition comports with the SEC's long-held view that an individual cannot be both a zealous legal advocate for management or the client company and, at the same time, maintain the objectivity and impartiality that are necessary for an audit.

The SEC recognizes that there may be implications for some foreign registrants. For example, in some jurisdictions it is mandatory that someone licensed to practice law perform tax work, and that an accounting firm providing such services, therefore, would be deemed to be providing legal services. Generally, the rules are not intended to prohibit foreign accounting firms from providing services that an accounting firm in the United States may provide.

In determining whether a service would impair the accountant's independence solely because the service is labeled a legal service in a foreign jurisdiction, the Commission will consider whether the provision of the service would be prohibited in the United States as well as in the foreign jurisdiction. Evaluating and determining whether services are permissible may require a comprehensive analysis of the facts and circumstances.

Expert Services

Clients retain experts to lend authority to their contentions in various proceedings by virtue of the expert's specialized knowledge and experience. In situations involving advocacy, the provision of expert services by the accountant makes the accountant part of the team that has been assembled to advance or defend the client's interests. The appearance of advocacy created by providing such expert services is sufficient to deem the accountant's independence impaired.

Thus, the SEC rules prohibit an accountant from providing expert opinions or other services to an audit client, or a legal representative of an audit client, for the purpose of advocating that client's interests in litigation or regulatory, or administrative investigations or proceedings.

Examples: Independence would be impaired if the auditor were engaged to provide forensic accounting services to the client's legal representative in connection with the defense of an investigation by the Commission's Division of Enforcement. Additionally, independence would be impaired if the audit client's legal counsel, in order to acquire the requisite expertise, engaged the accountant to provide such services in connection with a litigation, proceeding or investigation.

It can be seen that the prohibition on providing expert services covers engagements that are intended to result in the accounting firm's specialized knowledge and experience being used to support the audit client's positions in various adversarial proceedings.

In one sense, virtually all services provided by an accountant may be perceived to be expert services. But the prohibition only applies to those services that involve advocacy in proceedings and investigations and does not apply to other permitted non-audit services, such as tax services.

Thus, the rules do not preclude an audit committee or, at its direction, its legal counsel, from engaging the accountant to perform internal investigations or fact finding engagements. These types of engagements may include, among others, forensic or other fact-finding work that results in the issuance of a report to the audit client. The involvement by the accountant in this capacity generally requires performing procedures that are consistent with, but more detailed or more comprehensive than, those required by GAAS.

Performing such procedures is consistent with the role of the independent auditor and should improve audit quality. If, subsequent to the completion of such an engagement, a proceeding or investigation is initiated, accountants may allow their work product to be utilized by the audit client and its legal counsel without impairing their independence. The accountant, however, may not then provide additional services, but may provide factual accounts or testimony about the work performed.

It follows that the rules would not prohibit an accountant from assisting the audit committee in fulfilling its responsibilities to conduct its own investigation of a potential accounting impropriety. For example, if the audit committee is concerned about the accuracy of the inventory accounts at a subsidiary, it may engage the auditor to conduct a thorough inspection and analysis of those accounts, the physical inventory at the subsidiary, and related matters without impairing the auditor's independence.

Furthermore, independence is not impaired if, in an investigation or proceeding, an accountant provides factual accounts or testimony describing work it performed. Similarly, independence is not impaired if an accountant explains the positions taken or conclusions reached during the performance of any service provided for the audit client.

The SEC is aware that auditors have obligations under Exchange Act Section 10A to search for fraud that is material to corporate financial statements and to make sure the audit committee and others are informed of their findings. Auditors should conduct these procedures whether they become aware of a potential illegal act as a result of audit, review or attestation procedures they have performed or as a result of the audit committee expressing concerns about a part of the company's operations or compliance with the company's financial reporting system.

In these situations, the SEC assures that the auditor may conduct the procedures, with the approval of the audit committee, and provide the reports that the auditor deems appropriate. Should litigation arise or an investigation commence during the time period that the auditors are conducting such procedures, the SEC would not deem the completion of these procedures to be prohibited expert services so long as the auditors remain in control of their work and the work does not become subject to the direction or influence of the company's legal counsel.

But note that an auditor's independence would be impaired if its assistance to the audit committee included defending, or helping to defend, the audit committee or the company generally in a shareholder class action or derivative lawsuit, other than as a fact witness.

Tax Services

One of the most controversial issues taken up by Congress and the SEC during the corporate reform process was whether an accountant's provision of tax services for an audit client can impair independence. Ultimately, Congress decided not to prohibit the provision of tax services by the external auditor.

The Sarbanes-Oxley Act specifically recognizes that accountants may engage in non-audit related tax services subject to audit committee pre-approval. This language in Section 201 reveals a congressional intent that auditor independence is not impaired by an accountant providing traditional tax preparation services to an audit client or its affiliate.

Tax services are unique among non-audit services for a variety of reasons. Detailed tax laws must be consistently applied, and the Internal Revenue Service has discretion to audit any tax return. Moreover, accounting firms have historically provided a broad range of tax services to their audit clients. Indeed, the provision of tax services by accountants to their audit clients existed and continued without change when Congress formulated the securities laws in the 1930s.

After the enactment of Sarbanes-Oxley, the SEC reiterated its long-standing position that an accounting firm can provide tax services to its audit clients without impairing the firm's independence. While the agency does not define "tax services," the Commission understands that tax services can include a range of activities including:

- The preparation of tax returns;
- Tax compliance;
- Tax planning;
- Tax recovery; and
- Other tax-related services.

In addition, many engagements will require that an auditor review the tax accrual that is included in the financial statements. Reviewing tax accruals is part of audit services and is not, in and of itself, a tax compliance service.

Accordingly, accountants may continue to provide tax services such as tax compliance, tax planning, and tax advice to audit clients, subject to the normal audit committee pre-approval requirements. The SEC also requires companies to disclose the amount of fees paid to the accounting firm for tax services.

Cautionary note

Merely labeling a service as a tax service will not necessarily eliminate its potential to impair independence. Audit committees should understand that providing certain tax services to an audit client could, in certain circumstances, impair the auditor's independence.

Specifically, accountants would impair their independence by representing an audit client before a tax court, district court, or federal court of claims.

Similarly, it would not be appropriate to provide a prohibited service, label it a tax service, and argue that it is therefore permissible. For example, an accountant seeking to provide a brokerage service and arguing that, because there are tax implications of certain brokerage activities, the service is permissible would be attempting to improperly circumvent the list of prohibited services.

Best practices

Audit committees should carefully scrutinize the retention of an accountant in a transaction initially recommended by the accountant, the sole business purpose of which may be tax avoidance and the tax treatment of which may be not supported in the Internal Revenue Code.

An accounting firm should not be providing novel and debatable tax strategies and products that involve income tax shelters and extensive offshore partnerships or affiliates to audit clients. (See The Conference Board Commission on Public Trust and Private Enterprise, Findings and Recommendations, January 9, 2003, p. 37.)

Test

As a general matter, the SEC urges the audit committee to be aware of three basis principles when evaluating whether a proposed non-audit service is an allowable tax service or constitutes a prohibited legal service or expert service. (Release No. 33-8154.) The auditor cannot: (1) audit his or her own work; (2) function as a part of management; or (3) serve in an advocacy role for the client.

For example, an accountant providing representation before a tax court would be serving as the client's advocate and independence would be impaired.

Another example would be the formulation of tax strategies, such as tax shelters, designed to minimize a company's tax obligations. The provision of these types of services may require accountants to audit their own work, to become an advocate for the client's position on novel tax issues, or to assume a management function.

It can thus be seen that the audit committee must carefully scrutinize the impact on an auditor's independence of any transaction that is recommended by the auditor that is unrelated to the company's business plans or operations. Such transactions often have the sole purpose of tax avoidance and may not be supported in specific Internal Revenue Code provisions. Further, these transactions may be viewed as being initiated by the auditor, not the company, and might result in the auditor performing a management function. They also may result in an auditor auditing the results of a transaction that, but for the auditor bringing the transaction to the company, the company would not have entered into or even considered. This might be viewed as resulting in an auditor auditing the results of his or her own transaction. (See memorandum of Scott Taub, SEC Deputy Chief Accountant, Office, attached to letter from SEC Chairman William Donaldson to five consumer groups, July 11, 2004).

In some circumstances, even the provision of traditional tax services, such as preparing the company's tax returns, might impair an auditor's independence. One such circumstance may be when the service results in the auditor recommending abusive tax shelters to the company.

Thus, the audit committee should not summarily approve such services, even if the auditor routinely has provided them to the company for years. Rather, the SEC staff advises that each service should be evaluated annually to assure that it is, in fact, a tax service and to identify any concerns with proposed tax services that would lead a reasonable investor to question the integrity of the audit or the reliability of the company s financial statements. For example, audit committees should consider whether the auditor inappropriately has supplanted the role of management and the board in this area. (See memorandum from Scott Taub, SEC Deputy Chief Accountant, attached to letter from SEC Chairman William Donaldson to five consumer groups, July 11, 2004).

SEC Chief Accountant Donald Nicolaisen has emphasized that audit committees, in approving any audit or non-audit services, should be aware that any agreement that provides for the possible additional payment of a value-added fee based on the results of the an audit firm's performance of a tax or other service would be seen as impairing the firm's independence. In his view, the audit committee should carefully consider the impact on an accounting firm's independence of the possibility of even a completely voluntary payment of a value-added fee by an audit client. (See letter of Chief Accountant Donald Nicolaisen to the AICPA Professional Ethics Executive Committee, May 21, 2004).

Tax Shelters and Tax Services to Executives

Since the SEC issued its new rules, two types of tax services have raised serious concerns among investors, auditors, and regulators on the independence of accounting firms that provide both auditing and tax services. First, the Internal Revenue Service and the Department of Justice have brought a number of cases against accounting firms in connection with the marketing of tax shelter products. Second, audit firms have been criticized for providing tax services, including tax shelter products, to senior executives of their public company audit clients.

The provision of tax services to the executives of an audit client is not expressly addressed in either the Sarbanes-Oxley Act or in the SEC's rules. But the SEC staff has advised audit committees to review the provision of those services to assure that reasonable investors would conclude that the auditor providing such services is capable of exercising objective and impartial judgment on all issues within the audit engagement. (See memorandum from Scott Taub, SEC Deputy Chief Accountant, attached to letter from SEC Chairman William Donaldson to five consumer groups, July 11, 2004).

Exercising its authority under the Sarbanes-Oxley Act, the PCAOB has proposed Rule 3523 to provide that an auditor would not be considered independent if it provided any tax service to an officer in a financial reporting oversight role at the client company. Similarly, the Board would prohibit the auditor's provision of tax services in connection with tax shelters and aggressive tax transactions (Proposed Rule 3522).

In addition the PCAOB has proposed a rule designed to strengthen the auditor's responsibilities in seeking pre-approval of tax services. Proposed Rule 3524 would require an auditor seeking such pre-approval to provide the committee with detailed documentation of the nature and scope of the proposed tax service, discuss with the committee the potential effects of the tax service on the firm's independence, and document the firm's discussion with the committee.

The proposed rule would also require the auditor to provide the audit committee with an engagement letter that includes descriptions of the scope of any tax service under review and the fee structure for the engagement. Similarly, the audit committee would be given any amendment to the engagement letter or any other oral or written agreement relating to the service between the firm and the client company.

¶ 704 Administration of Audit Engagement

Historically, management retained the accounting firm, negotiated the audit fee, and contracted with the accounting firm for other services. The Sarbanes-Oxley Act changed that paradigm by requiring audit committees to be directly responsible for the appointment, compensation, and oversight of the work of auditors, and requiring auditors to report directly to the audit committee.

Both Sarbanes-Oxley and the SEC rules recognize the critical role that audit committees can play in the financial reporting process and in helping accountants maintain their independence from audit clients. An effective audit committee may enhance the accountant's independence by, among other things, providing a forum apart from management where the accountants may discuss their concerns. It may facilitate communications among the board of directors, management, internal auditors and independent accountants. An audit committee also may enhance auditor independence from management by appointing, compensating and overseeing the work of the independent accountants.

In that light, Sarbanes-Oxley Act Section 202 (see ¶ 2002) requires that audit committees pre-approve both audit services and permitted non-audit services of the accounting firm.

SEC rules require that the audit committee pre-approve all permissible non-audit services and all audit, review or attest engagements required under the securities laws. The rules require that before the accountant is engaged by the company to render the service, the engagement is:

- Approved by the audit committee; or

- Entered into pursuant to pre-approval policies and procedures established by the audit committee, provided the policies and procedures are detailed as to the particular service, the audit committee is informed of each service, and such policies and procedures do not include delegation of the audit committee's responsibilities to management.

The SEC rules thus embody the concept that the audit committee may pre-approve audit and non-audit services based on policies and procedures. Both explicit approval and approval based on policies and procedures are equally acceptable.

As provided in the Sarbanes-Oxley Act, the rules recognize audit services to be broader than those services required to perform an audit pursuant to GAAS. For example, the Act identifies as audit services those services related to the issuance of comfort letters in connection with securities underwriting and related to statutory audits required for insurance companies for purposes of state law. The SEC recognizes that domestically and internationally there are various requirements for statutory audits. Thus, such engagements are viewed as audit services in the context of the rules.

Furthermore, audit services also would include services performed to fulfill the accountant's responsibility under GAAS. For example, in some situations, a tax partner may be involved in reviewing the tax accrual that appears in the company's financial statements. Since that is a necessary part of the audit process, the activity constitutes an audit service.

Likewise, complex accounting issues may require that the firm engage in consultation with its national office or other technical reviewers to reach an audit judgment. Whether or not the firm separately charges for that consultation, the activity constitutes an audit service since it is a necessary procedure used by the accountant in reaching an opinion on the financial statements.

This would contrast with a situation where a company is evaluating a proposed transaction and asks the independent accountant to evaluate the accounting for the proposed transaction. After research and consultation, the accounting firm provides an answer to the company and bills for those services. In considering the nature of the services, these services would not be considered to be audit services.

The rules require that the audit committee pre-approve all services. In doing so, Sarbanes-Oxley permits the audit committee to establish policies and procedures for pre-approval provided they are detailed as to the particular service and designed to safeguard the continued independence of the accountant.

For example, the Act allows for one or more audit committee members who are independent board directors to pre-approve the service. Decisions made by the designated audit committee members must be reported to the full audit committee at each of its scheduled meetings.

Sarbanes-Oxley allows the audit committee to pre-approve a service at any time in advance of the activity. The SEC expects that audit committees will establish policies for the maximum period in advance of the activity the approval may be granted.

De Minimis Exception

Consistent with Sarbanes-Oxley, the SEC rules reflect a de minimis exception solely related to the provision of non-audit services. This exception waives the pre-approval requirements for non-audit services provided that:

- all such services do not aggregate to more than five percent of total revenues paid by the audit client to its accountant in the fiscal year when services are provided;

- were not recognized as non-audit services at the time of the engagement, and

- are promptly brought to the attention of the audit committee and approved prior to the completion of the audit by the committee or one or more designated representatives.

Investment Companies

The SEC rules limit an investment company's audit committee pre-approval responsibility to those services provided directly to the investment company and those services provided to an entity in the investment company complex where the nature of the services provided have a direct impact on the operations or financial reporting of the company. The investment company's audit committee could assess and determine before the work is conducted the impact that the services might reasonably have on the investment company accountant's independence as it relates to the audits of the company's financial statements.

In addition, only the service providers that provide ongoing services to the investment company must have their non-audit services pre-approved. Thus, the rules would limit the number of instances where pre-approval would be sought from multiple audit committees in the complex.

Although it may not be practical or feasible for the investment company audit committee to pre-approve all services provided to the fund complex, the SEC believes that the audit committee should be aware of all services the accountant is providing to entities in the complex. As a result, the rules require that the accountant disclose to the audit committee all services provided to the investment company complex, including the fees associated with those services.

In the SEC's view, the calculation of the de minimis exception should not relate solely to the level of services provided to the investment company. Thus, the rules provide that the threshold will be determined based on the services provided to the investment company complex that were subject to the pre-approval requirements for the investment company's audit committee.

Interaction with ICA Section 32(a)

Investment Company Act Section 32(a) requires that independent auditors of registered investment companies be appointed by majority vote of the disinterested directors. To reconcile the new auditor independence rules with Section 32(a), the investment company's audit committee must separately approve the independent auditor.

¶704

Shareholder ratification

In 2001, the SEC adopted Rule 32a-4 (reproduced at ¶ 3004) exempting mutual funds from the Investment Company Act's requirement that shareholders vote on the selection of the fund's independent public accountant so long as the fund has an audit committee composed wholly of independent directors. The rule permits continuing oversight of the fund's accounting and auditing processes by an independent audit committee, in place of the shareholder vote. Commenters agreed that the shareholder ratification has become largely perfunctory, and that an independent audit committee could exercise more meaningful oversight. (See Release No. IC-24816 (SEC 2001), 2000-01 CCH Dec. ¶ 86,411.)

Under the rule, a fund is exempt from having to seek shareholder approval of its independent public accountant if:

- The fund establishes an audit committee composed solely of independent directors that oversees the fund's accounting and auditing processes;

- The fund's board of directors adopts an audit committee charter setting forth the committee's structure, duties, powers, and methods of operation, or sets out similar provisions in the fund's charter or bylaws; and

- The fund maintains a copy of such an audit committee charter.

The rule permits the fund either to adopt an audit committee charter or to set forth audit committee provisions in the fund's charter or bylaws.

The rule does not require, nor does the SEC intend, that an audit committee perform daily management or supervision of a fund's operations. The SEC recognizes that audit committees function may vary from company to company and that firms need flexibility to determine all of the specific duties and functions of their audit committees.

Staff Interpretations

In can thus be seen that the SEC's rules include three requirements that must be followed in the audit committee's use of pre-approval through policies and procedures.

- The policies and procedures must be detailed as to the particular services to be provided.

- The audit committee must be informed about each service.

- The policies and procedures cannot result in the delegation of the audit committee's authority to management.

Pre-approval policies and procedures that do not comply with all three of these requirements are in contravention of the Commission's rules. Therefore, the SEC staff believes that monetary limits cannot be the only basis for the pre-approval policies and procedures. The establishment of monetary limits would not, alone, constitute policies that are detailed as to the particular services to be provided and would not, alone, ensure that the audit committee would be informed about each service. (See FAQ of August 23, 2003).

According to the SEC staff, any pre-approval policies adopted by the audit committee must be designed to ensure that the committee knows precisely what specific services it is being asked to pre-approve so that it can make a well-reasoned assessment of the impact of the service on the auditor's independence. (See FAQ of August 23, 2003). Thus, any designation of broad categories, or any attempt to provide blanket approvals of large groups of services, is not permitted. (See memorandum from Scott Taub, SEC Deputy Chief Accountant, attached to letter from SEC Chairman William Donaldson to five consumer groups, July 11, 2004).

The determination of the appropriate level of detail for the pre-approval policies will differ depending upon the facts and circumstances of the company. However, in the SEC staff's view, a key requirement is that the policies cannot result in a delegation of the audit committee's responsibility to management. As such, if a member of management is called upon to make a judgment as to whether a proposed service fits within the pre-approved services, then the pre-approval policy would not be sufficiently detailed as to the particular services to be provided. (See FAQ of August 23, 2003).

Similarly, pre-approval policies must be designed to ensure that the audit committee knows precisely what services it is being asked to pre-approve so that it can make a well-reasoned assessment of the impact of the service on the auditor's independence. For example, if the audit committee is presented with a schedule or cover sheet describing services to be pre-approved, that schedule or cover sheet must be accompanied by detailed back-up documentation regarding the specific services to be provided. (See FAQ of August 23, 2003).

Many of the pre-approval policies provide for an annual review of audit and non-audit services by the audit committee, which includes review of a schedule, or budget, of non-audit services anticipated in the coming year. The SEC staff believes that any schedule or cover sheet for a category of services provided to the committee for its administrative convenience must be accompanied by detailed backup documentation that spells out the terms of each non-audit service to be provided by the auditor that is being pre-approved by the audit committee. Such documentation should be so detailed that there should never be any doubt as to whether any particular service was brought to the audit committee's attention and was considered and pre-approved by the committee. (See memorandum from Scott Taub, SEC Deputy Chief Accountant, attached to letter from SEC Chairman William Donaldson to five consumer groups, July 11, 2004).

For example, a cover sheet may indicate that the audit committee is pre-approving the preparation of federal, state and local corporate tax returns. To comply with the rules regarding pre-approval, the backup documentation, however, must clearly identify each return and provide sufficient information for the audit committee to evaluate the impact of the filing of that return on the auditor's independence. This would require information on each jurisdiction where a return is filed, the type or types of tax (income, property etc) owed in each jurisdiction, how often each return is prepared and filed and any other appropriate information. (See memorandum from Scott Taub, SEC Deputy Chief Accountant, attached to letter from SEC Chairman William Donaldson to five consumer groups, July 11, 2004).

The SEC staff has also advised that an audit committee of the parent company can function as the audit committee of the wholly-owned subsidiaries for purposes of satisfying the pre-approval requirements. In this situation, the subsidiary's disclosure should include both the pre-approval policies and procedures of the subsidiary and of the parent. However, this view does not extend to the fund industry in a manner that would permit an adviser's audit committee to pre-approve non-audit work on behalf of the funds. (See FAQ of August 23, 2003).

Under the PCAOB's auditing standard for internal controls, the auditor cannot accept an engagement to provide internal control-related services to a client company unless that engagement has been specifically pre-approved by the audit committee. The standard does not use the terms audit or non-audit services.

But the PCAOB staff has advised that the pre-approval requirement applies to any internal control-related services, regardless of whether they are classified as audit or non-audit services for proxy disclosure purposes or otherwise. Every proposed engagement by the auditor to provide internal control-related services merits specific attention by the audit committee so that the audit committee can determine whether the performance of the services would impair the auditor's independence and whether management's involvement in the services is substantive and extensive. (See FAQ of June 23, 2004).

¶ 705 Disclosure

The SEC believes that disclosure of the procedures the audit committee uses to pre-approve audit services, as well as the disclosure of all non-audit services by category, including those meeting the de minimis exception, will provide investors valuable information that may be used to evaluate the relationships that exist between the accountant and the audit client.

Thus, the company must disclose the audit committee's pre-approval policies and procedures. Additionally, to the extent that the audit committee has applied the de minimis exception, the company must disclose the percentage of the total fees paid to the independent accountant where the de minimis exception was used. This information should be provided by category.

Companies are expected to provide clear, concise and understandable descriptions of the policies and procedures. Alternatively, they could include a copy of those policies and procedures with the information delivered to investors and filed with the Commission. Either method should allow shareholders to obtain a complete and accurate understanding of the audit committee's policies and procedures.

The SEC expects the policies and procedures to address auditor independence oversight functions in a prudent and responsible manner. Moreover, the procedures would describe, if applicable, the specific processes in place that monitor activities where the de minimis exception is invoked.

The disclosures must be included in a company's annual report. In addition, because this information is relevant to a decision to vote for a particular director or to elect, approve or ratify the choice of an independent public accountant, the disclosure must also be included in a company's proxy statement on Schedule 14A or information statement on Schedule 14C. Since the information is included in Part III of annual reports on Forms 10-K and 10-KSB, domestic companies are able to incorporate the required disclosures from the proxy or information statement into the annual report.

The SEC's intent is that this information should be made available to investors of all companies. But not all companies must file proxy statements. Thus, companies that do not issue proxy statements must include appropriate disclosures in their annual filing included in Form 10-K, Form 10-KSB, 20-F,

Form 40-F and Form N-CSR as appropriate. Asset-backed issuers and unit investment trusts are exempt from these disclosure requirements.

Investment Companies

Investment companies must disclose separately those audit and non-audit fees from services provided directly to the investment company and those non-audit fees from services provided to all other entities in the investment company complex where the services were subject to pre-approval by the investment company's audit committee.

Like an operating company, the investment company would be required to disclose the percentage of fees for each category of fees that were pre-approved pursuant to the exception. Disclosure is required of the total non-audit fees paid to the accountant, regardless of whether those fees were pre-approved by the investment company's audit committee, by the investment company, its adviser, and any entity controlling, controlled by, or under common control with the investment adviser that provides ongoing services to the fund.

SEC rules also require the investment company to disclose if the audit committee has considered whether the provision of non-audit services provided to the fund's adviser and its related parties that were not subject to the investment company audit committee's pre-approval is compatible with maintaining the principal accountant's independence.

¶ 706 Business Judgments

Although the rules may serve to direct the attention of audit committees to the potential for independence issues arising from non-audit services, any action taken by audit committees will be business judgments. Nonetheless, the rules should help audit committees carry out their existing responsibilities by codifying the key legal requirements that may bear on an audit committee's exercise of its business judgment.

The SEC believes that audit committees, as well as management, should engage in active discussions of independence-related issues with the outside auditors. As with discussions over the quality and acceptability of management's judgments, audit committees can be useful in considering whether assertions of independence rest on conservative or aggressive readings of the independence rules. Similarly, audit committees may wish to consider whether to adopt formal or informal policies concerning when or whether to engage the company's auditing firm to provide non-audit services.

Guiding Factors

In this connection, the SEC has noted that the O'Malley Panel recommended certain guiding factors for audit committees to consider in making business judgments about particular non-audit services. According to the O'Malley Panel, one guiding principle should be whether the service facilitates the performance of the audit, improves the client's financial reporting process, or is otherwise in the public interest. Other considerations include:

- Whether the service is being performed principally for the audit committee;

- The effects of the service, if any, on audit effectiveness or on the quality and timeliness of the entity's financial reporting process;

- Whether the service would be performed by specialists (e.g., technology specialists) who ordinarily also provide recurring audit support;

- Whether the service would be performed by audit personnel and, if so, whether it will enhance their knowledge of the entity's business and operations;

- Whether the role of those performing the service (e.g., a role where neutrality, impartiality and auditor skepticism are likely to be subverted) would be inconsistent with the auditor's role

- Whether the audit firm's personnel would be assuming a management role or creating a mutuality of interest with management

- Whether the auditors, in effect, would be auditing their own numbers

- Whether the project must be started and completed quickly

- Whether the audit firm has unique expertise in the service

- The size of the fee(s) for the non-audit service(s)

These factors expand on the four factors in the Preliminary Note to SEC Rule 2-01, which sets forth the general standard of auditor independence. The preliminary note states that the Commission looks in the first instance to whether a relationship or the provision of a service: (1) creates a mutual or conflicting interest between the accountant and the audit client; (2) places the accountant in the position of auditing his or her own work; (3) results in the accountant acting as management or an employee of the audit client; or (4) places the accountant in a position of being an advocate for the audit client.

The SEC cautions that these factors are general guidance only and their application may depend on particular facts and circumstances. For that reason, Rule 2-01 provides that, in determining whether an accountant is independent, the Commission will consider all relevant facts and circumstances.

Although it is easy for one to merely put non-audit services into what former SEC Chief Accountant Lynn Turner called a "good bucket" or a "bad bucket," investors will be better served by an audit committee, using the reasoned guidance provided by the O'Malley Panel, asking pertinent questions and making sound, reasoned business judgments. Such a process will inexorably lead to decisions by some audit committees to approve certain non-audit services and by some not to approve those services. But it will be a private sector self-governance, self-regulatory approach that now has the necessary information to make informed decisions and is well equipped to serve investor interests. (Remarks of SEC Chief Accountant Lynn Turner before the Colorado Society of CPAs, Dec. 15, 2000.)

Although the SEC welcomes active oversight by audit committees with respect to auditor independence, the agency does not believe that this oversight obviates the need for auditor independence rules. Audit committees bring business judgment to bear on the financial matters within their purview. Their purpose is not to set the independence standards for the profession, and the SEC is not attempting to saddle them with that responsibility. On the other hand, Sarbanes-Oxley and the SEC rules do facilitate the work of audit committees by establishing clear legal standards that audit committees can use as benchmarks against which to exercise business judgment.

¶706

AUDIT PARTNER ROTATION

¶ 801 In General

Sarbanes-Oxley Act Section 301 (reproduced at ¶ 2006) specifies that the audit committee has the responsibility for appointment, compensation, and oversight of the work of the company's audit firm. In that capacity, the audit committee has the responsibility for evaluating and determining that the audit engagement team has the competence necessary to conduct the audit engagement in accordance with GAAS.

The Act also requires rotation of certain audit partners on a five-year basis in order to continue to provide audit services for a company. Section 203 (reproduced at ¶ 2003) clearly specifies that the lead audit partner and reviewing partner should serve on the engagement in that capacity for no more than five consecutive years. SEC rulemaking has clarified the five-year rotation requirement specified in Sarbanes-Oxley.

Sarbanes-Oxley specifies that, at a minimum, two partners be subject to rotation: the lead audit partner and the concurring partner. The SEC rules require the lead and concurring partners to rotate after five years and, upon rotation, be subject to a five-year "time out" period. Because of the importance of achieving a fresh look to the independence of the audit function, the SEC believes that a five-year time out period is appropriate for these two partners.

Although the lead partner and the concurring partner perform critical functions that affect the engagement's conduct and effectiveness, many larger engagements include more than just the lead partner and the concurring partner. Often, these other partners on the engagement team play a significant role in the conduct of the audit and maintaining ongoing relationships with the client.

In the SEC's view, the partner rotation requirements must strike a balance between the need to achieve a fresh look on the engagement and a need for the audit engagement team to be composed of competent accountants. The proper balance is one that weighs the responsibility for decisions on accounting and financial reporting issues impacting the financial statements with the level of the relationship with the client's senior management. Such a balancing clearly would include the lead and concurring partners.

In addition, the lead partner at significant operating units has a high involvement with senior management and, for significant operations, responsibility for decisions on accounting matters that affect the financial statements. Likewise, other audit partners have a high involvement with senior management and some responsibility for accounting matters to be included in the financial statements.

In contrast, partners at smaller operating units and specialty partners typically have a low level of involvement with senior management and their responsibility for the overall presentation in the financial statements is relatively low. Specialty partners consult with others on the audit engagement team during the audit, review or attestation engagement regarding technical or industry-specific issues. For example, such partners would include tax specialists and valuation specialists.

In an effort to attain the proper balance, the SEC has extended the partner rotation requirements beyond the lead and concurring partner mandated by Sarbanes-Oxley, but not so deeply as to adversely affect audit quality.

¶ 802 "Audit Partner" Defined

The SEC has applied the partner rotation requirements to "audit partners." In addition to the lead and concurring partners, the term audit partners includes partners on the audit engagement team who have responsibility for decision-making on significant auditing, accounting, and reporting matters affecting the financial statements or who maintain regular contact with management and the audit committee. (See 17 CFR 210.2-01(f)(7)(ii).)

In particular, audit partners would include all those who serve the client at the company or parent level, other than specialty partners. Further, the lead partner on company subsidiaries whose assets or revenues constitute 20 percent or more of the consolidated assets or revenues are included within the definition of audit partner.

The term audit partner does not extend to all partners on the audit engagement team. For example, partners serving on subsidiaries that constitute less than 20 percent of the company's assets and revenues would not be audit partners and, thus not be subject to rotation. Likewise, partners on subsidiaries above the 20-percent threshold, other than the lead partner on those subsidiaries, are not subject to rotation.

Audit partners also would exclude specialty partners because they typically do not have significant interaction with management on an ongoing basis regarding significant audit, accounting, and reporting matters. It is the lead partner who has the ultimate responsibility for the audit.

In many cases, complex business transactions and other situations may require that the engagement team consult with the accounting firm's national office or others on technical issues. Partners assigned to national office duties who may be consulted on specific accounting issues related to a client are not audit partners even though they may periodically consult on client matters.

Although these partners play an important role in the audit process, they serve, primarily, as a technical resource for audit team members. Because they are not involved in the audit per se and do not routinely interact or develop relationships with the audit client, it is not necessary to rotate the involvement of these personnel.

Audit partners, other than the lead and concurring partner, will rotate after no more than seven years and be subject to a two-year time-out. In this way, a partner could serve either as the lead partner on a significant subsidiary or as an audit partner at the parent or issuer level for a period of time, such as two years, prior to becoming the lead or concurring partner on the engagement and still be able to serve in that lead or concurring role for five years.

An audit partner who starts in a position other than the lead or concurring partner and subsequently moves to the lead or concurring partner cannot serve the client in an audit partner capacity for more than seven consecutive years.

For example, a person serving as the lead partner on a significant subsidiary for a period of four years who then becomes the lead partner on the company would be able to serve in that capacity for three additional years before reaching a total of seven years as an audit partner on that client.

Small Firm Exemption

Addressing concerns that application of the rotation requirements to smaller firms would render them unable to provide audit services, the SEC exempted firms with fewer than five audit clients and fewer than ten partners from audit partner rotation. (See 17 CFR 210.2-01(c)(6)(ii).) The exemption is conditioned, however, on the Public Company Accounting Oversight Board conducting a review of all of the firm's engagements subject to the rotation rules at least once every three years. This special review will focus on the overall quality of the audit and, in particular, the independence and competence of the key personnel on the audit engagement teams.

¶ 803 Investment Companies

In the SEC's view, the rotation requirements with regard to investment companies should prohibit the rotation of partners between different investment companies in the same investment company complex. It is not necessary, however, for the rules to prohibit accountants from rotating to other entities in the investment company complex.

Consequently, the rules do not allow audit partners to satisfy the partner rotation requirements by rotating between investment companies in the same investment company complex. (See 17 CFR 210.2-01(c)(6)(iii).) The individual required to rotate and the applicable periods for rotation and time-out from the audit client will be applied in the same manner to investment companies as to other companies.

Lead and concurring partners will be required to rotate after a total of five consecutive years in either role. At a minimum, all audit partners that audit investment companies will be required to rotate after a total of seven years of consecutive service on any of the investment companies in the same investment company complex. Lead and concurring partners will be required to observe a time out period for five years before returning to the investment company and all other audit partners will be subject to a two year time out period.

The unique structure of investment company complexes allows for many different fiscal year-ends within the same investment company complex. In order to allow a partner to serve the total number of allowable periods on any one investment company audit in the complex, while still requiring partners to rotate off an investment company complex at the end of their specific periods, the SEC defined consecutive years of service for investment companies.

Thus, a consecutive year of service for audit partners includes all fiscal year-end audits of investment companies in the same investment company complex that are performed in a continuous twelve-month period. This would allow audit partners auditing multiple investment companies in the same investment company complex to audit each investment company for five or seven complete fiscal years, as appropriate.

¶ 804 Auditor Rotation and Internal Controls

Sarbanes-Oxley Act Section 404 (reproduced at 2007), as well as the Commission's rules, require the accounting firm to attest to management's report on the company's internal controls. Both a timely review engagement and an attestation engagement require the accounting firm to be independent with respect to the company. Accordingly, the Commission's rules for partner rotation extend to partners who serve on the engagement team that conducts the timely review of the interim financial information as well as the engagement team that conducts the attest engagement on management's report on the company's internal controls.

The attestation and report required by Section 404 must comply with standards for attestation engagements issued or adopted by the Public Company Accounting Oversight Board. On April 25, 2003, the SEC approved the PCAOB's adoption of the auditing and attestation standards in existence as of April 16, 2003 as interim standards. For a full discussion of auditor attestation of management's report on the company's internal control over financial reporting, see ¶ 309.

Chapter 9

Improper Influence on Audits

¶ 901 In General

Sarbanes-Oxley Act Section 303 prohibits any corporate officer or director, or any person acting under the direction, to take any action to fraudulently influence, coerce, manipulate, or mislead an independent accountant engaged in the performance of an audit of the company's financial statements for the purpose of rendering such financial statements materially misleading.

As mandated, the SEC adopted rules to implement the statutory prohibition. (See Release No. 34-47890 (SEC 2003), Fed. Sec. Law Rep. ¶ 86,921.) The rules, in combination with the existing rules under Regulation 13B-2, are designed to ensure that management makes open and full disclosures to, and has honest discussions with, the auditor of the financial statements. The rules prohibit corporate officers or directors, or persons acting under their direction, from subverting the auditor's responsibilities to investors to conduct a diligent audit of the financial statements and to provide a true report of the auditor's findings.

The SEC rules prohibit a company's officers or directors, or persons acting under their direction, from subverting the auditor's responsibilities to investors to conduct a diligent audit of the financial statements and to provide a true report of the auditor's findings. The new rules supplement the rules currently in Regulation 13B-2, which address the falsification of books, records and accounts and false or misleading statements, or omissions to make certain statements, to accountants.

As amended, Rule 13b2-2(b)(1) specifically prohibits officers and directors, and persons acting under their direction, from coercing, manipulating, misleading, or fraudulently influencing the auditor of the financial statements when the officer, director or other person knew or should have known that the action, if successful, could result in rendering the financial statements materially misleading.

Rule 13b2-2(b)(2) provides examples of actions that improperly influence an auditor that could result in rendering the financial statements materially misleading. Rule 13b2-2(c) applies similar provisions to audits of investment companies' financial statements.

For these purposes, the terms "coerce" and "manipulate" imply compelling the auditor to act in a certain way through pressure, threats, trickery, intimidation or some other form of purposeful action. Regarding the term "mislead," pre-existing Rule 13b2-2 for many years has prohibited officers and directors from directly or indirectly making or causing to be made materially misleading statements to auditors. Causing misleading statements to be made to auditors has included, and will continue to include, an officer or director entering into an arrangement with a third party to send a misleading confirmation or to provide other misleading information or data to the auditor of the issuer's financial statements.

The new rules do not alter this approach. A primary purpose of the Sarbanes-Oxley Act is to restore investor confidence in the integrity of financial reports. Such a purpose would not be served by imposing what would amount to a new scienter requirement on the pre-existing provision prohibiting officers and directors from causing misleading statements or omissions to be made to auditors.

¶ 902 Prohibited Conduct

Types of conduct that the Commission believes could constitute improper influence (if the person engaged in that conduct knows or should know that the conduct, if successful, could result in rendering the issuer's financial statements materially misleading) include, but are not limited to, directly or indirectly:

- Offering or paying bribes or other financial incentives, including offering future employment or contracts for non-audit services,
- Providing an auditor with an inaccurate or misleading legal analysis,
- Threatening to cancel or canceling existing non-audit or audit engagements if the auditor objects to the issuer's accounting,
- Seeking to have a partner removed from the audit engagement because the partner objects to the issuer's accounting,
- Blackmailing, and
- Making physical threats.

The facts and circumstances of each case would be relevant to determining whether the conduct would violate the new rule.

Further, in the appropriate circumstances and upon satisfying the criteria in the rules, each of the following actions could result in improper influence on the auditor: (1) knowingly providing to the auditor inadequate or misleading information that is key to the audit; (2) transferring managers or principals from the audit engagement; and (3) when predicated by an intent to defraud, engaging in verbal abuse, creating undue time pressure on the auditors, not providing information to auditors on a timely basis, and not being available to discuss matters with auditors on a timely basis.

Although an officer or director providing misleading information to an internal auditor would be relevant to the status of the company's internal accounting controls or disclosure controls, it would not appear to be related to the purpose of Sarbanes-Oxley Act Section 303, which is to protect and enhance the independent audit function. To the extent that the internal auditor's work is used by the independent auditor in conducting an audit or review of the financial statements, however, misleading or inaccurate information provided to the internal auditor may be deemed to be provided to the independent auditor.

¶ 903 Rendering Financial Statements Misleading

One prerequisite to liability for improper influence on an auditor is that the improper influence, if successful, could result in rendering the financial statements materially misleading. Because management prepares the financial statements and the auditor conducts an audit or review of those statements, the auditor would not directly render them misleading. Rather, the auditor might be improperly influenced to, among other things, issue an unwarranted report on the financial statements, including suggesting or acquiescing in the use of inappropriate accounting treatments or not proposing adjustments required for the financial statements to conform with generally accepted accounting principles.

Not Communicating to Audit Committee

An auditor also might be coerced, manipulated, misled, or fraudulently influenced not to perform audit or review procedures that, if performed, might divulge material misstatements in the financial statements. Other examples of activities that would fall within the rule would be for an officer, director, or person acting under an officer or director's direction, to improperly influence an auditor either not to withdraw a previously issued audit report when required by generally accepted auditing standards, or not to communicate appropriate matters to the audit committee. Sarbanes-Oxley Act Section 204 (reproduced at ¶ 2004) requires each registered public accounting firm to report certain matters to the audit committee.

Interim Financial Statements

New rule 13b2-2(b)(2) makes it clear that subparagraph (b)(1) would apply in such circumstances. The rule is not limited to the audit of the annual financial statements, but would include, among other things, improperly influencing an auditor during a review of interim financial statements or in connection with the issuance of a consent to the use of an auditor's report. Conducting reviews of interim financial statements and issuing consents to use past audit reports are sufficiently connected to the audit process, and improper influences during those processes are sufficiently connected to the harms that Sarbanes-Oxley seeks to prevent, that they should fall within the rule's scope. The list of examples in the rule is only illustrative; other actions also could result in rendering the financial statements materially misleading.

CHAPTER 10

ATTORNEY REPORTING DUTY

¶ 1001 Introduction

Sarbanes-Oxley Act Section 307 requires the SEC to prescribe minimum standards of professional conduct for attorneys appearing and practicing before the Commission in any way in the representation of issuers. The standards must include a rule requiring an attorney to report evidence of a material violation of securities laws or breach of fiduciary duty or similar violation by the company or any of its agents to the company's chief legal counsel or chief executive officer. If the CLO or CEO does not respond appropriately to the evidence, the attorney must report the evidence to the audit committee, another committee of independent directors, or the full board of directors.

The SEC has responded to the statutory mandate with a broad and detailed regulatory reporting regime covering both inside and outside corporate counsel that is designed to improve the accuracy and reliability of corporate disclosures made pursuant to the securities laws and foster investor confidence in the securities markets. In turn, this may lower the cost of capital. In addition, the rules should, in some instances, prevent or mitigate illegal conduct and hasten the apprehension of wrongdoers whose misconduct injures investors.

Audit committees are an integral part of the reporting process under the SEC rules. They are one rung on the up-the-ladder reporting ladder. In addition, the rules provide as an alternative to up-the-ladder reporting, that the attorney can report to a board committee called the qualified legal compliance committee. A company can designate the audit committee as the qualified legal compliance committee if company does not want to set up a new committee. Thus, it is imperative that audit committee members be aware of the details of the up-the-ladder reporting requirements.

The SEC rules are intended to assure that attorneys representing companies before the Commission are governed by standards of conduct that increase disclosure of potential impropriety within a company so that prompt intervention and remediation can take place. Doing so should boost investor confidence in the financial markets, enhance proper market functioning, and promote efficiency by reducing the likelihood that illegal behavior would remain undetected and unremedied for long periods of time. Since the rules would apply to all issuers and attorneys appearing before the Commission, they are unlikely to affect competition.

The SEC believes that the rules will deter corporate misconduct and fraud. Corporate wrongdoers at the lower or middle levels of the hierarchy will know that an attorney who becomes aware of their misconduct is obligated under the rules to report it up-the-ladder to the highest levels of the company. Similarly, in the event that wrongdoing or fraud exists at the highest corporate levels, those committing the misconduct will know that the company's attorneys are obligated to report any misconduct of which they become aware up-the-ladder to the board and its independent directors.

The attorney reporting rules are also an effort to improve corporate governance. By mandating up-the-ladder reporting of violations, the rules help ensure that evidence of material violations will be addressed and remedied within the company, rather than misdirected or "swept under the rug."

¶ 1002 Covered Attorneys

The SEC's attorney reporting rules define "attorney" to mean any person who is admitted, licensed, or otherwise qualified to practice law in any jurisdiction, domestic or foreign. The term broadly applies equally to lawyers employed in-house by a company and attorneys retained to perform legal work on behalf of a company, and covers persons who hold themselves out as attorneys, even if they are not in fact admitted, licensed, or otherwise qualified to practice law. The definition of "attorney" also covers lawyers licensed in foreign jurisdictions, whether or not they are also admitted to practice in the United States. (17 CFR § 205.2(c).)

Commenters argued that the proposed rule's definition of attorney applied to a large number of individuals employed by companies who are admitted to practice, but who do not serve in a legal capacity. By significantly narrowing the definition of the term "appearing and practicing" before the Commission, the SEC addressed concerns over the application of the rule to individuals admitted to practice who are employed in non-legal positions and do not provide legal services.

Foreign Attorneys

The proposal drew no distinction between the obligations of United States and foreign attorneys. Commenters suggested that it was inappropriate to apply the rule to foreign attorneys, arguing that foreign attorneys, and attorneys representing or employed by multijurisdictional firms, are subject to statutes, rules, and ethical standards in those foreign jurisdictions that are different from, and potentially incompatible with, the requirements of the rules.

To address these concerns, the SEC added the definition "non-appearing foreign attorney," which describes a person who does not appear and practice before the Commission for purposes of the rules. The definition excludes from up-the-ladder reporting foreign attorneys who do not hold themselves out as practicing or giving legal advice regarding U.S. law and who conduct activities that would constitute appearing and practicing before the Commission only incidentally to a foreign law practice, or in consultation with U.S. counsel. (17 CFR § 205.2(j).)

This definition effectively excludes many, but not all, foreign attorneys from the rule's coverage. Foreign attorneys who provide legal advice regarding U.S. securities law, other than in consultation with U.S. counsel, are subject to the rule if they conduct activities that constitute appearing and practicing before the Commission.

¶ 1003 Issuer as Client

Attorneys appearing and practicing before the Commission in the representation of a company owe their professional and ethical duties to the company as an organization. The fact that attorneys may work with and advise corporate officers, directors, or employees in the course of representing the company does not make such individuals their clients. (17 CFR § 205.3(a).)

The SEC recognizes that it is the client company, acting through its management, who chooses the objectives the lawyer must pursue, even when unwise, so long as they are not illegal or unethical. However, when an individual associated with the organization is violating a legal duty, and the behavior is likely to result in substantial injury to the organization, the SEC believes it is appropriate for counsel to act in the company's best interests by reporting up-the-ladder.

Issuer Defined

In defining "issuer," the rules adopt the definition set forth in Sarbanes-Oxley Act Section 2(a)(7), which in turn incorporates the definition contained in the Exchange Act. Under the Exchange Act, an issuer is one whose securities are registered under Section 12 or that must file reports under Section 15(d), or that files or has filed a registration statement that has not yet become effective under the Securities Act of 1933. (17 CFR § 205.2(h).)

The definition has been modified in two ways. First, the definition excludes foreign government issuers. Secondly, the definition clarifies that, for purposes of appearing and practicing before the Commission and in the representation of an issuer, the term "issuer" includes any person controlled by an issuer (such as a wholly-owned subsidiary), where the attorney provides legal services to that person for the benefit of, or on behalf of, an issuer.

Appearing and practicing

The rules broadly define the term "appearing and practicing" before the Commission to include:

• Transacting any business with the Commission, including communications in any form;

• Representing an issuer in a Commission administrative proceeding or in connection with any Commission investigation, inquiry, information request, or subpoena;

• Providing advice in respect of the securities laws or the SEC's rules or regulations thereunder regarding any document that the attorney has notice will be filed with or submitted to, or incorporated into any document that will be filed with or submitted to, the Commission, including the provision of such advice in the context of preparing, or participating in the preparation of, any such document; or

• Advising an issuer as to whether information or a statement, opinion, or other writing is required under the U.S. securities laws or the SEC's rules or regulations thereunder to be filed with or submitted to, or incorporated into any document that will be filed with or submitted to, the Commission. (17 CFR § 205.2(a).)

The term does not include an attorney who conducts these activities in other than in the context of providing legal services to an issuer with whom the attorney has an attorney-client relationship or is a non-appearing foreign attorney.

Under the rules, attorneys who advise that, under the federal securities laws, a particular document need not be incorporated into a filing, registration statement or other submission to the Commission will be covered by the definition. In addition, attorneys must have notice that a document they are preparing or assisting in preparing will be submitted to the Commission to be deemed to be "appearing and practicing." The SEC has clarified that preparation of a document (such as a contract) that the attorney never intended or had notice would be submitted to the Commission, or incorporated into a document submitted to the Commission, but which subsequently is submitted as an exhibit to or in connection with a filing, does not constitute appearing and practicing before the Commission.

Attorneys need not serve in the company's legal department to be covered by the rule, but they must be providing legal services to the company within the context of an attorney-client relationship. An attorney-client relationship may exist even in the absence of a formal retainer or other agreement. Moreover, in some cases, an attorney and a company may have an attorney-client relationship within the rule's meaning even though the attorney-client privilege would not be available with respect to communications between the attorney and the company.

Representation of an Issuer

The rules include a broad definition of what constitutes "in the representation of an issuer," which means providing legal services as an attorney for an issuer, regardless of whether the attorney is employed or retained by the issuer. The SEC believes that the broad definition is essential to protect investors. Accordingly, the term is defined to cover attorneys providing any legal services at the request of, or for the benefit of, an issuer. (17 CFR § 205.2(g).)

Taken together, the definitions for "appearing and practicing" and "in the representation of an issuer" recognize that attorneys interact with the SEC in a number of ways on behalf of issuers, and that such conduct should be covered by the rule.

¶ 1004 Reporting Duty

Section 205.3 lies at the core of the Commission's regime for attorney reporting. It sets out the rule on an attorney's duty to report evidence of a material violation of securities law or breach of fiduciary duty or similar violation by the company or any of officers, directors, employees, or agents as required by Sarbanes-Oxley. It also sets out related provisions addressing an attorney's obligations to the company. It also provides that, by communicating such information to the company's officers or directors, an attorney does not reveal client confidences or secrets or privileged or otherwise protected information related to the attorney's representation of a company. (17 CFR § 205.3(b).)

Initial Report

The first step to be taken by attorneys who become aware of evidence of a material violation by the company or any of its officers, directors, employees, or agents is to report such evidence to the company's chief legal officer or to both the CLO and chief executive officer. Subordinate attorneys comply with the rule if they report evidence of a material violation to their supervisory attorney, who is then responsible for complying with the rule's requirements. A subordinate attorney may also take the other steps described in the rule if the supervisor fails to comply. (If the company has a qualified legal compliance committee, an alternative reporting route is available.) (17 CFR § 205.3(b)(1).)

Reporting to Directors

A reporting attorney who reasonably believes that the chief legal officer or the chief executive officer has not provided an appropriate response, or has not responded within a reasonable time, must report the evidence of a material violation to the company's audit committee, another independent board committee, or the full board if there is no independent committee. (17 CFR § 205.3(b)(3).)

Providing no response at all within a reasonable time may be equivalent to not providing an appropriate response and no response may, under certain circumstances, require the attorney to report to a higher level of corporate authority when, for example, a filing or submission that the attorney reasonably believes contains a misstatement of material fact is to be made the next day.

Note that the direction that the attorney must report up-the-ladder is to the audit committee, if there is one; if there is no audit committee, then to another independent board committee, if there is one; and if there is no such committee, then to the full board of directors. This process is intended to implement the statutory language on reporting up-the-ladder while at the same time avoiding a situation in which one attorney might report some evidence of a material violation to one committee of directors while another attorney might report other evidence of a material violation to a second committee. This type of scattered reporting could obscure the full, cumulative significance of reported evidence.

In the SEC's view, an attorney does not reveal client confidences or secrets by communicating information related to the attorney's representation of a company to its officers or directors. Information related to the company's affairs communicated to the attorney is effectively communicated to the company. The officer or employee thus cannot have any reasonable expectation of confidentiality against the company regarding such information, and the attorney breaches no confidence in communicating the information to the issuer's CLO, CEO, or directors.

Evidence of Material Violation

Although the scope of attorney conduct covered by the reporting regime is broad, the definition of other terms limit the instances when an attorney has a reporting duty to those situations where it is appropriate to protect investors. Attorneys are obligated to report evidence of a material violation, which the rules define as credible evidence, based on which it would be unreasonable, under the circumstances, for a prudent and competent attorney not to conclude that it is reasonably likely that a material violation has occurred, is ongoing, or is about to occur. This is an objective standard designed to facilitate the effective operation of the rule and encourage the reporting of evidence of material violations. (17 CFR § 205.2(e).)

The term "evidence of a material violation" defines the trigger for an attorney's obligation to report up-the-ladder within a company. The revised

¶1004

definition confirms that the Commission intends an objective, rather than a subjective, triggering standard.

Evidence of a material violation must first be credible evidence. An attorney is obligated to report when, based on that credible evidence, it would be unreasonable, under the circumstances, for a prudent and competent attorney not to conclude that it is reasonably likely that a material violation has occurred, is ongoing, or is about to occur. This formulation, while intended to adopt an objective standard, also recognizes that there is a range of conduct in which an attorney may engage without being unreasonable.

The circumstances referred to in the definition are the circumstances at the time an attorney decide whether there is a duty to report the information. These circumstances may include, among others, the attorney's professional skills, background and experience, the time constraints under which the attorney is acting, the attorney's previous experience and familiarity with the client, and the availability of other lawyers with whom the lawyer may consult. An attorney is not required or expected to report gossip, hearsay, or innuendo, the SEC has noted, nor is the rule's reporting obligation triggered by a combination of circumstances from which the attorney, in retrospect, should have drawn an inference.

"Reasonably Likely" Discussed

Under the rules, evidence of a material violation must be reported in all circumstances in which it would be unreasonable for a prudent and competent attorney not to conclude that it is reasonably likely that a material violation has occurred, is ongoing, or is about to occur. To be reasonably likely a material violation must be more than a mere possibility, but it need not be more likely than not.

The Commission intends that the definition of "reasonably likely" will be consistent with the discussion of the term included in the adopting release for the final rules governing disclosure of off-balance sheet arrangements, enacted pursuant to Sarbanes-Oxley Act Section 401(a). (See Release No. 33-8182 (SEC 2003) 2000 CCH Dec. ¶ 86,821.)

Reasonably likely is the threshold the SEC applies to MD&A disclosure because it best promotes the utility of the disclosure requirements by reducing the possibility that investors will be overwhelmed by voluminous disclosure of insignificant and possibly unnecessarily speculative information. The SEC believes that the reasonably likely standard focuses on the information most important to an understanding of a company's off-balance sheet arrangements and their material effects on the firm's financial condition, changes in financial condition, revenues or expenses, results of operations, liquidity, capital expenditures or capital resources. Further, the SEC has indicated that the assessment must be objectively reasonable, viewed as of the time the determination is made. See Release No. 33-8182.

In a January 2002 release, the SEC indicated that reasonably likely is a lower disclosure threshold than more likely than not. Release No. 33-8056.

If a material violation is reasonably likely, an attorney must report evidence of this violation. Moreover, the term "reasonably likely" qualifies each of the three instances when a report must be made. Thus, a report is required when it is reasonably likely a violation has occurred, when it is reasonably likely a violation is ongoing or when reasonably likely a violation is about to occur.

¶1004

Materiality

After proposing a definition of "material," the SEC finally decided not to define the word "material," because the term already has a well-established meaning under the federal securities laws and the Commission intends for that same meaning to apply in the attorney reporting context. The Commission cited U.S. Supreme Court precedent defining "materiality" as dispositive.

According to the Supreme Court, materiality depends on the significance that a reasonable investor would place on the withheld or misrepresented information. There must be a substantial likelihood that, under all the circumstances, the omitted or misrepresented fact would have assumed actual significance in a reasonable investor's investment decision. Stated differently, there must be a substantial likelihood that reasonable investors would have viewed disclosure of the fact omitted or misrepresented as having substantially altered the total mix of information made available. Finally, in the case of contingent or speculative events, materiality depends on a balancing of both the indicated probability that the event will occur and the anticipated magnitude of the event in light of the totality of the company activity. (*TSC Industries, Inc. v. Northway, Inc.* (US Sup. Ct. 1976), 1976-77 CCH Dec. ¶ 95,615; *Basic, Inc. v. Levinson* (US Sup. Ct. 1988), 1987-88 CCH Dec. ¶ 93,645.)

"Material Violation"

Material violation means a material violation of an applicable United States federal or state securities law, a material breach of fiduciary duty arising under U.S. federal or state law, or a similar material violation of any U.S. federal or state law. This definition resolves an ambiguity in the statutory language and clarifies that only evidence of instances of material misconduct will trigger the reporting obligation. In addition, material violations must arise under United States law, and thus do not include violations of foreign law. (17 CFR § 205.2(i).)

The rules define the term material violation to clarify that the term material modifies all three succeeding references to violations, namely violation of securities law, breach of fiduciary duty, and similar violation, and that only evidence of material misconduct triggers the rule's reporting obligation.

The rules do not define what constitutes a violation of securities law since the term is well-understood. The Commission believes that the term covers violations of the federal securities laws, as well as violations of state securities laws.

The rules separately define "breach of fiduciary duty" to cover any breach of fiduciary or similar duty to the company recognized under an applicable federal or state statute or at common law, including but not limited to misfeasance, nonfeasance, abdication of duty, abuse of trust, and approval of unlawful transactions. In this definition, the SEC clarifies that breaches of fiduciary duties imposed by federal and state statutes are covered by the rule. (17 CFR § 205.2(d).)

Scope of Duty

The rules are not intended to impose on an attorney, whether employed or retained by the company, a duty to investigate evidence of a material violation or to determine whether in fact there is a material violation. But the rules do not discourage any such inquiry. And, it is axiomatic that attorneys cannot ignore evidence of material violations of which they are aware.

¶1004

In addition, the SEC has stated that the attorney's reporting obligation is not triggered until counsel can be sure that the corporate officer or employee will actually pursue an illegal course of action. This means that the Commission does not intend to inhibit the consultative process between a company and its attorney. The duty to report up the ladder does not arise from a consultation in which an attorney advises a corporate officer or employee that the law regarding a proposed course of action is unsettled and there is some possibility that a court might hold in the future that the action violated the securities laws.

The rules define "reasonable" or "reasonably" as denoting the conduct of a reasonably prudent and competent attorney. The definition is taken from Rule 1.0(h) of the ABA's Model Rules of Professional Conduct. (17 CFR § 205.2(l).)

"Reasonably believes" means that an attorney believes the matter in question and that the circumstances are such that the belief is not unreasonable. (17 CFR § 205.2(m).) This definition is based on the definition of "reasonable belief" or "reasonably believes" in Rule 1.0(i) of the ABA's Model Rules of Professional Conduct, modified to emphasize that the range of possible reasonable beliefs regarding a matter may be broad—limited for the purposes of this rule by beliefs that are unreasonable. Because the definition no longer is used in connection with the definition of "evidence of a material violation," the proposal's attempt to exclude the subjective element in reasonable belief has been abandoned. (See 17 CFR § 205.2(m).)

Investment Companies

The rules require that the committee of a registered investment company's board of directors to which an attorney is allowed to report evidence of a material violation must exclude "interested persons" as defined in Investment Company Act Section 2(a)(19). This is intended to assure that the report will go to independent directors. That exclusion has the same rationale here as does excluding "interested persons" from an investment company's QLCC. (17 CFR § 205.3(b)(3)(ii).)

Usually, a director who is not employed directly or indirectly by the company is an independent director of the company. However, registered investment companies constitute an important group of issuers that typically are managed externally. As a result, a director of a registered investment who is not employed directly or indirectly by the investment company but is employed by the investment company's investment adviser may well not be independent. Independent directors of a registered investment company thus cannot include any "interested person" of the investment company.

¶ 1005 Contemporaneous Record

The final rules eliminated requirements that reports and responses be documented and maintained for a reasonable period. Under the proposal, lawyers would have been required to document their report of evidence of a material violation; the CLO would have been required to document any inquiry in response to a report; reporting attorneys would have been required to document when they received an appropriate response to a report; and attorneys who believed they did not receive an appropriate response to a report would have been required to document that response.

The final rules now provide that any report or contemporaneous record of it, or any response to it may be used by attorneys in connection with any investigation, proceeding, or litigation in which their compliance with the attorney reporting rules is in issue. (17 CFR § 205.3(d)(1).)

¶ 1006 CLO's Investigatory Duty

The SEC rules do not impose on reporting attorneys a duty to independently investigate the evidence before making their reports. This is because attorneys employed by the company or retained as outside counsel are often not in a position to conduct such an inquiry. In many cases, they may lack the experience, resources, and access to records and to other employees necessary to conduct an appropriate inquiry. In addition, such an inquiry may be beyond the scope of outside counsel's representation.

The company's chief legal officer, however, is in a position to conduct an internal inquiry when appropriate. Moreover, a CLO has a clear duty to protect the company in every possible way. Thus, the rules expressly make the CLO responsible for having an inquiry conducted in response to a report unless the CLO makes a reasonable determination that it is not necessary to do so.

Specifically, chief legal officers must cause an inquiry into the evidence of a material violation as they reasonably believe is appropriate to determine whether the material violation described in the report has occurred, is ongoing, or is about to occur. A CLO who determines that no material violation has occurred, is ongoing, or is about to occur, must notify the reporting attorney and advise the reporting attorney of the basis for such determination.

Unless the CLO reasonably believes that no material violation has occurred, is ongoing, or is about to occur, he or she must take all reasonable steps to cause the company to adopt an appropriate response, and advise the reporting attorney thereof. In lieu of causing an inquiry, a chief legal officer may refer a report of evidence of a material violation to a qualified legal compliance committee if the company has duly established such a committee prior to the report of evidence of a material violation. (17 CFR § 205.3(b)(2).)

Futility Exception

The rules provide that an attorney who reasonably believes that it would be futile to report evidence of a material violation to the company's chief legal officer and chief executive officer may report the evidence of a material violation up-the-ladder. Thus, in the interest of expediting any required corrective action within the company, the rules allow, but do not require, an attorney to bypass the CLO or CEO and report evidence of a material violation directly to appropriate directors: first, to the audit committee, if there is one; and if there is not, then to another independent board committee, if there is one; and if there is not, then to the full board of directors, when the attorney reasonably believes that it is likely to be futile to report the evidence to the CLO or CEO. (17 CFR § 205.3(b)(4).)

Attorneys Retained to Investigate or Litigate

An attorney retained or directed by the company to investigate evidence of a reported material violation will be deemed to be appearing and practicing before the Commission. Directing or retaining an attorney to investigate reported evidence of a material violation does not relieve corporate officers or directors to whom the evidence of a material violation has been reported of the duty to respond to the reporting attorney. (17 CFR § 205.3(b)(5).)

The above provision has two components. First, since the investigating attorneys would themselves be appearing and practicing before the Commission, they would be bound by the requirements of the reporting regime. Second, the officer or directors who caused them to investigate will remain obligated to respond to the attorney who initially reported the evidence of a material violation. Either the company's officer or directors or, under the officer's or directors' instructions, the investigating attorneys would make reporting attorneys aware of the inquiry to keep them from concluding mistakenly that the required response was unreasonably delayed.

¶ 1007 Assessment of Company's Response

Under the SEC rules, attorneys fully comply with the reporting scheme when they have reported evidence of a material violation and reasonably believe that the company's response to that reported evidence is appropriate. (17 CFR § 205.3(b)(8).)

The rules also provide for circumstances in which attorneys do not receive an appropriate response to the evidence they have reported or do not receive any response in a reasonable time. Attorneys who do not reasonably believe that the company has made an appropriate response within a reasonable time to their reports must explain their reasons therefor to the chief legal officer, the chief executive officer, and directors to whom they reported the evidence of a material violation. (17 CFR § 205.3(b)(9).)

The SEC believes it would be truly extraordinary for an attorney reporting evidence of a material violation to receive an inappropriate response, for example one that simply asserted that the reported evidence is no cause for concern without any hint of evaluation or inquiry, or to receive no response at all within a reasonable time. But, if that unlikely scenario should unfold, the rules provide that attorneys believing that the response to evidence of a material violation is not appropriate or is unreasonably delayed are obligated to explain to the responsible officers or directors they so believe.

Appropriate Response

An attorney's duty to report up-the-ladder depends on whether he or she has received an appropriate response, which the rules define as a response to evidence of a reported material violation that provides a basis for an attorney reasonably to believe that no material violation is occurring, has occurred, or is about to occur; or that the company has adopted remedial measures that can be expected to stop any material violation that is occurring, prevent any material violation that has yet to occur, and rectify any material violation that has already occurred. (17 CFR § 205.2(b).)

It is also an appropriate response if the attorney reasonably believes that the company, with the consent of its board, has retained or directed an attorney to review the reported evidence of a material violation and either has substantially implemented any remedial recommendations made by such attorney after a reasonable investigation and evaluation of the reported evidence or has been advised that such attorney may assert a colorable defense on the company's behalf in any investigation or judicial or administrative proceeding relating to the reported evidence of a material violation.

The definition of appropriate response emphasizes that an attorney's evaluation of, and the appropriateness of a company's response to, evidence of material violations will be measured against a reasonableness standard. The

Commission's intent is to permit attorneys to exercise their judgment as to whether a response to a report is appropriate so long as their determination of what is an appropriate response is reasonable.

This standard requires the attorney to reasonably believe either that there is no material violation or that the company has taken proper remedial steps.

In providing that the attorney's belief that a response was appropriate be reasonable, the Commission is allowing the attorney to take into account, and the Commission to weigh, all attendant circumstances. The circumstances reporting attorneys might weigh in assessing whether they could reasonably believe that a response was appropriate would include the amount and weight of the evidence of a material violation, the severity of the apparent material violation, and the scope of the investigation into the report.

¶ 1008 Retaliatory Discharge

The SEC rules authorize attorneys to notify the company's board of directors or any board committee if they reasonably believe that they were discharged for reporting evidence of a material violation. This provision is an important corollary to the up-the-ladder reporting requirement. It is designed to ensure that a chief legal officer is not permitted to block a report to the board or other committee by discharging a reporting attorney. (17 CFR § 205.3(b)(10).)

¶ 1009 Qualified Legal Compliance Committee

As an alternative to up-the-ladder reporting, the rules allow attorneys to report evidence of a material violation to a qualified legal compliance committee (QLCC), if the company has formed such a committee. Attorneys reporting evidence of a material violation to a qualified legal compliance committee will have satisfied their obligation to report evidence of a material violation within the company and are not required to assess the company's response to the reported evidence of a material violation. They need take no further action regarding the evidence of a material violation.

Similarly, a chief legal officer may refer a report of evidence of a material violation to a qualified legal compliance committee in lieu of causing an inquiry to be conducted under the rules. Thereafter, the qualified legal compliance committee is responsible for responding to the evidence of a material violation reported to it.

This alternative to the reporting requirements would allow, but not require, an attorney to seek expedited assessment of reported evidence of a material violation. It would also relieve reporting attorneys of any further obligation once they reported the evidence to the company's QLCC. The SEC believes that this provision may well encourage attorneys to report evidence of a material violation more promptly, since reporting attorneys would not have to worry that they might ultimately be obliged to decide whether the company response was appropriate. Junior attorneys employed by a company might be especially concerned about having to second-guess their superiors, and yet those junior attorneys might also be the first to find evidence of a material violation that the company would want to know about.

Definition and Role

The QLCC is a committee of the company's board of directors with special authority and special responsibility. It is responsible for carrying out all the steps required by Sarbanes-Oxley Act Section 307. The QLCC must consist of at least three members, one of whom must also be a member of the audit committee, or if the company has no audit committee, a member from an equivalent committee of independent directors. The other two or more members cannot be directly or indirectly employed by the company, and, in the case of a registered investment company, cannot be "interested persons" as defined in Investment Company Act Section 2(a)(19). (17 CFR § 205.2(k).)

The QLCC must notify the CLO and CEO of the report of evidence of a material violation (except where such notification would have been excused as futile). The QLCC must then determine if an investigation is necessary regarding the report of evidence of a material violation by the company, its officers, directors, employees or agents. If the committee decides that an investigation is necessary, it must notify the audit committee or the full board of directors and initiate the investigation, which may be conducted either by the CLO or by outside attorneys. The QLCC has the authority to retain such additional expert personnel as it deems necessary.

At the investigation's conclusion, the QLCC may recommend, by majority vote, that the company implement an appropriate response to evidence of a material violation and to inform the CLO, the CEO, and the board of directors of the results of any the investigation and the appropriate remedial measures to be adopted. The QLCC may also take, by majority vote, all other appropriate action, including notifying the SEC in the event that the company fails in any material respect to implement an appropriate response that it has recommended.

Note that, while the QLCC has a duty to recommend that a company implement an appropriate response to evidence of a material violation, the QLCC is not required to direct the company to take action. Responding to commenters, the SEC reasoned that giving the QLCC explicit authority to compel the board to take remedial action would conflict with established corporate governance models.

More broadly, the QLCC is designed to institutionalize the process of reviewing reported evidence of a possible material violation, which the SEC views as a welcome development in itself. It is also envisioned that this new committee will produce broader synergistic benefits, such as heightening awareness of the importance of early reporting of possible material violations so that they can be prevented or stopped.

The most important respect in which the QLCC reporting route differs from up-the-ladder reporting is that using the alternative approach relieves an attorney who has reported evidence of a material violation to a QLCC from any obligation to assess the company's response to the reported evidence of a material violation.

The QLCC must adopt written procedures for the receipt, retention, and consideration of reports of evidence material violations.

Audit Committee as QLCC—Majority Vote

The final rules provide that an audit or other committee of the company may serve as the QLCC. Thus, the company is not required to form a QLCC as a new corporate structure, unless it wishes to, so long as another board committee meets all of the requisite criteria for a QLCC and agrees to function as a QLCC in addition to its separate duties. This provision recognizes that companies should have to create a new committee to serve as a QLCC so long as an existing committee contains the required number of independent directors.

The proposal did not specify whether the QLCC could act if its members did not all agree. In response to comments expressing concern over this point, the SEC clarified that the QLCC's decisions and actions must be made and taken based on majority vote. Unanimity is not required for a QLCC to operate; nor should an individual member of a QLCC act contrary to the collective decision of the committee. Thus, the rules specify that a QLCC may make its recommendations and take other actions by majority vote.

¶ 1010 Disclosure of Confidences

The rules authorize a covered attorney to reveal to the Commission confidences or secrets relating to the attorney's representation of a company before the Commission to the extent the attorney reasonably believes it necessary to:

- prevent the company from committing a material violation likely to cause substantial harm to the financial interest or property of the company or investors;

- prevent the company from perpetrating a fraud on the Commission; or

- rectify the consequences of the company's illegal act that the attorney's services had furthered. (17 CFR § 205.3(d)(2).)

¶ 1011 Sanctions and Remedies

If an attorney violates the reporting rules, the SEC nay bring a civil action seeking injunctive and other equitable relief, as well as civil money penalties under Exchange Act Section 21(d). Alternatively, the SEC may bring a cease-and-desist proceeding against the violator under Exchange Act Section 21C. But such a violation, by itself, will not meet the standard for imposing criminal penalties under Exchange Act Section 32(a). (17 CFR § 205.6(a).)

Private Actions

The Commission has expressly provided that no private right of action exists based on compliance or non-compliance with the rules. In addition, an attorney who complies in good faith with the rules will not be subject to discipline or otherwise liable under an inconsistent state standard. Moreover, the rules will not require attorneys to withdraw or report to the Commission, but will only require reporting to the Commission in the rare circumstances occurring when a majority of a QLCC determines that a company has failed to take remedial action that was directed by the QLCC.

Parallel State Proceedings

The SEC may discipline violators of the reporting rules without regard to whether a separate state proceeding is underway for the same conduct. Thus, if an attorney's conduct violates the reporting rules as well as a state ethics rule, and the state in question brings proceedings against the attorney, the SEC may still initiate its own disciplinary action. An SEC administrative proceeding for violation of the reporting rules may result in the attorney's censure, or in temporary or permanent denial of the privilege of practicing before the Commission. (17 CFR § 205.6(b).)

Good Faith Compliance

The SEC rules provide a limited safe harbor from state disciplinary proceedings for attorneys who comply in good faith with the reporting regime. (17 CFR § 205.6(c).) The safe harbor applies only to an attorney's liability for violating *inconsistent* state standards. The provision, therefore, is not available when the state imposes additional requirements that are consistent with the SEC's rules. Further, the safe harbor will not operate to preclude disciplinary actions brought by the SEC.

CHAPTER 11

Best Practices and Guidance

¶ 1101 Introduction

As the audit committee's role has increased in prominence, a number of best practices for audit committees have developed from various sources. Many of these best practices have been recommended to audit committees by either the SEC or its chief accountants (see ¶ 1104).

Two important sources for best practices are the report of the Blue Ribbon Committee on Improving the Effectiveness of Corporate Audit Committees (see ¶ 1103) and the Report of the Panel on Audit Effectiveness, i.e., the "O'Malley Panel" (see ¶ 1102). But going even further back, the Treadway Commission provided guidance for audit committees as well (see ¶ 1106).

As a general matter, due diligence and documentation provide the support for the best practices and work of an active, vigilant audit committee. (Remarks of former SEC Chief Accountant Lynn Turner, Seminar on Corporate Accountability, Scottsdale, Ariz., March 10, 2001.)

¶ 1102 O'Malley Report

The report by the Panel on Audit Effectiveness, commonly referred to as the O'Malley Panel, contained a number of best practice recommendations. The report, issued in 2000, was the work product of knowledgeable committee members, including former SEC Commissioners Aulana Peters and Bevis Longstreth, and the Chair, Shaun O'Malley, a former Chair of Price Waterhouse.

In January 2001, SEC Chairman Levitt sent a letter to the audit committee chairs of 5,000 public companies to be sure that the O'Malley Panel report was brought to the attention of audit committees, and that they had the opportunity to give consideration to the panel's recommendations.

Internal Controls

A company's internal controls is something an audit committee cannot ignore and is the subject of a best practice.

The ultimate responsibility for the numbers rests squarely on the shoulders of a company's chief financial officer. The CFO is the person who sets the tone and policies for the entire financial organization and it is the CFO who ensures the quality of the financial information provided to investors. A key component of any quality financial reporting process is the establishment of internal controls that provide reasonable assurance that the financial statements have been prepared in accordance with generally accepted accounting principles. (Remarks of SEC Chief Accountant Lynn Turner before the Colorado Society of CPAs, Dec. 15, 2000.)

That is why the O'Malley Panel recommended that audit committees obtain from management a report on the effectiveness of the company's internal controls. Former SEC Chief Accountant Lynn Turner strongly supported that recommendation and encourages both CFO's and audit committees to implement it. (Remarks of SEC Chief Accountant Lynn Turner before the Colorado Society of CPAs, Dec. 15, 2000.) The Sarbanes-Oxley Act now requires annual reports to contain an internal control report containing management's assessment of the effectiveness of the internal controls (see Chapter 3). Also, the independent auditor must attest to and report on the assessment.

Sarbanes-Oxley thus transformed what had previously been a best practice into a statutory duty. This is a sound policy in light of the Committee of Sponsoring Organizations' Report that highlighted the breakdown of internal controls at the management level in most financial fraud cases.

Auditor Independence

The O'Malley Panel also had recommendations that, in Mr. Turner's view, every audit committee should consider. These included the recommendation on internal controls, as well as guidance for audit committees regarding auditor's independence. For example, the panel recommended that audit committees pre-approve non-audit services over a specified threshold and that the audit committee consider a list of ten factors in making those determinations. (Remarks of SEC Chief Accountant Lynn Turner before the Colorado Society of CPAs, Dec. 15, 2000.)

According to Mr. Turner, audit committees and their CFO's should find that guidance to be timely and useful as they consider the issue of auditor independence. In its final rule on auditor independence, the Commission looked to audit committee oversight to play an important role in maintaining investor confidence. Audit committees asking the tough questions and making reasonable business judgments about the auditor's independence is a goal that must be achieved, he emphasized. (Remarks of SEC Chief Accountant Lynn Turner before the Colorado Society of CPAs, Dec. 15, 2000.)

The Sarbanes-Oxley Act now requires audit committees to pre-approve audit and non-audit services, as discussed in Chapter 7.

The O'Malley Panel recommended that in determining the appropriateness of a service, an audit committee should consider the following ten factors:

- Whether the service is being performed principally for the audit committee.

- The effects of the service, if any, on audit effectiveness or on the quality and timeliness of the entity's financial reporting process.

- Whether the service would be performed by specialists (e.g., technology specialists) who ordinarily also provide recurring audit support.

- Whether the service would be performed by audit personnel, and if so, whether it will enhance their knowledge of the entity's business and operations.

- Whether the role of those performing the service would be inconsistent with the auditors' role (e.g., a role where neutrality, impartiality and auditor skepticism are likely to be subverted).

- Whether the audit firm personnel would be assuming a management role or creating a mutual or conflicting interest with management.

Other Recommendations

Former SEC Chief Accountant Lynn Turner noted other recommendations of the O'Malley Panel as important to improving the audit process and quality of financial reporting. Specifically, the audit committee should: (1) review annually the performance of external and internal auditors; (2) be advised of plans to hire personnel of the audit firm into high level positions; and (3) ensure that factors, such as time pressures on auditors, are addressed so as not to negatively impact the credibility of audits. (Remarks of former SEC Chief Accountant Lynn Turner, Securities Regulation Institute, Northwestern University School of Law, January 24, 2001.)

¶ 1103 Blue Ribbon Committee

The Report of the Blue Ribbon Committee on Improving the Effectiveness of Corporate Audit Committees sets forth not only recommendations, but also lists best practices for audit committees. These best practices are set forth in five principles that address the audit committee's oversight role and responsibility, including the need to: oversee both the internal and external audit functions; ensure independent communication with the internal and external auditors; engage in a robust, candid, and probing discussion of the quality of the company's financial reporting and disclosure practices; and adopt measures to ensure the outside auditor's objectivity.

A former SEC Chief Accountant strongly urges every audit committee that is serious about the quality of the financial reporting of their company to seriously consider these best practices. (Remarks by SEC Chief Accountant Lynn Turner at seminar on Corporate Accountability, Scottsdale, Arizona, March 10, 2001.)

While the recommendation of these best practices pre-dates the Sarbanes-Oxley Act, they do seem to have a continuing value and efficacy.

Key Monitoring Role

Principle One discusses the audit committee's key role in monitoring the other component parts of the audit. In this pivotal role, aptly described as the first among equals, the committee oversees management who has and must accept the primary responsibility for the financial statements, the external auditors on whom investors rely to provide an unbiased, robust examination of the numbers to ensure their credibility and integrity, and where they exist, internal auditors who provide a source of advice and information on the processes and safeguards that exist. It is important that this oversight role be timely, robust, diligent and probing.

The audit committee should encourage procedures promoting accountability among management and the internal and external auditors. The audit committee should ensure that management develops a sound system of internal controls, that the internal auditor objectively assesses management's accounting practices and internal controls, and that the outside auditors assess management and the internal auditor's practices.

The audit committee should learn the roles and duties of each of these participants in the financial reporting process so that it will be in a position to ask the right questions as to how each participant carries out its functions. Finally, these questions should not be merely a checklist of standard questions, but should be tailored to a company's particular circumstances.

Audit Committee and Internal Auditor

Principle Two states the importance of independent communication and information flow between the audit committee and the internal auditor. The internal auditor should have an unobstructed and clear communication channel to the audit committee. This is especially important today as the internal auditor can evaluate and report to the audit committee on the adequacy and effectiveness of a company's internal controls.

In today's electronic world, the design and operation of effective internal accounting controls is more important than ever. And yet with increasing frequency, as the 1999 Committee of Sponsoring Organizations of the Treadway Commission (COSO) Report entitled, "Fraudulent Financial Reporting: 1987-1997," notes, financial frauds often involve the override of internal controls by a company's chief executive officer or chief financial officer.

The audit committee must establish a culture promoting disclosure by the internal auditor and a recognition that internal auditors who identify a problem and cannot obtain management's support have a duty to the audit committee, the full board, and ultimately the shareholders to disclose the information to the audit committee.

But as the blue ribbon panel so aptly observes, the internal auditor is in a unique position; employed by management while at the same time expected to review the conduct of management. This role can create significant tension since the internal auditor must have independence to objectively assess management's actions while at the same time being dependent on management for employment.

With this in mind, a best practice would be for the audit committee to put in place a formal mechanism to facilitate confidential exchanges between itself and the internal auditor. This mechanism could take the form of regular meetings independent of management or regular confidential reports circulated only to the audit committee. The regularity of the meetings is important since, in the panel's view, this will help independent dialogue between the audit committee and the internal auditor lose its "taboo" nature and no longer imply "treason against management."

Audit Committee and Outside Auditor

Principle Three stresses the need for independent communication and information flow between the audit committee and the outside auditors. The BRC report states that integral to this reliance is the requirement that the outside auditors perform their service without being affected by economic or other interests that would call into question their objectivity and, accordingly, the reliability of their attestation. Every audit committee should adopt additional voluntary measures to ensure outside auditors' objectivity.

The audit committee should develop regularly scheduled meetings with the outside auditors, independent of management. In addition, the audit committee should promote a culture that values objective and critical analysis of management and the internal auditor. In this regard, the audit committee should ensure that the outside auditors have given it the information that would be required to be disclosed by generally accepted auditing standards.

Candid Discussions

Principle Four is one of the cornerstones of the foundation of high quality financial reporting. That principle requires candid discussions with management, the internal auditor, and outside auditors regarding issues implicating judgment and impacting quality. The blue ribbon committee sketches the following scenario and order for these candid discussions.

Management should apprise the audit committee of its system for internal controls and provide an explanation of the company's financial statements. Specifically, management should provide periodic reviews of financial statements before SEC filing; presentations on any changes in accounting principles or financial reporting policies from a prior year; accounting treatment of significant transactions; and any significant variations between budgeted and actual numbers in a particular account. Management should also give audit committees information on any second opinion sought from an outside auditor with regard to the accounting treatment of a particular event or transaction. Finally, the audit committee should be informed of management's response to the assessments provided by the internal and outside auditors.

Once management has provided this basic financial knowledge, the audit committee should use the internal and outside auditors to verify management's compliance with procedures and seek additional input on any significant judgments. The audit committee should dialogue with the internal and external auditors to ensure that it has received all pertinent information.

The blue ribbon committee also advises the audit committee to have a checklist of questions to review with management and the internal and external auditors. While the checklist cannot be a substitute for the audit committee's own investigation and analysis, the questions could cover: the accounting implications of significant transactions; changes in elective accounting principles and the methods of applications of such principles; the use of reserves and accruals; significant estimates and judgments used in preparing financials; auditor methods for risk assessment and changes in the audit's scope as a result of the assessments; the emergence or elimination of high risk areas; and the results of external environmental factors on financial reporting and the audit process.

Diligent Committee Membership

Principle Five is diligent and knowledgeable committee membership. It goes without saying, you have to know what you are doing before you can do it, and to do any job right you need the right tools.

In this regard, the blue ribbon committee asks audit committees to consider training and education programs to ensure that its members have the proper background and knowledge as to relevant developments in accounting and finance. While training may be conducted by professionals inside the company, the audit committee should have the ability to also engage outside advisers for educational training. In order to determine their needs, members should analyze their weaknesses and ask for the views of management and the auditors on any gaps in members' knowledge.

¶ 1104 Additional Best Practices

Former SEC Chief Accountants Robert K. Herdman and Lynn Turner have given expert advice and best practices guidance to audit committees that, although pre-dating the passage of Sarbanes-Oxley, continues to have value. Both officials have also noted with approval certain practices recommended by leading investor, Warren Buffett. These best practices are discussed separately below.

Herdman's Remarks

Mr. Herdman has distilled 30 years of experience into three key qualities designed to ensure audit committee effectiveness. An effective audit committee will: (1) control the agenda; (2) be diligent; (3) take the time. (Remarks of SEC Chief Accountant Robert K. Herdman at the Tulane Corporate Law Institute, March 7, 2002.)

Controlling the agenda

According to Mr. Herdman, the audit committee must control the agenda when dealing with the following matters:

- Competence and independence of auditors;
- Internal controls;
- Audit scope and fees; and
- Corporate codes of conduct.

On this point, he also emphasized that the audit committee must have direct, unfettered, independent access to management, internal audit, and external auditors. The audit committee must be able to communicate in confidence with these three groups independently of each other.

Diligence

One of the most important aspects of diligence is to be proactive. Audit committees should not only rely on what is put before them as "the gospel truth," emphasized Former Chief Accountant Herdman, they should "take it and analyze it, throw a couple of rocks at it and see if they puncture it or bounce off."

A good place to start with being proactive is with respect to discussing and understanding the companies critical accounting policies. The SEC wants audit committees to engage in proactive discussions with company management and outside auditors regarding key accounting judgments. It is essential that the audit committee be actively, not passively, engaged.

Audit committee members should ask the tough questions about these policies. The rules of engagement should encourage comprehensive and con-structive questions that get to the root of the biggest issues facing the company's financial presentation and disclosure.

Taking the time

Audit committee members must take the time to achieve an adequate understanding of what the company's financials represent, to have enough time to consult with outside counsel and experts if necessary, to ask the tough and incisive questions, and to obtain answers that make sense. As such, an effective audit committee requires a commitment of time as follows:

- quality time to give the critical corporate governance and accounting and disclosure issues their full attention;
- quantity of time to allow thorough deliberations and discussion;
- time for proper up-front planning;
- time to conduct deliberate and frequent meetings;
- time for follow-up.

Turner's Remarks

Former SEC Chief Accountant Lynn Turner has listed best practices that he believes will improve the performance of audit committees and also improve the quality of companies' public information and financial reporting. (Remarks of SEC Chief Accountant Lynn Turner, Seminar on Corporate Accountability, Scottsdale, Ariz., March 10, 2001.)

Regularly scheduled meetings

The COSO Report noted that many financial frauds occurred in companies where audit committees met infrequently. Too often, committees meet maybe one to three times a year, often for a few minutes over breakfast or just before the regular board meetings. Such practices cannot foster the type of in-depth, robust dialogue the BRC called for. Sound advice from the auditors, both internal and outside will be short-changed, if presented at all, and there can be no in-depth probing into the quality of financial reporting done by management.

With this in mind, Mr. Turner strongly encouraged audit committees to meet no fewer than four to six times a year. Additional or extended meetings may very well be needed when events such as material acquisitions occur or for training provided by management to new committee members on the company's accounting practices and business operations. This basic understanding is fundamental to the ability of audit committee members to adequately fulfill their responsibilities.

Reviewing relationships

Just as the audit committee has responsibilities, so does the external auditor. According to the blue ribbon committee, it is imperative to the integrity and effectiveness of the audit committee's oversight process that all parties recognize that the audit committee and full board, as the representatives of shareholders, are the ultimate entities to which auditors are accountable.

This being so, the former chief accountant believes that the audit committee should review on a regular basis the relationships between management and the internal and external auditors.

It is critical that the external audit engagement partner clearly understand that he or she is responsible to and serving the investors and the audit committee, not management. It is the audit committee that hires auditors, evaluates their performance and, when necessary, fires them.

A best practice in this respect is for the auditor to issue the audit engagement letter directly to the audit committee and for the audit partner and committee to have a clear understanding of the engagement's terms, the audit's scope, and the auditor's responsibilities for reporting to the audit committee.

Management letter comments

Auditors often identify improvements that can or should be made to a company's internal controls, policies and financial disclosures. The auditor typically communicates these observations to management and the audit committee in what is referred to as a management letter, which is a valuable and integral part of each audit.

¶1104

However, the SEC staff has noted circumstances where the auditors, sometimes at the request of management, did not provide a copy of the management letter to the audit committee. In some of these circumstances, significant financial reporting issues arose. The issues were documented by the auditors in their workpapers and management letter but, unfortunately, had not been appropriately communicated to the audit committee.

Every audit committee should request from the auditor a copy of all management letter comments. It is important that these be obtained on a timely basis at the completion of each audit. In some cases, auditors may also provide management letter comments as they complete their interim audit procedures or their reviews of the quarterly financial statements. In addition to obtaining a copy of the management comment letter, audit committees should have an in-depth discussion with the internal and external auditors regarding what changes or improvements should be made in internal controls, policies or financial reporting processes.

Then the audit committee should discuss with management how those changes or improvements will be implemented. A robust management letter and candid discussion of that letter can be of tremendous value to the company and its audit committee.

Fair compensation

The audit committee must also ensure that the auditors are compensated fairly for performing an effective and quality audit. Over the years, audit committees who considered negotiating the lowest possible audit fee to be their most important job, without regard for audit quality, have disappointed the SEC Chief Accountant. In the view of SEC staff, an audit committee that "brow beats" an auditor into an unrealistically low fee will have to share the blame if at a later date investors call into question the quality of the company's financial reports. Instead, audit committees should inquire about issues such as:

- The adequacy of the audit's staffing;
- The experience levels of the auditors assigned to the audit, including their experience with the company and its industry;
- The percentage of the total audit hours actually spent by the more experienced partner and manager (a small percentage may raise a red flag and risk for the audit committee that sufficient expertise is not being devoted to judgmental and risky business and financial reporting issues);
- The total number of hours spent on the engagement by the partner and manager;
- The adequacy of the total hours spent on areas that require significant judgment and that have the greatest inherent risk when it comes to the numbers; and
- The number of hours being spent by the partner and manager on the more judgmental and risky business and financial reporting issues.

Loss leader treatment

During public hearings the Commission held on auditor independence, some participants expressed concern that the audit has been used as a loss leader to attract management consulting fees. It is not in the public's interest for audit fees to be viewed as a burden, a service only worthy of loss leader status in order to expand the non-audit fees of the accounting firm. It certainly is not in the interest of the individual members of the audit committee or the board of directors.

Former SEC Chief Accountant Lynn Turner, therefore, strongly endorsed the following recommendations made during the SEC public hearings by a well known audit committee member:

- Audit committees should inquire about and ensure that the audit fee does not represent a loss leader being used to leverage the audit into other consulting engagements.

- Audit committees should inquire about the compensation scheme for the audit partner and determine if it is affected in any way by the cross-selling of consulting services.

(Remarks of SEC Chief Accountant Lynn Turner, Seminar on Corporate Accountability, Scottsdale, Ariz., March 10, 2001.)

ISB letters

Another communication audit committees will be receiving annually is what is referred to as the Independence Standards Board, or ISB, letter. This letter from the auditors is to spell out any matters or relationships between the auditor and client that may impact on the auditor's independence.

Upon receiving the ISB letter, the best practice would be for the audit committee to consider the services and relationships identified in the letter using the guidance provided by the O'Malley Panel. This would be facilitated if management would reconcile for the audit committee the matters, issues and amounts disclosed in the ISB letter to the billings for services disclosed in the proxy. For example, does the proxy disclosure of "other" fees paid to the auditor include any prohibited services or fees, such as bookkeeping or contingent fees?

The former SEC Chief Accountant encourages audit committees to inquire as to whether the ISB letter discusses not only all matters relevant to the firm in the United States, but also to its affiliates overseas. (Remarks of SEC Chief Accountant Lynn Turner, Seminar on Corporate Accountability, Scottsdale, Ariz., March 10, 2001.)

Unfortunately, the SEC staff is aware of actual violations of the independence rules relating to financial interests held, or prohibited services being performed, such as bookkeeping, that were not reported to the audit committee in the ISB letter as required. This appears to be a larger issue for those companies that have international operations and when those operations are audited by a foreign affiliate of the U.S. firm. Accordingly, to avoid future embarrassment, audit committees are encouraged to ask the engagement partner if appropriate steps have been taken and quality controls put in place to ensure the auditor's independence on a global basis.

Earnings releases

Former Chief Accountant Turner encourages audit committees to ask questions about the quality of the company's public earnings releases since in his view some of these press releases "seem to spin straw into gold." Too often press releases convey an incomplete or inaccurate picture to investors. For example, press releases have presented:

- Earnings before marketing costs.

¶1104

- Cash earnings per share that bear no relevance to cash flows but rather are merely earnings adjusted to eliminate amortization of selected costs.

- Earnings before losses from newly started businesses, such as a new Internet subsidiary, or

- Any one or combination of the above, but with one-time gains from sales of investments added back.

Audit committees should view with skepticism this biased and unbalanced approach to disclosure of financial information.

Annual self-review

An audit committee that follows best practices should elect to undergo an annual evaluation. Just as the board of directors evaluates the management team, the audit committee should perform an annual self-assessment of its performance and obtain input from the entire board of directors.

Financial statements

According to former Chief Accountant Turner, four key ingredients have gone into cooking the books. First and foremost is premature revenue recognition. This is main reason financial statements are restated. SEC research indicates that restatements for revenue recognition cause a greater reduction in market capitalization than any other type of restatement. (Remarks of SEC Chief Accountant Lynn Turner, Seminar on Corporate Accountability, Scottsdale, Ariz., March 10, 2001.)

In this regard, the SEC staff has urged CEOs and CFOs to ensure that they have adequate internal accounting controls in place to promote compliance with the four basic principles in Staff Accounting Bulletin No. 101 on revenue recognition. In order for these controls, policies and procedures to be effective, they need to be well documented, in a written format, and distributed to those responsible for their implementation and operation. This includes not only the accounting and finance group, but also those in sales, marketing, order management and shipping. Training of the appropriate personnel on a worldwide basis is also required to achieve effective internal controls that will ensure proper maintenance of the company's books and records.

A second particularly spicy ingredient in cooking the books is the improper recording of what are commonly referred to as "cushions," "reserves" or "loss accruals." GAAP is specific in noting that accruals or cushions for general "loss accruals" or "reserves" are not acceptable. Unfortunately, especially in business mergers, management has cooked the books using this form of earnings management. Again, the SEC staff recommends that companies establish internal controls and written policies and procedures that should be followed when accounting for such transactions. Consistent with the guidance of the AICPA, the SEC staff believes that this is a topic that audit committees would be well served to have both their internal and external independent auditors devote adequate resources to, and report back to the audit committee.

A third ingredient that seems to be used with increasing frequency, and is of concern to the SEC staff, is the use of changing estimates to make the numbers. While this may be perfectly acceptable when supported by real economic facts, too often the staff has been seeing companies changing estimates when the underlying economics of the business do not support the change, and without any disclosure to investors. As such, investors are unwarily using numbers for their investment decisions that lack transparency, consistency and comparability.

The former SEC Chief Accountant's advice to audit committees on this topic is once again to consider the AICPA's guidance. Audit committees should be sure to ask:

- Were there any changes in estimates made, such as: changes in depreciable lives of assets, changes in assumptions used to calculate pension or health care costs, or changes in estimates of loss accruals such as inventory valuation allowances, pending litigation, tax examinations, etc.?

- How large was the effect of those changes on the company's results?

- Are those changes reflected in and consistent with the company's budget and strategic plans and recent business and industry economic factors and developments?

- Are all such changes in estimates quantified and disclosed in the company's financial statements and the management's discussion and analysis section of the annual report to shareholder?

The fourth and last ingredient in cooking the books is that of deferring as an asset, expenses or costs that would otherwise typically be reflected as an expense in the current financial statements. In the past, costs of starting up plants and product lines, large advertising campaigns, or costs of other types of large one-time events have been improperly deferred. As a result, it is usually a good idea to identify such events and inquire of the CFO and external auditor if the accounting that has been applied is in conformity with GAAP.

Leading Investor's Views

As noted by both former SEC Chief Accountants Lynn Turner and Robert Herdman, Warren Buffet, perhaps the most widely recognized investor of our time, has also weighed in during the development of the BRC's recommendations. (See Remarks of SEC Chief Accountant Lynn Turner, Seminar on Corporate Accountability, Scottsdale, Ariz., March 10, 2001; Remarks by SEC Chief Accountant Robert Herdman at the Tulane Corporate Law Institute, March 7, 2002.) Mr. Buffett suggested an approach based on audit committees asking auditors three intriguing questions:

- If the auditor were solely responsible for preparation of the company's financial statements, would they have been prepared in any way different than the manner selected by management? The audit committee should inquire as to both material and nonmaterial differences. If the auditor would have done anything differently than management, an explanation should be made of management's argument and the auditor's response.

- If the auditor were an investor, would he have received the information essential to a proper understanding of the company's financial performance during the reporting period?

- Is the company following the same internal audit procedure that would be followed if the auditor himself were CEO? If not, what are the differences and why?

Mr. Buffet recommended that the audit committee document the responses to these questions in its minutes. The answers to these questions really indicate whether, if the auditor was running the company, the same financial statements and disclosures would have been published and the same internal controls would have been established. (Remarks of SEC Chief Accountant Lynn Turner, Seminar on Corporate Accountability, Scottsdale, Ariz., March 10, 2001.)

American Assembly on the Future of the Accounting Profession

A report issued as part of the 103rd American Assembly on the future of the accounting profession set forth a number of best practices for audit committees. Participants in the assembly included former Federal Reserve Board Chairman Paul Volcker, former SEC Chairmen David Ruder, Roderick Hills and Harold Williams, and current SEC Chairman William Donaldson, as well as PCAOB Chairman William McDonough. Although they participated in the assembly, the current regulators did not vote on the report. (Future of the Accounting Profession, 103rd American Assembly, November, 2003).

The new listing standards adopted by both the New York Stock Exchange and Nasdaq in response to the Sarbanes-Oxley Act establish exacting standards that audit committees must meet when it comes to both their composition and their activities. A key criterion for audit committee membership is financial literacy.

A number of the assembly participants suggested that companies and investors would be best served by audit committees whose members can understand the following:

- The transactions that require management to choose between accounting practices and/or use judgment in making an assumption or an estimate;

- The choices available to management when reporting such transactions;

- The choices made and the reasons for the choices; and

- Whether the choices made present, overall, a fair presentation of the transaction.

Adopting such standards need not be burdensome to audit committees since they can charge their auditors with identifying the assumptions, estimates and accounting practices that have been chosen by management. It is incumbent on audit committees, however, to engage in meaningful discussions with both management and auditors in order to ensure the financial positions of their companies are presented fairly.

The Sarbanes-Oxley Act also sets numerous mandates for audit committees. One such is the duty to pre-approve non-audit services not expressly prohibited by the Act. Thus, audit committees can exercise discretion in determining what non-audit services a company may decide to engage its auditors to provide.

Some audit committees have adopted a blanket prohibition on external auditors providing non-audit services, a trend that the assembly report regrets. Within limits, authorizing auditors to undertake complementary services can be beneficial to a company. However, since auditors cannot audit their own work, audit committees must remain vigilant and devote a greater degree of scrutiny in situations where non-audit services are being provided.

Audit committees must also continue to assert their central role in corporate governance. In this regard, committee members should invest the time necessary to develop a full understanding of the company's business. Accounting knowledge, unless it is accompanied by insight into the corporation and industry, will not suffice.

Moreover, audit committee members must develop and display a healthy degree of skepticism to prevent them from being lulled into a sense of false security by compelling presentations made by management or auditors. Audit committees also must strive to protect auditor objectivity.

The Sarbanes-Oxley Act requires that audit committees be responsible for retaining the company's external auditor, and stipulates that that auditor must report directly to the audit committee. For this relationship to work well, it must be nourished. Audit committee members must seek out their auditors and make clear to them that the committee is the client and that its members will support the auditors, even in the case of a conflict between auditors and management.

In short, audit committees must take charge of the audit, control the selection of both the audit firm and the partner engaged to lead it, and make the final decision when it comes time to set the audit fee. Above all else, they must protect the auditor's independence.

The audit committee must also be in charge of the internal audit function. While the chief internal auditor may report for administrative purposes to the CEO or CFO of the company, the audit committee must supervise the decisions to hire, compensate, and retain the personnel engaged in the internal audit. The committee must be responsible for determining bonuses for internal auditors and for protecting their career paths. Internal auditors can undertake their duties effectively within the company only if the audit committee assures them that they need not fear reprisals from those whom they audit.

Breeden Report

A report to the U.S. District Court for the SDNY on corporate governance for the future of MCI, Inc., commonly referred to as the Breeden Report, contained a number of best practices for audit committees. The report, issued in August of 2003, was the work of former SEC chairman Richard C. Breeden.

The Breeden Report posits that the chair of the audit committee bears enormous responsibility for the company's financial reporting, internal controls and the performance of both internal and external auditors. Obviously, it is in the company's interest to have an experienced audit committee chair who is up to speed on the issues.

But the report also recognizes a risk to the company if an individual serves too long as chairman, and is not as effective as might be desirable. Thus, the report recommends that the chairmanship of the committee rotate among its members not less than every three years. At the end of such rotation, the former chair may remain a member of the audit committee, and may even serve a non-consecutive term as chair again in the future. In addition, the chair of the audit committee should be reelected annually by the board.

In most companies there is additional compensation for service on audit committees, though the amount is typically relatively low. This is a problem in light of the work increasingly expected of audit committees and the special risks and responsibilities of serving. Since low compensation will ultimately mean that members of this vital committee may not devote enough time to the role, or that high quality members cannot be recruited, the report recommend that committee members receive a meaningful retainer of at least $50,000 for members and at least $75,000 for the chair.

Importantly, the report emphasized that there should be zero tolerance for conflicts or related party transactions between audit committee members and the company. Thus, the report recommends that no committee member should receive any form of compensation from the company other than board and committee retainer fees. Similarly, committee members should not receive any remuneration from or through shareholders with more than a one percent interest in the company.

The report also recommends that the audit committee review a report from the general counsel at least twice each year as to compliance with the company's prohibitions against any related party transactions between directors or employees and their families and the company or any of its affiliates. The committee should also receive copies of reports of all transactions in the company's stock by members of the board of directors and senior executives, and it should review such transactions for compliance with both legal and corporate standards, including advance public notice of all transactions.

Since the CFO occupies a uniquely sensitive role in financial reporting, disclosure and corporate governance, the report recommended that the audit committee conduct an annual review of the CFO's performance, including all transactions or payments of any kind between the CFO and the company or any of its affiliates, suppliers, vendors, customers, investors or entities affiliated with any such person, any employee or director or spouses or family members of any such persons. This annual review should include all business and investing activities of the CFO, which should be disclosed to the committee in connection with any such review.

The committee's annual CFO evaluation should verify the absence of related party transactions of any kind between the CFO and the company, compliance by the CFO with the company's code of conduct and the absence of any involvement in profit making activities outside the company other than investments in bona fide instruments or situations available to the public and wholly unrelated to the company.

In addition, such review should assess the CFO's record in the areas of achieving transparency in financial reports, establishment and enhancement of internal controls, and overall competence and expertise. The review should also examine the CFO's progress each year in the recruiting and training of a high quality finance department staff.

In light of its enormous responsibilities, the audit committee should identify and retain professional advisors to provide necessary analytic support to its work. In this regard, the report recommends that the committee identify and retain an independent law firm, as well as any independent analytic resources deemed beneficial. While such professionals need only be consulted as deemed useful by the committee, the report urges that these relationships be established in advance so that advice can be taken quickly.

The Breeden Report also recommends that the board establish and disclose annual training requirements for members of the audit committee as a qualification for continued service on the committee. These training refreshers should cover the requirements and obligations of audit committees, or cover issues of accounting principles, auditing standards, risk management or ethical

¶1104

compliance. Each new member of the committee should attend training in a program approved by the chair.

The quality of disclosure programs often suffers from inattention by audit committees. However, disclosure programs are a vital adjunct to accounting and auditing programs. Good disclosure can also significantly improve chances that misstated earnings or overvalued balance sheets will be discovered earlier than would otherwise be the case. The company's objective should be to provide maximum transparency for investors, not simply to meet the minimum legal requirements. This helps prevent fraud because the large numbers of outside financial managers who will be able to do a better analysis far exceed the resources of any audit committee.

Since outside users of financial reports are among the best persons to evaluate a company's disclosure quality, the Breeden Report recommends that the audit committee meet annually with shareholders, portfolio managers and analysts to solicit input and suggestions on means to improve the quality of the company's disclosure. It should also conduct at least one meeting annually with management and advisors to the audit committee specifically to review avenues for improving transparency in public disclosures.

The chairman of the audit committee should generally be expected to devote substantial time to the work of the committee, including meetings or discussions with internal financial personnel, external audit personnel, analysts or shareholders, experts for the committee or others.

In its oversight capacity, the committee should review efforts by management and outside auditors to enhance the company's internal controls and the quality of risk management programs at least twice each year. The committee should also meet not less than twice each year with the general counsel to review issues arising out of compliance activities and the company's ethics office, as well to assess contingent legal and regulatory risks to the company.

In addition, the committee should regularly meet with the external auditors to review the annual audit plan, the annual testing of internal controls by outside auditors, management letters issued by such auditors, accounting policy issues, including review of all technical accounting issues under discussion between the audit engagement team and the firm's national or other technical and quality control offices. The committee should also review all invoices submitted by the external auditors before payment.

U.K. Corporate Governance Code

The U.K. Combined Code on Corporate Governance contains many best practices for audit committees. These best practices require that every board should consider in detail what arrangements for its audit committee are best suited for its particular circumstances. Audit committee arrangements need to be proportionate to the task, and will vary according to the size, complexity and risk profile of the company. The code rests on the overarching principle that the audit committee has a special role to act independently from the executive to ensure that the interests of shareholders are properly protected in relation to financial reporting and internal control.

The code emphasizes that it is not the duty of audit committees to carry out functions that properly belong to others, such as the company's management in the preparation of the financial statements or the auditors in the planning or conducting of audits. To do so could undermine the responsibility of management and auditors. Audit committees should, for example, satisfy themselves that there is a proper system and allocation of responsibilities for the day-to-day monitoring of financial controls, but should not seek to do the monitoring themselves.

That does not mean, however, that the audit committee's oversight job is not a difficult or detailed one. Audit committees have wide-ranging, time consuming and intensive work to do. The audit committee must intervene if there are signs that something may be seriously amiss. For example, if the audit committee is uneasy about the explanations of management and auditors about a particular financial reporting policy decision, there may be no alternative but to grapple with the detail and perhaps to seek independent advice.

With regard to meetings, the code sets forth the following principles.

- The audit committee chairman, in consultation with the company secretary, should decide the frequency and timing of the committee meetings.

- There should be as many meetings as the audit committee's role and responsibilities require.

- There should be at least three meetings during the year, held to coincide with key dates within the financial reporting and audit cycle.

- No one other than audit committee members is entitled to be present at a meeting.

- It is for the audit committee to decide if non-members should attend for a particular meeting or a particular agenda item.

- It is expected that the external audit lead partner will be invited regularly to attend meetings, as well as the finance director.

- A sufficient interval should be allowed between audit committee meetings and main board meetings to allow any work arising from the audit committee meeting to be carried out and reported to the board.

- The audit committee should annually meet the external and internal auditors, without management present.

In addition to the remuneration paid to all independent directors, the code directs that audit committee members receive added remuneration to recompense them for their additional duties. In doing so, the code emphasized that consideration should be given to the time members are required to give to audit committee business, the skills they bring to bear and the onerous duties they take on, as well as the value of their work to the company.

The code states that training should be provided to members of the audit committee on an ongoing and timely basis and should include an understanding of the principles of and developments in financial reporting and related company law. In appropriate cases, it may also include understanding financial statements, applicable accounting standards and recommended practice; the regulatory framework for the company's business; the role of internal and external auditing and risk management. The training may take various forms, including attendance at formal courses and conferences, internal company talks and seminars, and briefings by external advisers.

Internal Audit Process

According to the code, the audit committee should monitor and review the effectiveness of the company's internal audit function and ensure that internal audit has the necessary resources and access to information. The audit committee should also approve the appointment or termination of the head of internal audit.

In reviewing the work of internal auditors, the audit committee should:

- ensure that the internal auditor has direct access to the board chairman and to the audit committee and is accountable to the committee;

- review and assess the annual internal audit work plan;

- receive periodic reports on the results of the internal auditors' work;

- monitor management's responsiveness to the internal auditor's findings and recommendations;

- meet annually with the head of internal audit without management present; and

- assess the role and effectiveness of internal audit in the overall context of the company's risk management system.

External Audit Function

As in the U.S., under the U.K. code the audit committee is the body responsible for overseeing the company's relations with the external auditor.

Generally, the code directs the audit committee to assess annually the qualification, expertise and resources, and independence of the external auditors and the effectiveness of the audit process. The assessment should cover all aspects of the audit service, including obtaining a report on the audit firm's own internal quality control procedures. If the external auditor resigns, the audit committee should investigate the issues giving rise to the resignation and consider whether any action is required.

The audit committee should approve the terms of engagement and the remuneration to be paid to the external auditor. As a corollary to the approval, the committee should satisfy itself that the fee to be paid for the audit services is appropriate and that an effective audit can actually be conducted for such a fee.

More specifically, the audit committee should review the engagement letter issued by the external auditor at the start of each audit, ensuring that it has been updated to reflect changes in circumstances arising since the previous year. Similarly, the scope of the external audit should be reviewed by the audit committee with the auditor. If the audit committee is not satisfied as to its adequacy it should arrange for additional work to be undertaken.

Importantly, the audit committee should establish procedures to annually ensure the independence of the external auditor. In this regard, the audit committee should annually seek from the external audit firm information about policies and processes for maintaining independence and monitoring compliance with relevant requirements, including the rotation of audit partners and staff.

The U.K. corporate governance code fully recognizes, as does the Sarbanes-Oxley Act, that the provision of non-audit services by the external auditor to the client company is fraught with peril for the maintenance of independence. Thus, the code directs the audit committee to ensure that the provision of non-audit services does not impair the external auditor's independence.

In this context, the audit committee should consider:

¶1104

- whether the skills and experience of the audit firm make it a suitable supplier of the non-audit service;

- whether there are safeguards in place to ensure that there is no threat from the non-audit services to an independent audit;

- the nature of the non-audit services, the related fee levels and the fee levels individually and in aggregate relative to the audit fee; and

- the criteria which govern the compensation of the individual auditors.

Using principles similar to the SEC's general principles of auditor independence, the U.K. code states that the audit committee should not approve non-audit services if the provision of the service would result in the:

- external auditor auditing its own work;

- external auditor making management decisions for the company;

- creation of a mutuality of interest; or

- external auditor being an advocate for the company.

Dutch Corporate Governance Code

Under the Dutch Corporate Governance Code (the Tabaksblat Code), the management board and the audit committee must annually report their dealings with the external auditor to the supervisory board. With regard to the external auditor's independence, for example, the report would discuss the desirability of rotating the responsible partners of an external audit firm that provides audit services, and the desirability of the same audit firm providing non-audit services to the company. In addition, at least once every four years, the supervisory board and the audit committee must conduct a thorough assessment of the functioning of the external auditor within the various entities and in the different capacities in which the external auditor acts. The main conclusions of this assessment must be communicated to the general meeting of shareholders for the purposes of assessing the nomination for the appointment of the external auditor.

A specific best practice under the code is that, when the need arises, the external auditor may request the chair of the audit committee for leave to attend the meeting of the audit committee. Another best practice is that the external auditor and the audit committee must be involved in drawing up the work schedule of the internal auditor. They must also take cognizance of the findings of the internal auditor.

With regard to financial reporting, the code specifies as a best practice that the audit committee must determine the involvement of the external auditor in the content and publication of financial reports other than the annual accounts. This best practice was inserted in the code to ensure that financial reports and press releases are included in the supervision without providing a rigid specification of the external auditor's role. It is also more broadly based on the recognition that financial reports and press releases issued by the management board often have considerable influence on the markets

In practical effect, the best practice means that the audit committee will receive such reports and press releases before they are issued and be given the chance to ask questions and make comments. Moreover, the audit committee will decide how and to what extent the external auditor should provide specific duties relative to the reports and press releases.

¶ 1105 Auditing Standards

Recommendation No. 8 of the Blue Ribbon Committee on Improving the Effectiveness of Corporate Audit Committees takes the position that generally accepted auditing standards require that a company's outside auditor discuss with the audit committee the auditor's judgments about the quality, not just the acceptability, of the company's accounting principles as applied in its financial reporting. The discussion should include such issues as the clarity of the company's financial disclosures and degree of aggressiveness or conservatism its accounting principles and underlying estimates and other significant decisions made by management in preparing the financial disclosure and reviewed by the outside auditors. This requirement should be written in a way to encourage open, frank discussion and to avoid boilerplate.

In response to Recommendation No. 8, in December of 1999 the Auditing Standards Board amended Statement of Auditing Standards No. 61 to require additional communications with audit committees of SEC clients. This amendment adopted a modified form of Recommendation No. 8 requiring that the independent auditor discuss with the audit committee the quality, not just the acceptability, of the entity's accounting principles as applied in its financial reporting. SAS 61 specifies that the discussion should involve management and include such matters as the consistency, clarity and completeness of accounting policies and disclosures.

Under SAS 61, the auditor is required to communicate a number of matters, including the quality of an entity's accounting principles, with the entity's audit committee. The purpose of communication with the audit committee is to provide the audit committee with information that may assist it in overseeing the entity's financial accounting, reporting and disclosure process. The auditor's attention to the accounting and financial knowledge of audit committee members, the timing of communications, and the delivery of appropriate content in the proper context will enable auditors to provide significant insight and assistance to the audit committee to fulfill its oversight role while observing a high standard of professional practice.

In February 2000, the AICPA published practice alert 2000-2, which is intended to provide auditors with information that will assist them in preparing for and participating in discussions with audit committees.

The practice alert is intended to assist firms in the identifying matters relevant to a discussion with an entity's audit committee of the quality of accounting principles used in the preparing an entity's financial statements.

The objective of Recommendation No. 8 is to educate and advise audit committee members so they may better carry out their oversight role on behalf of the board and ultimately public shareholders. This objective becomes more critical and sensitive in light of increasing expectations of the financial community with respect to audit committees.

The audit committee members benefit from the auditor's views regarding the quality of the entity's accounting principles as applied in its financial reporting. At the same time, management must be regarded as a critical participant in that discussion. The intimate knowledge of management concerning the day-to-day as well as non-recurring matters that influence the operations and financial reporting is essential to an understanding of the financial information.

¶ 1106 Treadway Commission

In 1987, the seminal Report of the National Commission on Fraudulent Financial Reporting, chaired by former SEC Commissioner James C. Treadway, Jr., set forth good practice guidelines for audit committees. The report generally concluded that audit committees need to be informed and vigilant, have their duties and responsibilities set forth in a written charter, and must be given resources and authority adequate to discharge their duties. In the course of its deliberations, the Treadway Commission developed some general guidelines for audit committees, as discussed below:

- *Size and term of appointment.* An audit committee normally should consist of not fewer than three independent directors. The maximum size may vary, but the committee should be small enough so that each member is an active participant. While the term of appointment is generally at the board's discretion, the Treadway Commission believes it is desirable to have terms arranged to maintain continuity consistent with bringing fresh perspectives to the committee's work.

- *Meetings.* The audit committee should meet on a regular basis and special meetings should be called as circumstances require.

- *Reporting to the board.* The audit committee should report its activities to the full board on a regular basis, such as after each meeting, so that the board is kept informed of its activities on a current basis.

- *Expand knowledge of company operations.* A systematic and continuing learning process for audit committee members will increase their effectiveness. One way is to review various financial aspects of the company on a planned basis.

- *Company counsel.* The audit committee should meet regularly with the company's general counsel, and outside counsel when appropriate, to discuss legal matters that may have a significant impact on the company's financial statements.

- *Audit plans.* The audit committee should review with the chief internal auditor and the independent public accountant their annual audit plans, including the degree of coordination of the respective plans. In addition, the committee should inquire as to the extent to which the planned audit scope can be relied upon to detect fraud or weaknesses in internal controls.

- *Electronic data processing.* The audit committee should discuss with the internal auditor and the independent public accountant what steps are planned for a review of the company's electronic data processing procedures and controls, and inquire as to the specific security programs to protect against computer fraud or misuse.

- *Other auditors.* The audit committee should inquire as to the extent to which independent public accountants other than the principal auditor are to be used and understand the rationale for using them. The committee should request that their work be coordinated and that an appropriate review of their work be performed by the principal auditor.

- *Officer expenses and perquisites.* The audit committee should review in-house policies and procedures for regular review of officers' expenses and perquisites, including any use of corporate assets, inquire as to the results of the review, and, if appropriate, review a summarization of the expenses and perquisites of the period under review.

- *Areas requiring special attention.* The audit committee should instruct the independent public accountant and the internal auditor that the committee expects to be advised if there are any areas that require its special attention.

- *Selection of independent public accountant.* The Treadway Commission concluded that a primary responsibility of the audit committee should be the selection of an independent public accountant for the company. The actual selection generally is proposed by management, with the audit committee confirming management's selection, and is ratified by the shareholders.

CHAPTER 12

OTHER CONSIDERATIONS

¶ 1201 Overview

Apart from the statutory and SEC rule requirements discussed in the preceding chapters, certain other considerations also affect the audit committee's actions and responsibilities. These are principles and standards that arise largely from the litigation context, developed by the courts. For example, the concept of "materiality" (see ¶ 1202) guides the audit committee in determining whether audited financial statements are reliable, a determination that requires assessing the materiality of any discovered misstatements or omissions.

Another such principle is the "business judgment rule" (see ¶ 1203), a common law doctrine that shields corporate directors from liability for actions taken in good faith and in the exercise of their business judgment. Still another concept developed by the courts is the standard for assessing an outside director's involvement in day-to-day operations, for purposes of determining whether he or she had knowledge of wrongdoing within the company (see ¶ 1204). Finally, the concept of "scienter," or fraudulent intent, is central to establishing whether an audit committee member—or any other person—is liable for securities fraud (see ¶ 1205).

¶ 1202 Materiality

The audit committee, in executing its responsibilities, should have a clear understanding of the concept of materiality. The SEC's original proposal for audit committee disclosure, consistent with the blue ribbon committee's recommendations, would have required the audit committee to disclose whether it became aware of material misstatements or omissions in the audited financial statements. (See Release No. 34-41987 (SEC 1999), 1999-2000 CCH Dec. ¶ 86,209.) The SEC modified this provision to require only that the audit committee state whether it recommended that the board include the financial statements in the annual report filed with the Commission. (See Item 306(a) of Regulation S-K, discussed at ¶ 502 and reproduced at ¶ 3001.)

Although the provision no longer mentions materiality, perhaps implicit in its disclosure requirement is the premise that the committee, in evaluating the reliability of audited financials, has considered the materiality of any misstatements or omissions that it discovers. Thus, in order to assess the financial statements properly and, in turn, recommend whether to include them in the company's annual report, the audit committee must understand and apply the concept of materiality.

The following discussion provides an overview of materiality standards, as articulated under federal securities law and under the accounting and auditing literature.

Federal Securities Law

In general, information is material under federal securities law if a reasonable investor would consider it important in making an investment decision. Materiality therefore depends on the significance that a reasonable investor would place on the misrepresented or withheld information. There must be a substantial likelihood that, under all the circumstances, the misstated or omitted fact would have assumed actual significance in a reasonable investor's investment decision. Stated differently, there must be a substantial likelihood that reasonable investors would have viewed disclosure of the fact omitted or misrepresented as having significantly altered the "total mix" of information made available. (*TSC Industries, Inc. v. Northway, Inc.* (US Sup. Ct. 1976), 1976-77 CCH Dec. ¶ 95,615; *Basic, Inc. v. Levinson* (US Sup. Ct. 1988), 1987-88 CCH Dec. ¶ 93,645.)

Background

Determining whether a fact is material requires consideration of all the surrounding circumstances. There is no "bright line" test for what a reasonable investor would consider significant in making an investment decision. Because of its fact-intensive nature, therefore, the determination is notoriously difficult. As one court noted:

> [S]ince the importance of a particular piece of information depends on the context in which it is given, materiality has become one of the most unpredictable and elusive concepts of the federal securities laws. The SEC itself has despaired of providing written guidelines to advise wary corporate management of the distinctions between material and non-material information, and instead has chosen to rely on an after-the-fact, case-by-case approach, seeking injunctive relief when it believes that the appropriate boundaries have been breached.

(*SEC v. Bausch & Lomb, Inc.* (CA-2 1977), 1977-78 CCH Dec. ¶ 96,186.)

More recently, the SEC has offered limited guidance on materiality. See Release No. 34-43154 (SEC 2000), 2000 CCH Dec. ¶ 86,319 (adopting Regulation FD). Although acknowledging the difficulty of making materiality judgments, the Commission stated, "[W]e do not believe an appropriate answer to this difficulty is to set forth a bright-line test, or an exclusive list of 'material' items." Quoting the Supreme Court in *Basic*, the SEC reasoned, "Any approach that designates a single fact or occurrence as always determinative of an inherently fact-specific finding such as materiality, must necessarily be over- or underinclusive." Nonetheless, the Commission did identify certain types of information or events that are potentially material:

- earnings information;

- mergers, acquisitions, tender offers, joint ventures, or changes in assets;

- new products or discoveries, or developments regarding customers or suppliers (e.g., the acquisition or loss of a contract);

- changes in control or in management;

- changes in auditors or auditor notification that the company can no longer rely on an auditor's audit report;

- events regarding the company's securities (e.g., defaults on senior securities, calls of securities for redemption, repurchase plans, stock splits

¶1202

or changes in dividends, changes to shareholder rights, or public or private sales of additional securities); and

- bankruptcies or receiverships.

(Release No. 34-43154, supra (citing for comparison purposes NASD Rule IM-4120-1).)

The SEC did not mean to imply that each of the items listed above is per se material. The information and events on the list still require determinations as to their materiality (although some determinations will come more easily than others). For example, the Commission noted, "some new products or contracts will be material to an issuer, yet that does not mean that all product developments or contracts will be material." This demonstrates why no bright-line standard or list of items can adequately address the range of situations that may arise, the SEC concluded. For the same reason, the Commission declined to create an exclusive list of events or information that have a higher probability of being material. (Release No. 34-43154, supra.)

Financial results

Financial results are subject to the same materiality standard under federal securities law as any other type of disclosure. Assessing the materiality of financial information therefore requires the same fact-intensive, case-by-case analysis that all other materiality judgments require. In short, there is no bright-line or formulaic standard for determining whether a financial disclosure is material. Companies therefore should not rely on a rule of thumb that defines as immaterial misstatements or omissions of financial information that fall below a certain quantitative threshold—for example, a five-percent deviation from actual results. This is true under federal securities law, discussed here, as well as under FASB accounting and auditing standards, discussed further below.

Rejecting a bright-line materiality standard for financial results, the Second Circuit, for example, held that a misstatement representing 1.7 percent of a company's pre-tax revenues was not immaterial as a matter of law. (*Ganino v. Citizens Utility Co.* (CA-2 2000), 2000-01 CCH Dec. ¶ 91,210.) There, a district court had concluded that alleged misrepresentations of the company's fees were immaterial as a matter of law because they amounted to only 1.7 percent of the firm's total revenues. Quoting a newspaper article, the district court stated, "[M]ost auditors—and their corporate clients—define materiality as any event or news that might affect a company's earnings, positively or negatively, by 3% to 10%." The Second Circuit disagreed, however, stating that reliance on a single numeric or percentage benchmark was erroneous. Materiality is a mixed question of law and fact, the appellate court reasoned, and "we have consistently rejected a formulaic approach to assessing the materiality of an alleged misrepresentation." The court added:

> A bright-line rule indeed is easier to follow than a standard that requires the exercise of judgment in the light of all the circumstances. But ease of application alone is not an excuse for ignoring the purposes of the Securities Acts and Congress' policy decisions. Any approach that designates a single fact or occurrence as always determinative of an inherently fact-specific finding such as materiality, must necessarily be overinclusive or underinclusive.

(*Ganino*, supra (quoting *Basic, inc. v. Levinson* (US Sup. Ct. 1988), 1987-88 CCH Dec. ¶ 93,645, n. 14).)

Accounting and Auditing Literature

The accounting and auditing literature contains standards of materiality that closely resemble the Supreme Court's standard under federal securities law. For example, the Financial Accounting Standards Board (FASB) states:

> The omission or misstatement of an item in a financial report is material if, in the light of surrounding circumstances, the magnitude of the item is such that it is probable that the judgment of a reasonable person relying upon the report would have been changed or influenced by the inclusion or correction of the item.

(Statement of Financial Accounting Concepts No. 2, Qualitative Characteristics of Accounting Information (FASB 1980).) This formulation, the SEC staff notes, "is in substance identical to the formulation used by the courts in interpreting the federal securities laws." (Staff Accounting Bulletin No. 99 (SEC 1999), FED. SEC. L. REP. ¶ 75,563.) Both standards focus on the effect of a statement or omission on the actions of a reasonable person who relies on the information. Moreover, both standards require consideration of the surrounding circumstances; not just the statement or omission itself.

Quantitative vs. qualitative considerations

The accounting and auditing literature does not define materiality by strictly quantitative measures. Although some companies and auditors have adopted rules of thumb that define as immaterial misstatements or omissions of financial information that fall below a certain quantitative threshold—for example, a five-percent deviation from actual results—the SEC staff concluded that such quantitative standards are not acceptable and have no support under the accounting and auditing literature. Staff Accounting Bulletin No. 99 (SEC 1999), FED. SEC. L. REP. ¶ 75,563.

The staff noted that "the FASB rejected a formulaic approach to 'discharging the onerous duty of making materiality decisions' in favor of an approach that takes into account all the relevant considerations." See Statement of Financial Accounting Concepts No. 2, Qualitative Characteristics of Accounting Information (FASB 1980), supra. "[M]agnitude by itself, without regard to the nature of the item and the circumstances in which the judgment has to be made, will not generally be a sufficient basis for a materiality judgment," FASB concluded.

The SEC staff believes that there are many situations where misstatements below five percent could well be material. Qualitative factors may cause misstatements of quantitatively small amounts to have a material effect, the staff explained. Such factors include whether the misstatement:

- arises from an item capable of precise measurement or whether it arises from an estimate (and, if so, the degree of imprecision inherent in the estimate);

- masks a change in earnings or other trends;

- hides a failure to meet analysts' consensus expectations for the enterprise;

- changes a loss into income or vice versa;

- concerns a segment or other portion of the company's business identified as playing a significant role in the company's operations or profitability;

- affects the company's compliance with regulatory requirements;
- affects the company's compliance with loan covenants or other contractual requirements;
- results in an increase in management's compensation3/43/4for example, by satisfying requirements for the award of bonuses or other forms of incentive compensation; and
- involves concealment of an unlawful transaction.

(SAB No. 99, supra.)

Another relevant, qualitative factor is the demonstrated price volatility of the company's securities in response to certain disclosures. Such volatility may provide guidance as to whether investors regard as material quantitatively small misstatements. For example, where management or the independent auditor expects that a known misstatement may result in a significant positive or negative market reaction, that expected reaction is relevant to the materiality determination. (SAB No. 99, supra.)

Also relevant is whether the misstatement is intentional. "While the intent of management does not render a misstatement material, it may provide significant evidence of materiality," the staff concluded. The evidence is particularly compelling where management has intentionally misstated financial information to "manage" reported earnings. In that instance, the staff noted, management "presumably has done so believing that the resulting amounts and trends would be significant to users of the registrant's financial statements." (SAB No. 99, supra.)

¶ 1203 Business Judgment Rule

Audit committee members, like other corporate directors, have available to them the broad protections of the business judgment rule. This rule is a common law doctrine that shields corporate directors from liability for certain actions taken in good faith and in the exercise of their business judgment. The SEC recognizes that audit committee members can avail themselves of the business judgment rule's broad embrace.

In adopting its audit committee proxy statement disclosure rules, the SEC said that the required disclosure is designed to help inform shareholders of the audit committee's oversight with respect to financial reporting and underscore the importance of that role. The SEC believes that, under state corporation law, the more informed the audit committee becomes through its discussions with management and the auditors, the more likely that the business judgment rule will apply and provide broad protection. Those discussions should serve to strengthen the information and reporting system that should be in place.

Under the business judgment rule, the decisions of directors and officers in managing the company may not be attacked so long as the directors acted in good faith and used their best business judgment. The rule is a presumption that in making a business decision the directors of a corporation acted on an informed basis, in good faith and in the honest belief that the action taken was in the best interests of the company. The rule contains five key elements:

- A business decision;
- Disinterestedness;
- Due care;
- Good faith; and

- No abuse of discretion.

An application of the traditional business judgment rule places the burden on the party challenging the board's decision to establish facts rebutting the presumption. If the business judgment rule is not rebutted, a court will not substitute its judgment for that of the board if the board's decision can be attributed to any rational business purpose.

The business judgment rule originated as a means of limiting the liability of corporate officers and directors for mere mistakes or errors of judgment, giving them a wide latitude in running the company. For many decades, the business judgment rule has served a legitimate purpose in shielding directors from liability for their conduct in running the company's business.

The rule has been stated in various forms in various jurisdictions, but it essentially provides that, absent bad faith or self-dealing, a court will not interfere with the judgment of a board of directors unless there is a showing of gross and palpable overreaching. Under the rule's protection, a board enjoys a presumption of sound business judgment and its decisions will not be disturbed if they can be attributed to any rational purpose.

The business judgment rule recognizes a fundamental tenet of corporation law, which is that directors are charged with managing the company's affairs. It is a presumption that, in making a business decision, directors act on an informed basis in good faith and honest belief that the action taken was in the company's best interest. The bedrock principle embodied in the rule is a judicial reluctance to substitute a court's judgment for that of a board if the board's decision can be attributed to any rational business purpose.

The duty of care requires a director to be diligent and prudent in managing the company's affairs, but directors have broad freedom of action. Thus, while they may be liable for any action that injures the company, whether it results from negligence or from participation in, approval of, or acquiescence in a wrongful act, they are not liable merely because, in the exercise of their valid business judgment, they chose a course of action that turned out badly for the business. Conduct that would be applauded if it succeeded does not merit punishment simply because it failed.

Courts have held that directors are left solely to their own honest and unselfish judgment. If directors exercise that judgment without fraud and free of conflicts of interest, a court will not second-guess them. The doctrine that bars judicial inquiry into actions taken by directors in good faith and in honest pursuit of the legitimate interests of the company is the business judgment rule. (*Galef v. Alexander* (CA-2 1980), 1979-80 CCH Dec. ¶ 97,259.)

The business judgment rule is process-oriented and informed by a deep respect for all good faith board decisions. A judge or jury considering a board's decision, or an audit committee's decision, after the fact may believe that it is substantively wrong, former Delaware Chancellor William Allen has noted, but that would not provide grounds for director liability so long as the court determines that the process used was rational or was used in good faith. A director's obligation includes a duty to attempt in good faith to assure that an adequate corporate information and reporting system exists, and that a failure to do so may, under some circumstances, render a director liable for losses caused by non-compliance with applicable legal standards. (*Caremark Int'l Inc. Derivative Litigation* (Del. Ch. 1996), 698 A.2nd 959.)

¶1203

Caremark also teaches that information and reporting systems can exist in an organization that are reasonably designed to provide to senior management and to the board itself timely, accurate information sufficient to allow management and the board, each within its scope, to reach informed judgments concerning both the company's compliance with law and its business performance.

The Delaware Supreme Court has said that the threshold issue in determining applicability of the business judgment rule is whether the directors exercised an informed business judgment. (*Smith v. Van Gorkom* (Del. S. Ct. 1985), 1984-85 CCH Dec. ¶ 91,921.) The determination of whether a business judgment is an informed one turns on whether the directors have informed themselves before making a business decision of all material information reasonably available to them.

There is no protection under the test for directors who have made an unintelligent or unadvised judgment. According to the Delaware court, fulfillment of the director's fiduciary function requires more than the absence of bad faith or fraud. Representation of the financial interests of others imposes on a director an affirmative duty to protect those interests and to proceed with a critical eye in assessing corporate information. The standard of care under Delaware law for purposes of determining the liability of directors under the business judgment rule is predicated upon concepts of gross negligence.

In some circumstances, most commonly when there is a charge that a director had a conflict of interest, courts have applied the primary purpose test is assessing the propriety of a director's conduct. Under this test, the court will typically examine whether the primary purpose of the director was properly a corporate purpose or one originating in personal or selfish considerations.

Not infrequently, courts have placed the burden of proving the propriety of an action on the directors if there has been a prima facie showing that the directors had a self interest in a particular corporate transaction. In several cases, courts have faulted directors for conduct that hurt the company's financial health or that was not in the interests of the shareholders despite assertions that the business judgment rule protected the directors from judicial interference.

For example, a federal appeals court, while agreeing that the business judgment rule affords directors a wide latitude in devising strategies to resist unfriendly advances nevertheless indicated that the rule governs only when the directors are not shown to have a self-interest in the transaction at hand. Once self interest or bad faith is shown, the burden shifts to the directors to prove that the transaction was fair and reasonable to the company. (*Norlin Corp. v. Rooney, Pace, Inc.* (CA-2 1984), 1984 CCH Dec. ¶ 91,564.)

¶ 1204 Outside Directors

Many if not most audit committee members are outside directors. When faced with securities fraud allegations in private federal court actions, a crucial element is whether they can retain their outsider status or whether the court will treat them essentially as inside directors because of their involvement with ongoing corporate activities. Essentially, the more closely a director participates in the company's day-to-day operations, the greater the likelihood a court will impute to that director personal knowledge of alleged wrongdoing.

One court held, for example, that directors who were members of the audit committee, but not company officers, were much closer to the position occupied by an inside director than they were to a typical outside director based on allegations that they had access to a substantial fund of information regarding the company and its financial condition, knew about many of the company's problems, and were responsible for reviewing the outside audits. (*AM Int'l, Inc. Securities Litigation* (SD NY 1985), 1984-85 CCH Dec. ¶ 92,057.)

Similarly, securities fraud charges were stated against members of an audit committee since it was alleged that they caused false financial statements to be issued with either actual knowledge or reckless disregard of the existence of the ongoing fraud said to have occurred at the company. In addition, on the facts pleaded, the audit committee members seemed much closer to the position of inside director than to that of the typical outside director. In any case, reliance on cases involving outside directors who had no awareness of fraud was improper given sufficient facts supporting an inference that the audit committee members either had knowledge of the ongoing fraud or recklessly disregarded its existence. (*Greenfield v. Professional Care, Inc.* (ED NY 1987), 1987-88 CCH Dec. ¶ 93,506.)

The liability of audit committee members for securities fraud seems to turn on the extent of their operational involvement in company affairs. Thus, one court dismissed securities fraud claims against audit committee members because they were not involved in the company's day-to-day operations. (*Sunbeam Securities Litigation* (SD Fla 1999), 1999-2000 CCH Dec. ¶ 90,735.)

Similarly, another court held that an outside director who was chairman of the audit committee was not an active director familiar with the company's day-to-day activities, and that there were no allegations sufficient to support a strong inference that he acted with fraudulent intent (discussed at ¶ 1205). There was no allegation that he was involved in the day-to-day corporate operations such that it would have been severely reckless for him to not have caught the accounting problems. (*Cheney v. Cyberguard* (SD Fla 2000), 2000-01 CCH Dec. ¶ 91,258.)

¶ 1205 Fraudulent Intent

Although allegations of negligence against audit committees may have had support in some instances, for example when they conducted ineffective monitoring of a company's accounting mechanisms, negligence is not a sufficient foundation for a securities fraud claim. The federal securities laws require a much greater degree of culpability to maintain a securities fraud action.

What is required is scienter, which is an intent to defraud, or can also be extreme recklessness, which courts have defined to be highly unreasonable omissions or misrepresentations involving not merely simple or even inexcusable negligence, but an extreme departure from the standards of ordinary care that presents a danger of misleading buyers or sellers that is either known to the defendant or is so obvious that the defendant must have been aware of it. (*Sunbeam Securities Litigation* (SD Fla 1999), 1999-2000 CCH Dec. ¶ 90,735.)

In one case, the court held that a complaint lacking any particularized allegations of scienter on the part of the audit committee members could not sustain a fraud charge. The court reasoned in part that the audit committee members' level of removal from the company's day-to-day operations severely weakened the impact of "red flag" allegations. (*Sunbeam*, supra.)

The fact, standing alone, that an audit committee member signed an annual report is not sufficient to show an intent to defraud. Similarly, conclusory allegations that individuals held positions on the company audit committee were insufficient to maintain a securities fraud action. (*Cheney v. Cyberguard* (SD Fla 2000), 2000-01 CCH Dec. ¶ 91,258; *Jacobs v. Coopers & Lybrand* (SD NY 1999), 1999 CCH Dec. ¶ 90,443.)

As a general matter then, the requisite scienter necessary to establish that fraud has been committed by an outside director may not be inferred against audit committee members merely from their status as directors. However, when corporate outsiders appear to be much closer to the position of inside directors than to a typical outside director, together with more specific allegations linking their position with knowledge of an alleged failure by the company to convey all material adverse information about the its financial condition to prospective investors, the pleading scienter requirement can satisfied.

Thus, a complaint alleged sufficiently particularized facts from which one could infer that audit committee members intentionally or recklessly acted to defraud investors when it alleged that, as members of the audit committee, each of the outside directors had the responsibility of reviewing the company's financial statements with management and the outside auditors prior to the publication of those statements and for reviewing the company's public disclosures. (*Prostic v. Xerox Corp.* (D Conn. 1991), 1991 CCH Dec. ¶ 96,196.)

Similarly, outside directors were more like corporate insiders when they served as members of the audit committee, in which capacity they were responsible, inter alia, for monitoring the company's internal and external audit functions, control systems, financial accounting and reporting, and adherence to applicable legal ethical and regulatory requirements. (*Greenfield v. Professional Care, Inc.* (ED NY 1987), 1987-88 CCH Dec. ¶ 93,506.)

Allegations that an audit committee essentially abdicated its responsibilities in certain areas and was aware of a laundry list of dubious accounting practices that should have caused it to investigate and to uncover fraud stated facts from which a reasonable jury could infer that committee members acted with scienter. It was no defense that each audit committee member held stock in the company when it collapsed, and thus had no motive to shut their eyes to the truth, since motive is not an essential component of scienter. (*JWP Inc. Securities Litigation* (SD NY 1996), 1996-97 CCH Dec. ¶ 99,293.)

SELECTED LAWS AND RULES

SARBANES-OXLEY ACT PROVISIONS

[¶2001]

Section 201 SERVICES OUTSIDE THE SCOPE OF PRACTICE OF AUDITORS

(a) PROHIBITED ACTIVITIES—Section 10A of the Securities Exchange Act of 1934 (15 U.S.C. 78j-1) is amended by adding at the end the following:

'(g) PROHIBITED ACTIVITIES—Except as provided in subsection (h), it shall be unlawful for a registered public accounting firm (and any associated person of that firm, to the extent determined appropriate by the Commission) that performs for any issuer any audit required by this title or the rules of the Commission under this title or, beginning 180 days after the date of commencement of the operations of the Public Company Accounting Oversight Board established under section 101 of the Sarbanes-Oxley Act of 2002 (in this section referred to as the 'Board'), the rules of the Board, to provide to that issuer, contemporaneously with the audit, any non-audit service, including—

'(1) bookkeeping or other services related to the accounting records or financial statements of the audit client;

'(2) financial information systems design and implementation;

'(3) appraisal or valuation services, fairness opinions, or contribution-in-kind reports;

'(4) actuarial services;

'(5) internal audit outsourcing services;

'(6) management functions or human resources;

'(7) broker or dealer, investment adviser, or investment banking services;

'(8) legal services and expert services unrelated to the audit; and

'(9) any other service that the Board determines, by regulation, is impermissible.

'(h) PREAPPROVAL REQUIRED FOR NON-AUDIT SERVICES—A registered public accounting firm may engage in any non-audit service, including tax services, that is not described in any of paragraphs (1) through (9) of subsection (g) for an audit client, only if the activity is approved in advance by the audit committee of the issuer, in accordance with subsection (i).'.

(b) EXEMPTION AUTHORITY—The Board may, on a case by case basis, exempt any person, issuer, public accounting firm, or transaction from the prohibition on the provision of services under section 10A(g) of the Securities Exchange Act of 1934 (as added by this section), to the extent that such exemption is necessary or appropriate in the public interest and is consistent with the protection of investors, and subject to review by the Commission in the same manner as for rules of the Board under section 107.

[¶2002]

Section 202 PREAPPROVAL REQUIREMENTS

Section 10A of the Securities Exchange Act of 1934 (15 U.S.C. 78j-1), as amended by this Act, is amended by adding at the end the following:

'(i) PREAPPROVAL REQUIREMENTS—

'(1) IN GENERAL—

'(A) AUDIT COMMITTEE ACTION—All auditing services (which may entail providing comfort letters in connection with securities underwritings or statutory audits required for insurance companies for purposes of State law) and non-audit services, other than as provided in subparagraph (B), provided to an issuer by the auditor of the issuer shall be preapproved by the audit committee of the issuer.

'(B) DE MINIMUS EXCEPTION—The preapproval requirement under subparagraph (A) is waived with respect to the provision of non-audit services for an issuer, if—

'(i) the aggregate amount of all such non-audit services provided to the issuer constitutes not more than 5 percent of the total amount of revenues paid by the issuer to its auditor during the fiscal year in which the nonaudit services are provided;

'(ii) such services were not recognized by the issuer at the time of the engagement to be non-audit services; and

'(iii) such services are promptly brought to the attention of the audit committee of the issuer and approved prior to the completion of the audit by the audit committee or by 1 or more members of the audit committee who are members of the board of directors to whom authority to grant such approvals has been delegated by the audit committee.

'(2) DISCLOSURE TO INVESTORS—Approval by an audit committee of an issuer under this subsection of a non-audit service to be performed by the auditor of the issuer shall be disclosed to investors in periodic reports required by section 13(a).

'(3) DELEGATION AUTHORITY—The audit committee of an issuer may delegate to 1 or more designated members of the audit committee who are independent directors of the board of directors, the authority to grant preapprovals required by this subsection. The decisions of any member to whom authority is delegated under this paragraph to preapprove an activity under this subsection shall be presented to the full audit committee at each of its scheduled meetings.

'(4) APPROVAL OF AUDIT SERVICES FOR OTHER PURPOSES—In carrying out its duties under subsection (m)(2), if the audit committee of an issuer approves an audit service within the scope of the engagement of the auditor, such audit service shall be deemed to have been preapproved for purposes of this subsection.'.

[¶2003]

Section 203 AUDIT PARTNER ROTATION

Section 10A of the Securities Exchange Act of 1934 (15 U.S.C. 78j-1), as amended by this Act, is amended by adding at the end the following:

'(j) AUDIT PARTNER ROTATION—It shall be unlawful for a registered public accounting firm to provide audit services to an issuer if the lead (or coordinating) audit partner (having primary responsibility for the audit), or the audit partner responsible for reviewing the audit, has performed audit services for that issuer in each of the 5 previous fiscal years of that issuer.'.

[¶2004]

Section 204 AUDITOR REPORTS TO AUDIT COMMITTEES

Section 10A of the Securities Exchange Act of 1934 (15 U.S.C. 78j-1), as amended by this Act, is amended by adding at the end the following:

'(k) REPORTS TO AUDIT COMMITTEES—Each registered public accounting firm that performs for any issuer any audit required by this title shall timely report to the audit committee of the issuer—

'(1) all critical accounting policies and practices to be used;

'(2) all alternative treatments of financial information within generally accepted accounting principles that have been discussed with management officials of the issuer, ramifications of the use of such alternative disclosures and treatments, and the treatment preferred by the registered public accounting firm; and

'(3) other material written communications between the registered public accounting firm and the management of the issuer, such as any management letter or schedule of unadjusted differences.'.

[¶2005]

Section 205 CONFORMING AMENDMENTS

(a) DEFINITIONS—Section 3(a) of the Securities Exchange Act of 1934 (15 U.S.C. 78c(a)) is amended by adding at the end the following:

'(58) AUDIT COMMITTEE—The term 'audit committee' means—

'(A) a committee (or equivalent body) established by and amongst the board of directors of an issuer for the purpose of overseeing the accounting and financial reporting processes of the issuer and audits of the financial statements of the issuer; and

'(B) if no such committee exists with respect to an issuer, the entire board of directors of the issuer.

[¶2006]

Section 301 PUBLIC COMPANY AUDIT COMMITTEES

Section 10A of the Securities Exchange Act of 1934 (15 U.S.C. 78f) is amended by adding at the end the following:

'(m) STANDARDS RELATING TO AUDIT COMMITTEES—

'(1) COMMISSION RULES—

'(A) IN GENERAL—Effective not later than 270 days after the date of enactment of this subsection, the Commission shall, by rule, direct the national securities exchanges and national securities associations to prohibit the listing of any security of an issuer that is not in compliance with the requirements of any portion of paragraphs (2) through (6).

'(B) OPPORTUNITY TO CURE DEFECTS—The rules of the Commission under subparagraph (A) shall provide for appropriate procedures for an issuer to have an opportunity to cure any defects that would be the basis for a prohibition under subparagraph (A), before the imposition of such prohibition.

'(2) RESPONSIBILITIES RELATING TO REGISTERED PUBLIC ACCOUNTING FIRMS—The audit committee of each issuer, in its capacity as a committee of the board of directors, shall be directly responsible for the appointment, compensation, and oversight of the work of any registered public accounting firm employed by that issuer (including resolution of disagreements between management and the auditor regarding financial reporting) for the purpose of preparing or issuing an audit report or related work, and each such registered public accounting firm shall report directly to the audit committee.

'(3) INDEPENDENCE—

'(A) IN GENERAL—Each member of the audit committee of the issuer shall be a member of the board of directors of the issuer, and shall otherwise be independent.

'(B) CRITERIA—In order to be considered to be independent for purposes of this paragraph, a member of an audit committee of an issuer may not, other than in his or her capacity as a member of the audit committee, the board of directors, or any other board committee—

'(i) accept any consulting, advisory, or other compensatory fee from the issuer; or

'(ii) be an affiliated person of the issuer or any subsidiary thereof.

'(C) EXEMPTION AUTHORITY—The Commission may exempt from the requirements of subparagraph (B) a particular relationship with respect to audit committee members, as the Commission determines appropriate in light of the circumstances.

'(4) COMPLAINTS—Each audit committee shall establish procedures for—

'(A) the receipt, retention, and treatment of complaints received by the issuer regarding accounting, internal accounting controls, or auditing matters; and

'(B) the confidential, anonymous submission by employees of the issuer of concerns regarding questionable accounting or auditing matters.

'(5) AUTHORITY TO ENGAGE ADVISERS—Each audit committee shall have the authority to engage independent counsel and other advisers, as it determines necessary to carry out its duties.

'(6) FUNDING—Each issuer shall provide for appropriate funding, as determined by the audit committee, in its capacity as a committee of the board of directors, for payment of compensation—

'(A) to the registered public accounting firm employed by the issuer for the purpose of rendering or issuing an audit report; and

'(B) to any advisers employed by the audit committee under paragraph (5).'.

[¶2007]

Section 404 MANAGEMENT ASSESSMENT OF INTERNAL CONTROLS

(a) RULES REQUIRED—The Commission shall prescribe rules requiring each annual report required by section 13(a) or 15(d) of the Securities Exchange Act of 1934 (15 U.S.C. 78m or 78o(d)) to contain an internal control report, which shall—

(1) state the responsibility of management for establishing and maintaining an adequate internal control structure and procedures for financial reporting; and

(2) contain an assessment, as of the end of the most recent fiscal year of the issuer, of the effectiveness of the internal control structure and procedures of the issuer for financial reporting.

(b) INTERNAL CONTROL EVALUATION AND REPORTING—With respect to the internal control assessment required by subsection (a), each registered public accounting firm that prepares or issues the audit report for the issuer shall attest to, and report on, the assessment made by the management of the issuer. An attestation made under this subsection shall be made in accordance with standards for attestation engagements issued or adopted by the Board. Any such attestation shall not be the subject of a separate engagement.

[¶2008]

Section 407 DISCLOSURE OF AUDIT COMMITTEE FINANCIAL EXPERT

(a) RULES DEFINING 'FINANCIAL EXPERT'—The Commission shall issue rules, as necessary or appropriate in the public interest and consistent with the protection of investors, to require each issuer, together with periodic reports required pursuant to sections 13(a) and 15(d) of the Securities Exchange Act of 1934, to disclose whether or not, and if not, the reasons therefor, the audit committee of that issuer is comprised of at least 1 member who is a financial expert, as such term is defined by the Commission.

(b) CONSIDERATIONS—In defining the term 'financial expert' for purposes of subsection (a), the Commission shall consider whether a person has, through education and experience as a public accountant or auditor or a principal financial officer, comptroller, or principal accounting officer of an issuer, or from a position involving the performance of similar functions—

(1) an understanding of generally accepted accounting principles and financial statements;

(2) experience in—

(A) the preparation or auditing of financial statements of generally comparable issuers; and

(B) the application of such principles in connection with the accounting for estimates, accruals, and reserves;

(3) experience with internal accounting controls; and

(4) an understanding of audit committee functions.

(c) DEADLINE FOR RULEMAKING—The Commission shall—

(1) propose rules to implement this section, not later than 90 days after the date of enactment of this Act; and

(2) issue final rules to implement this section, not later than 180 days after that date of enactment.

SEC Regulations

[¶ 3001]

Item 306 of Regulation S-K

(a) The audit committee must state whether:

(1) The audit committee has reviewed and discussed the audited financial statements with management;

(2) The audit committee has discussed with the independent auditors the matters required to be discussed by SAS 61 (Codification of Statements on Auditing Standards, AU § 380), as may be modified or supplemented;

(3) The audit committee has received the written disclosures and the letter from the independent accountants required by Independence Standards Board Standard No. 1 (Independence Standards Board Standard No. 1, Independence Discussions with Audit Committees), as may be modified or supplemented, and has discussed with the independent accountant the independent accountant's independence; and

(4) Based on the review and discussions referred to in paragraphs (a)(1) through (a)(3) of this Item, the audit committee recommended to the Board of Directors that the audited financial statements be included in the company's Annual Report on Form 10-K (17 CFR 249.310) (or, for closed-end investment companies registered under the Investment Company Act of 1940 (15 U.S.C. 80a-1 *et seq.*), the annual report to shareholders required by Section 30(e) of the Investment Company Act of 1940 (15 U.S.C. 80a-29(e)) and Rule 30d-1 (17 CFR 270.30d-1) thereunder) for the last fiscal year for filing with the Commission.

(b) The name of each member of the company's audit committee (or, in the absence of an audit committee, the board committee performing equivalent functions or the entire board of directors) must appear below the disclosure required by this Item.

(c) The information required by paragraphs (a) and (b) of this Item shall not be deemed to be "soliciting material," or to be "filed" with the Commission or subject to Regulation 14A or 14C (17 CFR 240.14a-1 *et seq.* or 240.14c-1 *et seq.*), other than as provided in this Item, or to the liabilities of section 18 of the Exchange Act (15 U.S.C. 78r), except to the extent that the company specifically requests that the information be treated as soliciting material or specifically incorporates it by reference into a document filed under the Securities Act or the Exchange Act.

(d) The information required by paragraphs (a) and (b) of this Item need not be provided in any filings other than a company proxy or information statement relating to an annual meeting of security holders at which directors are to be elected (or special meeting or written consents in lieu of such meeting). Such information will not be deemed to be incorporated by reference into any filing under the Securities Act or the Exchange Act, except to the extent that the company specifically incorporates it by reference.

[¶ 3002]

Item 7(d) of Schedule 14A

(d)(1) State whether or not the registrant has standing audit, nominating and compensation committees of the Board of Directors, or committees performing similar functions. If the registrant has such committees, however designated, identify each committee member, state the number of committee meetings held by each such committee during the last fiscal year and describe briefly the functions performed by such committees. Such disclosure need not be provided to the extent it is duplicative of disclosure provided in accordance with Item 401(i) of Regulation S-K (§ 229.401(i) of this chapter).

(2)(i) If the registrant does not have a standing nominating committee or committee performing similar functions, state the basis for the view of the board of directors that it is appropriate for the registrant not to have such a committee and identify each director who participates in the consideration of director nominees;

(ii) Provide the following information regarding the registrant's director nomination process:

(A) If the nominating committee has a charter, disclose whether a current copy of the charter is available to security holders on the registrant's website. If the nominating committee has a charter and a current copy of the charter is available to security holders on the registrant's website, provide the registrant's website address. If the nominating committee has a charter and a current copy of the charter is not available to security holders on the registrant's website, include a copy of the charter as an appendix to the registrant's proxy statement at least once every three fiscal years. If a current copy of the charter is not available to security holders on the registrant's website, and is not included as an appendix to the registrant's proxy statement, identify in which of the prior fiscal years the charter was so included in satisfaction of this requirement;

(B) If the nominating committee does not have a charter, state that fact;

(C) If the registrant is a listed issuer (as defined in § 240.10A-3) whose securities are listed on a national securities exchange registered pursuant to section 6(a) of the Act (15 U.S.C. 78f(a)) or in an automated inter-dealer quotation system of a national securities association registered pursuant to section 15A(a) of the Act (15 U.S.C. 78o-3(a)) that has independence requirements for nominating committee members, disclose whether the members of the nominating committee are independent, as independence for nominating committee members is defined in the listing standards applicable to the listed issuer;

(D) If the registrant is not a listed issuer (as defined in § 240.10A-3), disclose whether each of the members of the nominating committee is independent. In determining whether a member is independent, the registrant must use a definition of independence of a national securities exchange registered pursuant to section 6(a) of the Act (15 U.S.C. 78f(a)) or a national securities association registered pursuant to section 15A(a) of the Act (15 U.S.C. 78o-3(a)) that has been approved by the Commission (as that definition may be modified or supplemented), and state which definition it used. Whatever definition the registrant chooses, it must apply that definition consistently to all members of the nominating committee and use the independence standards of the same national securities exchange or national securities association for purposes of nominating committee disclosure under this requirement and audit committee disclosure required under paragraph (d)(3)(iv) of Item 7 of Schedule 14A (§ 240.14a-101);

(E) If the nominating committee has a policy with regard to the consideration of any director candidates recommended by security holders, provide a description of the material elements of that policy, which shall include, but need not be limited to, a statement as to whether the committee will consider director candidates recommended by security holders;

(F) If the nominating committee does not have a policy with regard to the consideration of any director candidates recommended by security holders, state that fact and state the basis for the view of the board of directors that it is appropriate for the registrant not to have such a policy;

(G) If the nominating committee will consider candidates recommended by security holders, describe the procedures to be followed by security holders in submitting such recommendations;

(H) Describe any specific, minimum qualifications that the nominating committee believes must be met by a nominating committee-recommended nominee for a position on the registrant's board of directors, and describe any specific qualities or skills that the nominating committee believes are necessary for one or more of the registrant's directors to possess;

(I) Describe the nominating committee's process for identifying and evaluating nominees for director, including nominees recommended by security holders, and any differences in the manner in which the nominating committee evaluates nominees for director based on whether the nominee is recommended by a security holder;

(J) With regard to each nominee approved by the nominating committee for inclusion on the registrant's proxy card (other than nominees who are executive officers or who are directors standing for re-election), state which one or more of the following categories of persons or entities recommended that nominee: security holder, non-management director, chief executive officer, other executive officer, third-party search firm, or other, specified source. With regard to each such nominee approved by a nominating committee of an investment company, state which one or more of the following additional categories of persons or entities recommended that nominee: security holder, director, chief executive officer, other executive officer, or employee of the investment company's investment adviser, principal underwriter, or any affiliated person of the investment adviser or principal underwriter;

(K) If the registrant pays a fee to any third party or parties to identify or evaluate or assist in identifying or evaluating potential nominees, disclose the function performed by each such third party; and

(L) If the registrant's nominating committee received, by a date not later than the 120th calendar day before the date of the registrant's proxy statement released to security holders in connection with the previous year's annual meeting, a recommended nominee from a security holder that beneficially owned more than 5% of the registrant's voting common stock for at least one year as of the date the recommendation was made, or from a group of security holders that beneficially owned, in the aggregate, more than 5% of the registrant's voting common stock, with each of the securities used to calculate that ownership held for at least one year as of the date the recommendation was made, identify the candidate and the security holder or security holder group that recommended the candidate and disclose whether the nominating committee chose to nominate the candidate, provided, however, that no such identification or disclosure is required without the written consent of both the security holder or security holder group and the candidate to be so identified.

Instructions to paragraph (d) (2) (ii) (L):

1. For purposes of Item 7(d) (2) (ii) (L), the percentage of securities held by a nominating security holder may be determined using information set forth in the registrant's most recent quarterly or annual report, and any current report subsequent thereto, filed with the Commission pursuant to this Act (or, in the case of a registrant that is an investment company registered under the Investment Company Act of 1940, the registrant's most recent report on Form N-CSR (§§ 249.331 and 274.128)), unless the party relying on such report knows or has reason to believe that the information contained therein is inaccurate.

2. For purposes of the registrant's obligation to provide the disclosure specified in Item 7(d) (2) (ii) (L), where the date of the annual meeting has been changed by more than 30 days from the date of the previous year's meeting, the obligation under that Item will arise where the registrant receives the security holder recommendation a reasonable time before the registrant begins to print and mail its proxy materials.

3. For purposes of Item 7(d) (2) (ii) (L), the percentage of securities held by a recommending security holder, as well as the holding period of those securities, may be determined by the registrant if the security holder is the registered holder of the securities. If the security holder is not the registered owner of the securities, he or she can submit one of the following to the registrant to evidence the required ownership percentage and holding period:

A. A written statement from the "record" holder of the securities (usually a broker or bank) verifying that, at the time the security holder made the recommendation, he or she had held the required securities for at least one year; or

B. If the security holder has filed a Schedule 13D (§ 240.13d-101), Schedule 13G (§ 240.13d-102), Form 3 (§ 249.103), Form 4 (§ 249.104), and/or Form 5 (§ 249.105), or amendments to those documents or updated forms, reflecting ownership of the securities as of or before the date of the recommendation, a copy of the schedule and/or form, and any subsequent amendments reporting a change in ownership level, as well as a written statement that the security holder continuously held the securities for the one-year period as of the date of the recommendation.

4. For purposes of the registrant's obligation to provide the disclosure specified in Item 7(d) (2) (ii) (L), the security holder or group must have provided to the registrant, at the time of the recommendation, the written consent of all parties to be identified and, where the security holder or group members are not registered holders, proof that the security holder or group satisfied the required ownership percentage and holding period as of the date of the recommendation.

Instruction to paragraph (d) (2) (ii): For purposes of Item 7(d) (2) (ii), the term "nominating committee" refers not only to nominating committees and committees performing similar functions, but also to groups of directors fulfilling the role of a nominating committee, including the entire board of directors.

(3) If the registrant has an audit committee:

(i) Provide the information required by Item 306 of Regulation S-K.

(ii) State whether the registrant's Board of Directors has adopted a written charter for the audit committee.

(iii) Include a copy of the written charter, if any, as an appendix to the registrant's proxy statement, unless a copy has been included as an appendix to the registrant's proxy statement within the registrant's past three fiscal years.

(iv) (A) If the registrant is a listed issuer, as defined in § 240.10A-3:

(*1*) Disclose whether the members of the audit committee are independent, as independence for audit committee members is defined in the listing standards applicable to the listed issuer. If the registrant does not have a separately designated audit committee, or committee performing similar functions, the registrant must provide the disclosure with respect to all members of its board of directors.

(*2*) If the listed issuer's board of directors determines, in accordance with the listing standards applicable to the listed issuer, to appoint a director to the audit committee who is not independent (apart from the requirements in § 240.10A-3) because of exceptional or limited or similar circumstances, disclose the nature of the relationship that makes that individual not independent and the reasons for the board of directors' determination.

(B) If the registrant, including a small business issuer, is not a listed issuer, disclose whether the registrant has an audit committee established in accordance with section 3(a)(58)(A) of the Act (15 U.S.C. 78c(a)(58)(A)) and, if so, whether the members of the committee are independent. In determining whether a member is independent, the registrant must use a definition for audit committee member independence of a national securities exchange registered pursuant to section 6(a) of the Act (15 U.S.C. 78f(a)) or a national securities association registered pursuant to section 15A(a) of the Act (15 U.S.C. 78o-3(a)) that has been approved by the Commission (as such definition may be modified or supplemented), and state which definition was used. Whichever definition is chosen must be applied consistently to all members of the audit committee.

(v) The information required by paragraph (d)(3) of this Item shall not be deemed to be "soliciting material," or to be "filed" with the Commission or subject to Regulation 14A or 14C 17 CFR 240.14a-1 et seq. or 240.14c-1 et seq.), other than as provided in this Item, or to the liabilities of section 18 of the Exchange Act (15 U.S.C. §78r), except to the extent that the registrant specifically requests that the information be treated as soliciting material or specifically incorporates it by reference into a document filed under the Securities Act or the Exchange Act. Such information will not be deemed to be incorporated by reference into any filing under the Securities Act or the Exchange Act, except to the extent that the registrant specifically incorporates it by reference.

(vi) The disclosure required by this paragraph (d)(3) need only be provided one time during any fiscal year.

(vii) Investment companies registered under the Investment Company Act of 1940 (15 U.S.C. §80a-1 *et seq.*), other than closed-end investment companies, need not provide the information required by this paragraph (d)(3).

[¶ 3003]

Item 9(e) of Schedule 14A

(e)(1) Disclose, under the caption *Audit Fees*, the aggregate fees billed for each of the last two fiscal years for professional services rendered by the principal accountant for the audit of the registrant's annual financial statements and review of financial statements included in the registrant's Form 10-Q (17 CFR 249.308a) or 10-QSB (17 CFR 249.308b) or services that are normally provided by the accountant in connection with statutory and regulatory filings or engagements for those fiscal years.

(2) Disclose, under the caption *Audit-Related Fees*, the aggregate fees billed in each of the last two fiscal years for assurance and related services by the principal accountant that are reasonably related to the performance of the audit or review of the registrant's financial statements and are not reported under paragraph (e)(1) of this section. Registrants shall describe the nature of the services comprising the fees disclosed under this category.

(3) Disclose, under the caption *Tax Fees*, the aggregate fees billed in each of the last two fiscal years for professional services rendered by the principal accountant for tax compliance, tax advice, and tax planning. Registrants shall describe the nature of the services comprising the fees disclosed under this category.

(4) Disclose, under the caption *All Other Fees*, the aggregate fees billed in each of the last two fiscal years for products and services provided by the principal accountant, other than the services reported in paragraphs (e)(1) through (e)(3) of this section. Registrants shall describe the nature of the services comprising the fees disclosed under this category.

(5)(i) Disclose the audit committee's pre-approval policies and procedures described in 17 CFR 210.2-01(c)(7)(i).

(ii) Disclose the percentage of services described in each of paragraphs (e)(2) through (e)(4) of this section that were approved by the audit committee pursuant to 17 CFR 210.2-01(c)(7)(i)(C).

(6) If greater than 50 percent, disclose the percentage of hours expended on the principal accountant's engagement to audit the registrant's financial statements for the most recent fiscal year that were attributed to work performed by persons other than the principal accountant's full-time, permanent employees.

(7) If the registrant is an investment company, disclose the aggregate non-audit fees billed by the registrant's accountant for services rendered to the registrant, and to the registrant's investment adviser (not including any subadviser whose role is primarily portfolio management and is subcontracted with or overseen by another investment adviser), and any entity controlling, controlled by, or under common control with the adviser that provides ongoing services to the registrant for each of the last two fiscal years of the registrant.

(8) If the registrant is an investment company, disclose whether the audit committee of the board of directors has considered whether the provision of non-audit services that were rendered to the registrant's investment adviser (not including any subadviser whose role is primarily portfolio

management and is subcontracted with or overseen by another investment adviser), and any entity controlling, controlled by, or under common control with the investment adviser that provides ongoing services to the registrant that were not pre-approved pursuant to 17 CFR 210.2-01(c)(7)(ii) is compatible with maintaining the principal accountant's independence.

Instruction to Item 9(e).

For purposes of Item 9(e)(2), (3), and (4), registrants that are investment companies must disclose fees billed for services rendered to the registrant and separately, disclose fees required to be approved by the investment company registrant's audit committee pursuant to 17 CFR 210.2-01(c)(7)(ii). Registered investment companies must also disclose the fee percentages as required by item 9(e)(5)(ii) for the registrant and separately, disclose the fee percentages as required by item 9(e)(5)(ii) for the fees required to be approved by the investment company registrant's audit committee pursuant to 17 CFR 210.2-01(c)(7)(ii).

[¶ 3004]

Investment Company Act Rule 32a-4

A registered management investment company or a registered face-amount certificate company is exempt from the requirement of section 32(a)(2) of the Act (15 U.S.C. 80a-32(a)(2)) that the selection of the company's independent public accountant be submitted for ratification or rejection at the next succeeding annual meeting of shareholders, if:

(a) The company's board of directors has established a committee, composed solely of directors who are not interested persons of the company, that has responsibility for overseeing the fund's accounting and auditing processes ("audit committee");

(b) The company's board of directors has adopted a charter for the audit committee setting forth the committee's structure, duties, powers, and methods of operation or set forth such provisions in the fund's charter or bylaws; and

(c) The company maintains and preserves permanently in an easily accessible place a copy of the audit committee's charter and any modification to the charter.

[¶ 3005]

Exchange Act Rule 10A-3

(a) Pursuant to section 10A(m) of the Act (15 U.S.C. 78j-1(m)) and section 3 of the Sarbanes-Oxley Act of 2002 (15 U.S.C. 7202):

(1) *National securities exchanges.* The rules of each national securities exchange registered pursuant to section 6 of the Act (15 U.S.C. 78f) must, in accordance with the provisions of this section, prohibit the initial or continued listing of any security of an issuer that is not in compliance with the requirements of any portion of paragraph (b) or (c) of this section.

(2) *National securities associations.* The rules of each national securities association registered pursuant to section 15A of the Act (15 U.S.C. 78o-3) must, in accordance with the provisions of this section, prohibit the initial or continued listing in an automated inter-dealer quotation system of any security of an issuer that is not in compliance with the requirements of any portion of paragraph (b) or (c) of this section.

(3) *Opportunity to cure defects.* The rules required by paragraphs (a)(1) and (a)(2) of this section must provide for appropriate procedures for a listed issuer to have an opportunity to cure any defects that would be the basis for a prohibition under paragraph (a) of this section, before the imposition of such prohibition. Such rules also may provide that if a member of an audit committee ceases to be independent in accordance with the requirements of this section for reasons outside the member's reasonable control, that person, with notice by the issuer to the applicable national securities exchange or national securities association, may remain an audit committee member of the listed issuer until the earlier of the next annual shareholders meeting of the listed issuer or one year from the occurrence of the event that caused the member to be no longer independent.

(4) *Notification of noncompliance.* The rules required by paragraphs (a)(1) and (a)(2) of this section must include a requirement that a listed issuer must notify the applicable national securities exchange or national securities association promptly after an executive officer of the listed issuer becomes aware of any material noncompliance by the listed issuer with the requirements of this section.

(5) *Implementation.*

(i) The rules of each national securities exchange or national securities association meeting the requirements of this section must be operative, and listed issuers must be in compliance with those rules, by the following dates:

(A) July 31, 2005 for foreign private issuers and small business issuers (as defined in § 240.12b-2); and

(B) For all other listed issuers, the earlier of the listed issuer's first annual shareholders meeting after January 15, 2004, or October 31, 2004.

(ii) Each national securities exchange and national securities association must provide to the Commission, no later than July 15, 2003, proposed rules or rule amendments that comply with this section.

(iii) Each national securities exchange and national securities association must have final rules or rule amendments that comply with this section approved by the Commission no later than December 1, 2003.

(b) *Required standards.*

(1) *Independence.*

(i) Each member of the audit committee must be a member of the board of directors of the listed issuer, and must otherwise be independent; provided that, where a listed issuer is one of two dual holding companies, those companies may designate one audit committee for both companies so long as each member of the audit committee is a member of the board of directors of at least one of such dual holding companies.

(ii) *Independence requirements for non-investment company issuers.* In order to be considered to be independent for purposes of this paragraph (b)(1), a member of an audit committee of a listed issuer that is not an investment company may not, other than in his or her capacity as a member of the audit committee, the board of directors, or any other board committee:

(A) Accept directly or indirectly any consulting, advisory, or other compensatory fee from the issuer or any subsidiary thereof, provided that, unless the rules of the national securities exchange or national securities association provide otherwise, compensatory fees do not include the receipt of fixed amounts of compensation under a retirement plan (including deferred compensation) for prior service with the listed issuer (provided that such compensation is not contingent in any way on continued service); or

(B) Be an affiliated person of the issuer or any subsidiary thereof.

(iii) *Independence requirements for investment company issuers.* In order to be considered to be independent for purposes of this paragraph (b)(1), a member of an audit committee of a listed issuer that is an investment company may not, other than in his or her capacity as a member of the audit committee, the board of directors, or any other board committee:

(A) Accept directly or indirectly any consulting, advisory, or other compensatory fee from the issuer or any subsidiary thereof, provided that, unless the rules of the national securities exchange or national securities association provide otherwise, compensatory fees do not include the receipt of fixed amounts of compensation under a retirement plan (including deferred compensation) for prior service with the listed issuer (provided that such compensation is not contingent in any way on continued service); or

(B) Be an "interested person" of the issuer as defined in section 2(a)(19) of the Investment Company Act of 1940 (15 U.S.C. 80a-2(a)(19)).

(iv) *Exemptions from the independence requirements.*

(A) For an issuer listing securities pursuant to a registration statement under section 12 of the Act (15 U.S.C. 78*l*), or for an issuer that has a registration statement under the Securities Act of 1933 (15 U.S.C. 77a *et seq.*) covering an initial public offering of securities to be listed by the issuer, where in each case the listed issuer was not, immediately prior to the effective date of such registration statement, required to file reports with the Commission pursuant to section 13(a) or 15(d) of the Act (15 U.S.C. 78m(a) or 78o(d)):

(*1*) All but one of the members of the listed issuer's audit committee may be exempt from the independence requirements of paragraph (b)(1)(ii) of this section for 90 days from the date of effectiveness of such registration statement; and

(*2*) A minority of the members of the listed issuer's audit committee may be exempt from the independence requirements of paragraph (b)(1)(ii) of this section for one year from the date of effectiveness of such registration statement.

(B) An audit committee member that sits on the board of directors of a listed issuer and an affiliate of the listed issuer is exempt from the requirements of paragraph (b)(1)(ii)(B) of this section if the member, except for being a director on each such board of directors, otherwise meets the independence requirements of paragraph (b)(1)(ii) of this section for each such entity, including the receipt of only ordinary-course compensation for serving as a member of the board of directors, audit committee or any other board committee of each such entity.

(C) An employee of a foreign private issuer who is not an executive officer of the foreign private issuer is exempt from the requirements of paragraph (b)(1)(ii) of this section if the employee is elected or named to the board of directors or audit committee of the foreign private issuer pursuant to the issuer's governing law or documents, an employee collective bargaining or similar agreement or other home country legal or listing requirements.

(D) An audit committee member of a foreign private issuer may be exempt from the requirements of paragraph (b)(1)(ii)(B) of this section if that member meets the following requirements:

(*1*) The member is an affiliate of the foreign private issuer or a representative of such an affiliate;

(*2*) The member has only observer status on, and is not a voting member or the chair of, the audit committee; and

(*3*) Neither the member nor the affiliate is an executive officer of the foreign private issuer.

(E) An audit committee member of a foreign private issuer may be exempt from the requirements of paragraph (b)(1)(ii)(B) of this section if that member meets the following requirements:

(*1*) The member is a representative or designee of a foreign government or foreign governmental entity that is an affiliate of the foreign private issuer; and

(*2*) The member is not an executive officer of the foreign private issuer.

(F) In addition to paragraphs (b)(1)(iv)(A) through (E) of this section, the Commission may exempt from the requirements of paragraphs (b)(1)(ii) or (b)(1)(iii) of this section a particular relationship with respect to audit committee members, as the Commission determines appropriate in light of the circumstances.

(2) *Responsibilities relating to registered public accounting firms.* The audit committee of each listed issuer, in its capacity as a committee of the board of directors, must be directly responsible for the appointment, compensation, retention and oversight of the work of any registered public accounting firm engaged (including resolution of disagreements between management and the auditor regarding financial reporting) for the purpose of preparing or issuing an audit report or performing other audit, review or attest services for the listed issuer, and each such registered public accounting firm must report directly to the audit committee.

(3) *Complaints.* Each audit committee must establish procedures for:

(i) The receipt, retention, and treatment of complaints received by the listed issuer regarding accounting, internal accounting controls, or auditing matters; and

(ii) The confidential, anonymous submission by employees of the listed issuer of concerns regarding questionable accounting or auditing matters.

(4) *Authority to engage advisers.* Each audit committee must have the authority to engage independent counsel and other advisers, as it determines necessary to carry out its duties.

(5) *Funding.* Each listed issuer must provide for appropriate funding, as determined by the audit committee, in its capacity as a committee of the board of directors, for payment of:

(i) Compensation to any registered public accounting firm engaged for the purpose of preparing or issuing an audit report or performing other audit, review or attest services for the listed issuer;

(ii) Compensation to any advisers employed by the audit committee under paragraph (b)(4) of this section; and

(iii) Ordinary administrative expenses of the audit committee that are necessary or appropriate in carrying out its duties.

(c) *General exemptions.*

(1) At any time when an issuer has a class of securities that is listed on a national securities exchange or national securities association subject to the requirements of this section, the listing of other classes of securities of the listed issuer on a national securities exchange or national securities association is not subject to the requirements of this section.

(2) At any time when an issuer has a class of common equity securities (or similar securities) that is listed on a national securities exchange or national securities association subject to the requirements of this section, the listing of classes of securities of a direct or indirect consolidated subsidiary or an at least 50% beneficially owned subsidiary of the issuer (except classes of equity securities, other than non-convertible, non-participating preferred securities, of such subsidiary) is not subject to the requirements of this section.

(3) The listing of securities of a foreign private issuer is not subject to the requirements of paragraphs (b)(1) through (b)(5) of this section if the foreign private issuer meets the following requirements:

(i) The foreign private issuer has a board of auditors (or similar body), or has statutory auditors, established and selected pursuant to home country legal or listing provisions expressly requiring or permitting such a board or similar body;

(ii) The board or body, or statutory auditors is required under home country legal or listing requirements to be either:

(A) Separate from the board of directors; or

(B) Composed of one or more members of the board of directors and one or more members that are not also members of the board of directors;

(iii) The board or body, or statutory auditors, are not elected by management of such issuer and no executive officer of the foreign private issuer is a member of such board or body, or statutory auditors;

(iv) Home country legal or listing provisions set forth or provide for standards for the independence of such board or body, or statutory auditors, from the foreign private issuer or the management of such issuer;

(v) Such board or body, or statutory auditors, in accordance with any applicable home country legal or listing requirements or the issuer's governing documents, are responsible, to the extent permitted by law, for the appointment, retention and oversight of the work of any registered public accounting firm engaged (including, to the extent permitted by law, the resolution of disagreements between management and the auditor regarding financial reporting) for the purpose of preparing or issuing an audit report or performing other audit, review or attest services for the issuer; and

(vi) The audit committee requirements of paragraphs (b)(3), (b)(4) and (b)(5) of this section apply to such board or body, or statutory auditors, to the extent permitted by law.

(4) The listing of a security futures product cleared by a clearing agency that is registered pursuant to section 17A of the Act (15 U.S.C. 78q-1) or that is exempt from the registration requirements of section 17A pursuant to paragraph (b)(7)(A) of such section is not subject to the requirements of this section.

(5) The listing of a standardized option, as defined in § 240.9b-1(a)(4), issued by a clearing agency that is registered pursuant to section 17A of the Act (15 U.S.C. 78q-1) is not subject to the requirements of this section.

(6) The listing of securities of the following listed issuers are not subject to the requirements of this section:

(i) Asset-Backed Issuers (as defined in § 229.1101 of this chapter);

(ii) Unit investment trusts (as defined in 15 U.S.C. 80a-4(2)); and

(iii) Foreign governments (as defined in § 240.3b-4(a)).

(7) The listing of securities of a listed issuer is not subject to the requirements of this section if:

(i) The listed issuer, as reflected in the applicable listing application, is organized as a trust or other unincorporated association that does not have a board of directors or persons acting in a similar capacity; and

(ii) The activities of the listed issuer that is described in paragraph (c)(7)(i) of this section are limited to passively owning or holding (as well as administering and distributing amounts in respect of) securities, rights, collateral or other assets on behalf of or for the benefit of the holders of the listed securities.

(d) *Disclosure.* Any listed issuer availing itself of an exemption from the independence standards contained in paragraph (b)(1)(iv) of this section (except paragraph (b)(1)(iv)(B) of this section), the general exemption contained in paragraph (c)(3) of this section or the last sentence of paragraph (a)(3) of this section, must:

(1) Disclose its reliance on the exemption and its assessment of whether, and if so, how, such reliance would materially adversely affect the ability of the audit committee to act independently and to satisfy the other requirements of this section in any proxy or information statement for a meeting of shareholders at which directors are elected that is filed with the Commission pursuant to the requirements of section 14 of the Act (15 U.S.C. 78n); and

(2) Disclose the information specified in paragraph (d)(1) of this section in, or incorporate such information by reference from such proxy or information statement filed with the Commission into, its annual report filed with the Commission pursuant to the requirements of section 13(a) or 15(d) of the Act (15 U.S.C. 78m(a) or 78o(d)).

(e) *Definitions.* Unless the context otherwise requires, all terms used in this section have the same meaning as in the Act. In addition, unless the context otherwise requires, the following definitions apply for purposes of this section:

(1)(i) The term *affiliate* of, or a person *affiliated* with, a specified person, means a person that directly, or indirectly through one or more intermediaries, controls, or is controlled by, or is under common control with, the person specified.

(ii)(A) A person will be deemed not to be in control of a specified person for purposes of this section if the person:

(*1*) Is not the beneficial owner, directly or indirectly, of more than 10% of any class of voting equity securities of the specified person; and

(*2*) Is not an executive officer of the specified person.

(B) Paragraph (e)(1)(ii)(A) of this section only creates a safe harbor position that a person does not control a specified person. The existence of the safe harbor does not create a presumption in any way that a person exceeding the ownership requirement in paragraph (e)(1)(ii)(A)(*1*) of this section controls or is otherwise an affiliate of a specified person.

(iii) The following will be deemed to be affiliates:

(A) An executive officer of an affiliate;

(B) A director who also is an employee of an affiliate;

(C) A general partner of an affiliate; and

(D) A managing member of an affiliate.

(iv) For purposes of paragraph (e)(1)(i) of this section, dual holding companies will not be deemed to be affiliates of or persons affiliated with each other by virtue of their dual holding company arrangements with each other, including where directors of one dual holding company are also directors of the other dual holding company, or where directors of one or both dual holding companies are also directors of the businesses jointly controlled, directly or indirectly, by the dual holding companies (and, in each case, receive only ordinary-course compensation for serving as a member of the board of directors, audit committee or any other board committee of the dual holding companies or any entity that is jointly controlled, directly or indirectly, by the dual holding companies).

(2) In the case of foreign private issuers with a two-tier board system, the term *board of directors* means the supervisory or non-management board.

(3) In the case of a listed issuer that is a limited partnership or limited liability company where such entity does not have a board of directors or equivalent body, the term board of directors means the board of directors of the managing general partner, managing member or equivalent body.

(4) The term *control* (including the terms *controlling, controlled by* and under *common control with*) means the possession, direct or indirect, of the power to direct or cause the direction of the management and policies of a person, whether through the ownership of voting securities, by contract, or otherwise.

(5) The term *dual holding companies* means two foreign private issuers that:

(i) Are organized in different national jurisdictions;

(ii) Collectively own and supervise the management of one or more businesses which are conducted as a single economic enterprise; and

(iii) Do not conduct any business other than collectively owning and supervising such businesses and activities reasonably incidental thereto.

(6) The term *executive officer* has the meaning set forth in § 240.3b-7.

(7) The term *foreign private issuer* has the meaning set forth in § 240.3b-4(c).

(8) The term *indirect* acceptance by a member of an audit committee of any consulting, advisory or other compensatory fee includes acceptance of such a fee by a spouse, a minor child or stepchild or a child or stepchild sharing a home with the member or by an entity in which such member is a partner, member, an officer such as a managing director occupying a comparable position or executive officer, or occupies a similar position (except limited partners, non-managing members and those occupying similar positions who, in each case, have no active role in providing services to the entity) and which provides accounting, consulting, legal, investment banking or financial advisory services to the issuer or any subsidiary of the issuer.

(9) The terms *listed* and *listing* refer to securities listed on a national securities exchange or listed in an automated inter-dealer quotation system of a national securities association or to issuers of such securities.

Instructions to § 240.10A-3.

1. The requirements in paragraphs (b)(2) through (b)(5), (c)(3)(v) and (c)(3)(vi) of this section do not conflict with, and do not affect the application of, any requirement or ability under a listed issuer's governing law or documents or other home country legal or listing provisions that requires or permits shareholders to ultimately vote on, approve or ratify such requirements. The requirements instead relate to the assignment of responsibility as between the audit committee and management. In such an instance, however, if the listed issuer provides a recommendation or nomination regarding such responsibilities to shareholders, the audit committee of the listed issuer, or body performing similar functions, must be responsible for making the recommendation or nomination.

2. The requirements in paragraphs (b)(2) through (b)(5), (c)(3)(v), (c)(3)(vi) and Instruction 1 of this section do not conflict with any legal or listing requirement in a listed issuer's home jurisdiction that prohibits the full board of directors from delegating such responsibilities to the listed issuer's audit committee or limits the degree of such delegation. In that case, the audit committee, or body performing similar functions, must be granted such responsibilities, which can include advisory powers, with respect to such matters to the extent permitted by law, including submitting nominations or recommendations to the full board.

3. The requirements in paragraphs (b)(2) through (b)(5), (c)(3)(v) and (c)(3)(vi) of this section do not conflict with any legal or listing requirement in a listed issuer's home jurisdiction that vests such responsibilities with a government entity or tribunal. In that case, the audit committee, or body performing similar functions, must be granted such responsibilities, which can include advisory powers, with respect to such matters to the extent permitted by law.

4. For purposes of this section, the determination of a person's beneficial ownership must be made in accordance with § 240.13d-3.

TOPICAL INDEX

References are to paragraph numbers.

A

Advisors
. audit committees
.. authority to engage 206

Asset-backed issuers
. audit committees
.. audit committee financial expert 402
.. exemption from listing requirements 210

Attorney reporting duty
. assessment of company response 1007
. audit committee involvement 1001
. covered attorneys 1002
. disclosure of issuer confidences 1010
. investigatory duties 1006
. issuer as client 1003
. qualified legal compliance committee 1009
. reporting duty 1004
. retaliatory discharge 1008
. sanctions and remedies 1011

Audit committees
. advisors
.. authority to engage 206
. asset-backed issuers
.. exemption from listing requirements 210
. attorney reporting duty
.. audit committee involvement 1001
.. qualified legal compliance committee 1009
. auditor disclosure of fraud 103
. auditor independence
.. actuarial services 703
.. appraisal services 703
.. audit committee approval of services 704
.. bookkeeping services 703
.. brokerage and advisory services 703
.. business judgments 706
.. disclosure of pre-approval policies and
         procedures 705
.. expert services 703
.. financial information systems 703
.. human resources 703
.. internal audits 703
.. investment companies 704
.. legal services 703
.. management functions 703
.. pre-approval by audit committee 702
.. prohibited services 702
.. tax services 703

Audit committees—continued
. auditor independence—continued
.. waiver of pre-approval requirement 702
. auditor report to audit committee
.. alternative accounting treatments 603
.. critical accounting policies 602
.. investment companies 606
.. material written communications 604
.. timeliness 605
. business judgment
.. auditor independence 706
. charters 503
. compensation 203
. composition 202
. fees 203
. funding 207
. general description 101
. independence
.. affiliated person 203
.. ceasing to be independent 211
.. compensation 203
.. de minimis exception 203
.. exemption for new issuers 203
.. exemptive requests 203
.. fees 203
.. foreign private issuers 203
.. look back provisions 203
.. no-action letters 203
.. overlapping board memberships 203
.. safe harbor 203
.. third party representative 203
. intent to defraud 1205
. internal controls
.. auditor attestation 302; 309
.. auditor independence 303
.. control framework 302
.. disclosure controls and procedures 311
.. evaluation methods 305
.. financial reporting 312
.. foreign private issuers 307
.. generally 301
.. impact on audit committees 301
.. investment companies 310
.. location of management's report 306
.. material weakness 304
.. oversight 301
.. quarterly evaluations 307
. oversight of independent auditor 202; 204
. oversight role generally 102
. procedures for handling complaints 205